HISTORY AND
PSYCHOANALYSIS

By the same author

Pius XII and the Third Reich
Knopf, 1966

Prelude to Downfall: Hitler and the United States, 1939–1941
Knopf, 1967

Kurt Gerstein
Knopf, 1969

Réflexions sur l'avenir d'Israël
Le Seuil, 1969, 1971

L'Antisémitisme Nazi: Histoire d'une psychose collective
Le Seuil, 1971

With Mahmoud Hussein:
Arabs & Israelis: A Dialogue
Holmes & Meier, 1975

HISTORY AND PSYCHOANALYSIS

An Inquiry into the Possibilities and Limits of Psychohistory

by Saul Friedländer

translated by Susan Suleiman

Holmes & Meier Publishers, Inc.

New York ● London

First published in the United States of America 1978 by
Holmes & Meier Publishers, Inc.
30 Irving Place
New York, New York 10003

Published in Great Britain by:
Holmes & Meier Publishers, Ltd.
Hillview House
1, Hallswelle Parade, Finchley Road
London NW11 ODL

Originally published as *Histoire et Psychanalyse: Essai sur les
   possibilités et les limites de la psychohistoire*
Copyright © 1975 by Editions du Seuil
LIBRARY OF CONGRESS CATALOGING IN PUBLICATION DATA

Friedländer, Saul, 1932–
   History and psychoanalysis.

   Translation of Histoire et psychanalyse.
   Bibliography: p.
   1. Psychohistory.   I.   Title.
D16.16.F7413 1978   155   77-18524
ISBN 0-8419-0339-5

MANUFACTURED IN THE UNITED STATES OF AMERICA

Contents

Publisher's Note

When *Histoire et psychoanalyse* was completed in the spring of 1975, many recognized this work as a significant study in a field that was fast becoming one of the most important avenues of interdisciplinary research. As a result, Holmes & Meier undertook to translate Saul Friedländer's work for the English-speaking world.

The remarkable proliferation of psychohistorical inquiry over the past two years testifies to its potential for incisive explication of historical events. This makes Saul Friedländer's overview of the methodological problems, limitations and innovations of psychohistory increasingly important. More than shedding new light on traditional problems, Friedländer envisions the future of this growing discipline, anticipating problems and exploring guidelines for subsequent study in a work which is certain to provide historians with a conceptual and methodological model for years to come.

To the memory of my students
Shaul Shalev and Avi Shmueli,
fallen in the Yom Kippur War

Introduction

Despite the recent growth of a kind of history that is oriented more toward the study of material conditions than of human motivations—that is, despite the recent appearance on the scene of a "history without people"—the great majority of historians still concur with Marc Bloch's statement that "historical facts are in essence psychological facts." In reality, the importance accorded to the historical study of psychological phenomena is increasing at the same time as the other aspects of what can henceforth be considered as an attempt to attain a "total" history. But to recognize the importance of a domain is not enough; one must also agree on a method of investigation, a way of proceeding. As far as the history of psychological phenomena is concerned, two divergent attitudes are possible: one can limit oneself to description alone, or one can go a step further and aim for theoretical explanation.

In his *Combats pour l'histoire,* Lucien Febvre launched an eloquent and often-cited appeal in favor of the theoretical study of psychological phenomena: "If we maintain," he wrote, "always and above all, a contact with the research done by psychologists and with the results they obtain; if we make it a rule never to engage in such psychological research applied to history, or in history attempting to reconstitute the evolution of psychological principles, without first familiarizing ourselves with the latest state of research on the question; . . . if we rely heavily, and from the beginning, on the latest results obtained by the experimental and critical labor of our colleagues the psychologists—then we shall be able, I think, to undertake a series of works that we are greatly in want of; and as long as we are in want of them, *there will be no history worthy of the name.*"[1] Yet, if one reads the works of Lucien Febvre or Marc Bloch, for example, one is struck by their strictly descriptive character. In his *Luther,* furthermore, Febvre treats psychoanalysis with a sovereign sarcasm, even though he obviously lacks familiarity with the subject. The number of contemporary historians who follow in this tradition is legion.

The aim of the present book is simple: to examine the extent to which the present-day historian can already go beyond the description of psychological

facts and attempt a theoretical interpretation that seems objectively necessary for historical research and that appears, in principle, realizable.

Where psychological phenomena are concerned, the interpretation favored
by traditional historians implies a recourse to intuition, to empathy, to
"common sense." The fact is, however, that as soon as we are faced with
complex psychological problems, as soon as we abandon the domain of
rationality, our intuition risks abandoning us too—or worse still, risks leading
us to the most foolish platitudes. As Frank Manuel recently wrote, Dilthey's
interpretation of Schleiermacher's religious thought has universal implications, but his analysis of Hölderlin's madness smacks of musical comedy.[2]
Indeed, some of the most curious fantasies are occasionally paraded as "explanations." Lucien Febvre holds up to ridicule Abbé Velly, who "explained"
the fall of Childeric in a well-turned phrase: "Born with a tender heart, he
abandoned himself too much to love; it was the cause of his downfall."
"Poppycock," adds Febvre.[3] Poppycock, indeed, but is it very different from a
recent "explanation" of the expansion of Christianity, the popularity of the
Crusades and the explosion of modern nationalisms as the result of . . . a
snowball effect produced by the initial success of a small group?[4] "Common
sense" is all too often the hallmark of Bouvard and Pécuchet; and even if it
were that of La Fontaine or La Rochefoucauld, it would still not be capable of
explaining the phenomenon of collective murder or even the relationship
between master and slave.

It might be objected that no character is more complex than the heroes of
Dostoevsky or Proust, and yet neither of these authors relied on any kind of
systematization or, *a fortiori,* on any specific psychological theory. Why
should the historian not emulate them? Because, I would argue, the procedures of literary or artistic creation are totally different from those followed
by the historian: in the former, the creative imagination dominates, giving rise
to affective states that are not subject to documentary analysis or textual
(factual) constraints; in the latter, the dominant mode is necessarily that of
rigorous, rational, and critical progression.[5]

Let me not be misunderstood: I am in no way suggesting that we banish
"everyday" psychology and intuition from the field of historical investigation.
The observation of human beings has been going on for thousands of years; to
say that man focused his interest on the complexity of human behavior well
before the rise of scientific psychology would be a simple truism.[6] Contemporary psychologists would certainly admit that one part of their theories is
essentially no more than an abstract classification of the unmediated facts of
experience and of behavior. But it is precisely this classification, this striving
for abstraction, that is necessary for patterns to become perceptible, for
general hypotheses to be formulated—in short, for the development of a
conceptual framework utilizable and applicable not only by psychologists
themselves, but by all those who are engaged in disciplines bearing on the
study of man. *It is not a question of eliminating description and intuition; it is
a question of carrying them through, of completing them.*

The theoretical arguments that buttress the possibility of systematization in the historical study of psychological phenomena can be traced back to one of the positions in the "great debate" that has dominated modern historiography since the end of the 19th century—since the time when the German critical school sought to establish a fundamental difference between the sciences of man and the natural sciences, between the idiographic sciences and the nomothetic sciences. Let us, in what follows, simply make our own position clear.

We should note first of all, with Jean Piaget, that more and more of the new scientific disciplines are related, by their subject matter as well as by the concepts they employ, both to the natural sciences and the social sciences.[7] One can go even further by adopting—and at the same time slightly modifying— the argument advanced by Carl Hempel, according to which the logic of any explicative undertaking is *necessarily* the same in the physical sciences as in the social sciences, especially in history.[8] According to Hempel, any proposition concerning an event can, on the one hand, be deduced from propositions concerning previous or contemporaneous events and, on the other hand, be inferred from certain general laws that are empirically verifiable. Now, if we replace the "general law" by a number of more or less probable causal series, and if instead of concentrating on the universal character of the general law we limit ourselves to studying certain observable regularities endowed with varying coefficients of probability and manifesting themselves in specific sociocultural contexts, then we have moved from the domain of physics to that of the social sciences.[9] The historian thus arrives at the partial explanation of partial series of events. Complementing what Paul Veyne has called "weak explanation," which does not go beyond the narrative level, we find—again in Veyne's words—the possibility not of determining laws *of* history, but of admitting laws *in* history.[10]

It is true that not all aspects of historical inquiry lend themselves equally well to the implicit or explicit use of generalizations: the historian's work includes sequences with "weak explanation," which are essentially descriptive and in which no significant generalizations are to be perceived, and sequences with "strong explanation," in which such generalizations are perceivable. When the historian "explains" Hitler's attack on Russia in 1941–to cite an example used by Raymond Aron to cast doubt on the validity of the Hempelian model[11]—he relies on "weak explanation"; but if he turns to the Wall Street crash of 1929, it is the "strong explanation" that appears.

Many have argued that it is the aims of the historian that distinguish him from the physical scientist and the social scientist: the natural and social sciences attempt to discover laws, whereas "the aim of the historian is . . . not to abstract from the real world the variables necessary for establishing general laws, but rather to grasp each concrete process in all its complexity, and consequently in its irreducible originality."[12] On this point everyone is doubtless agreed, but it does not at all follow that, in order to describe the "irreducible originality of an event," the historian cannot or must not have recourse to a whole series of generalizations whose bases the social sciences are capable of providing him. Besides, the uniqueness of a phenomenon cannot logically be conceived except in relation to a generalization; understanding the one necessarily implies grasping the other.[13]

Thus, the method that the German critical school assigned to history—namely, the exclusive use of intuitive understanding (*Verstehen*) as opposed to explanation (*Erklären*)—is not really applicable. In fact, the attempt to rely exclusively on the method of "intuitive understanding" has led its proponents to irresolvable contradictions or else to the formulation of totally unverifiable hypotheses—such as postulating, for example, the unconscious hereditary transmission of experiences accumulated over several generations, or invoking the existence of an "objective mind." If the "objective mind" is invariable, it cannot explain how we understand what is particular and changing; if it is variable, then it cannot enable us to have an intuitive grasp of the past. . . .[14]

The position we have been defending is not at all new, and many historians accept it without qualms: a recourse to economics, demography, or sociology for the enrichment of historical explanation presents no problems for them. But the minute one turns to psychology—especially to psychoanalysis, for as we shall see the other branches of modern psychology do not lend themselves well to historical investigation—one finds that strong reservations are expressed. To be sure, changes in outlook have occurred here too in recent years,[15] but the opposition to systematic psychological history, and especially to the use of psychoanalysis, can still count on a vast and determined majority.

When William L. Langer, then president of the American Historical Association, declared in 1957 that the integration of the principles of modern psychology (i.e., psychoanalysis) into historical investigation was the "next assignment" that historians must undertake,[16] the only reaction he encountered was astonishment. And when Sir Lewis Namier had recourse to psychoanalytic concepts in seeking to understand the behavior of certain English political figures of the 18th century, or when E. R. Dodds used these concepts in elucidating the mentality of vast strata of Greek society during the Hellenistic period,[17] historians simply shrugged their shoulders. Why?

The reticence of historians as far as psychoanalysis is concerned has been attributed variously to ignorance or to an exaggerated sense of professional pride, the latter being but a smokescreen for a growing feeling of insecurity in the face of the expansion of more prestigious disciplines in the contemporary academic world.[18] The application of psychoanalysis not to history but to historians is too easy a way, however, of overcoming an opposition based on more solid ground than that of a hypothetical clannish jealousy.

It is possible, first of all, that many historians have simply found unsatisfactory a few historical studies written by well-known psychoanalysts such as Erikson, for example.[19] Similarly, the efforts of a small number of historians working in this field may have produced no better an impression. Some historians refuse to grant any scientific validity to psychoanalysis itself—without always having very clear notions on the subject. But there is more to it than that, and Jacques Barzun recently summed up, in a caustic article, the essential grounds for opposition in the profession against the application of psychoanalysis to history—in other words, against the discipline that is coming to be known as psychohistory—as a new direction in historiography.[20]

According to Barzun, psychohistory is in no way a novelty; it is but "the latest in a succession of waves that began with historiography itself," every one of which claimed, from Plutarch to Lytton Strachey, to furnish a systematic explanation for the human behavior that it is the task of the historian to describe and explain.[21] A curious argument, which in fact reinforces the position of psychohistory: does not the existence of these diverse waves, from Plutarch to our own day, prove that, since during all this time historians have felt the need for a systematic explanation of human behavior, they can never be content with mere description? But the fact that Plutarch attempted to explain the behavior of his heroes does not mean that his implicit theories had the same scope and import as Freud's. As for Strachey and the "new biographers" of the 1920's, they were influenced by psychoanalysis, and in a sense the rise of psychoanalytic biography can be traced to the years immediately following the First World War; in a limited sense only, however, for many historians consider Lytton Strachey and his imitators to have been, first and foremost, writers of fiction. Is *Elizabeth and Essex* a work of history? No, it is a novel.

Barzun cites certain works of psychohistory that contain hardly any other explanations than those one finds in historiography in general, the only difference being in their use of a few technical terms. The examples he chooses are not very representative, however, and it is not the presence of a technical vocabulary that matters. Psychohistory can, as we shall see, open up avenues that simple common sense would have difficulty in discovering. Barzun himself recognizes this, even while using it as one of his principal arguments against psychohistory. He writes: "Suppose a more intensive and systematic application to history of Freudian ideas about motive. . . . If this were done . . . we should have to say that we had in hand, not a piece of historiography of a new kind, but a piece of psychology—or sociology or anthropology. The method of the discipline would have yielded its proper fruit: the formulation of a determinism. The novelty of the effort would be in having established a generality with historical instead of living material."[22]

The above argument leads straight back into the polemic concerning the nature of history—indeed, Barzun's concluding pages address themselves directly to that polemic—and affirms the extreme traditionalist position. But the fact is that a successful application of Freudian notions to history would not give rise to a new determinism and would not produce a work of psychology rather than of history; rather, it would (to repeat once again) lead to a partial explanation of a partial series of events. It would, in other words, enrich, not hinder, history in its chronological narration of concrete events (to cite the terms in which Barzun defines history in general).

Two fundamental questions remain: how is the historian to choose between the multiple theories of contemporary psychology? How can one make sure that psychohistorical explanation is verifiable, that it does not replace facts by hypotheses or by fiction?

As early as 1941, Sidney Rattner noted that the multiplicity of contemporary psychological theories doubtless discouraged many historians.[23] Barzun, basing himself on Woodworth and Sheehan's textbook of psychology, mentions the existence of seven different schools.[24] By grouping some of the latter together, one could arrive at what Carl Rogers saw as the three main orientations of American psychology in the early sixties: experimental psychology, theories basically psychoanalytic in inspiration, and finally a third direction, that of phenomenological or existential psychology.[25]

It is evident that contemporary psychology is not a unified discipline.[26] It is equally evident that, beneath the apparent chaos of multiple theories, one can find overlapping areas and links of various kinds—between psychoanalysis and phenomenological psychology on the one hand, and between both of these and experimental psychology on the other.

The problem of psychohistorical explanation and of its verification criteria remains, however, and it is a major one; indeed, it is one of the central issues to which the present work will address itself. But many other questions exist as well, questions that Barzun did not even come close to perceiving. . . .

The preceding pages may have given the impression that we ourselves have no doubts about the possibilities offered by the application of psychoanalysis to history. In fact, however, the present study is as much concerned with a critique of psychohistory as with an examination of the new perspectives it could open up. The "objective limits" of this discipline become apparent rather quickly, and we shall have to define them clearly: they are the limits of psychoanalytic explanation in general, but also of psychohistorical explanation in particular, both on the level of theory and on the more concrete levels of biographical interpretation and the analysis of collective behavior.

The lacunae of psychoanalytic theory have often been noted, and we shall refer to them throughout our study. They are especially apparent outside the therapeutic context, and it is a great temptation to reject the whole body of Freudian theories because of their most evident shortcomings. For those who consider, however, that Freud's contribution remains sufficiently rich and coherent to be used despite its weak points, the problem will be that of selection, adaptation, and synthesis. Now a great many psychoanalysts—regardless of the "school" they belong to—consider their interpretation of Freud's thought to be an unimpeachable, monolithic whole, and any attempt to be selective is met with a ferocious opposition more appropriate to the members of a religious sect than to the representatives of a still-evolving scientific discipline.

The task of the historian must in fact be to reexamine psychoanalytic theory in the light of historical evidence, not to overlook the historical givens for the sake of preserving intact all the elements of the theory. Perhaps the historian will even be able to suggest certain theoretical innovations, as the anthropologists did in their time, thanks to the accumulation of convergent documentary data. In any case, whenever psychoanalytic theory proves insufficient, the historian will be obliged to complete his explanation by means of description and intuitive evaluation. Let us repeat once again: systematic explanation must not exclude the intuitive process, it must give it a framework.

The problem of proof, or of the verification criteria of psychohistorical explanation, is directly linked to the preceding question: the ambiguous and metaphoric character of many psychoanalytic concepts, as well as certain inconsistencies within Freudian theory in general, allow one—especially outside the clinical context—to formulate divergent and even contradictory explanations for the same series of events. If we add to that the fact that any explanation in psychohistory must, by its very nature, be founded essentially on a theoretical construct that the historical facts cannot directly confirm, we become aware of the irresistible attraction of imaginary constructs. One is reminded of the Sempé cartoon which shows a tourist standing before the tiny remnants of a classical column and reconstituting in his mind a temple overflowing with people, the forum where they are greeting Caesar, the roads covered with marching legions, the whole city as well as the hills surrounding it, and finally, pell-mell, the Discus-thrower, the Apollo of Belvedere, and Diogenes in his tub! One will easily admit therefore that the problem of verification criteria in psychohistorical explanation becomes fundamental. These criteria must be defined, and their application demonstrated at every stage of the investigation.

The application of these criteria leads necessarily to a reexamination of the relative importance of the various subjects treated by psychohistory; this reexamination should arrive, notably, at a more critical conception of psychoanalytic biography, which has until now been the *pièce de résistance* in this new discipline. As for the psychohistorical analysis of collective phenomena, we shall have to reconsider its whole field of application.

Finally, we must emphasize the general methodological stance that a study such as ours seems to impose: in the debate concerning the position of history in relation to the natural and the social sciences, we have clearly opted for the unity of the scientific domain and the integration of history with the social sciences; but today, the very term "social sciences" generally implies the use of quantitative methods and, as far as possible, experimental rigor. Psychoanalysis cannot claim to possess such verification criteria. (We shall discuss the reasons for this in chapter 1.) Traditional historians will therefore criticize psychohistory for its schematicism and its tendency toward systematization, while the social scientists will reject it for its lack of rigor. Nevertheless, one can envisage a method founded on the systematic search for coherent structures, verified by a comparative study of cases. The rapid rise of structuralism, despite all its hazards, is a good indication of the possibilities of a middle road, which psychohistory can also follow. (This is not to equate structuralism and psychohistory, however, for in the case of the latter, a genetic—therefore historical—demonstration tends to confirm the validity and the compatibility of the structures as they are defined. We will return to these questions later.)

Due to the absence, to date, of general works devoted to psychohistory,[27] and in particular to the problems we have mentioned, the present book has been cast in a rather systematic mold. We hope that even if the answers are only tentative, the questions at least will have been clearly formulated. We hope above all to present enough material to enable one to formulate a judgment about the possibilities and the limits of this new discipline.

1. The Theoretical Framework

Psychohistory, then, is the utilization of a systematic psychology—in this instance, of psychoanalysis—in the framework of historical investigation. Such a method implies the possibility of demonstrating that a certain configuration of historical facts is susceptible to psychoanalytic interpretation outside a therapeutic context. It is evident that the very definition of psychohistory raises a series of major questions, of which the first is obviously this one: Why, given the great number of modern psychological theories, should the choice have fallen on psychoanalysis? Is the latter a sufficiently solid, sufficiently "scientific" theory to allow the historian to rely on its hypotheses?

The Choice of a Theory

In considering the range of contemporary psychological theories, the historian soon realizes that he must limit his choice to the domain of theories of the personality. Physiological psychology concerns him only to the degree that it gives rise to certain psychiatric concepts; the applicability of the latter is extremely limited, however, unless they form part of a general theory of the personality. Phenomenological psychology has its most significant application in the theories of the personality derived from it. As for the various hypotheses of experimental psychology, be it in the field of experimental social psychology, learning theory, motivation theory, etc., the phenomena they deal with occur on the level of elementary processes that are extremely far removed from the complex situations that preoccupy the historian. Certain of these hypotheses are relevant to political science or the study of international relations, but for the historian, whose field of inquiry is not the immediate present and who cannot have recourse to questionnaires or laboratory experiments, their relevance is at best secondary.[1]

We should also mention Piaget's genetic epistemology, which Robert Coles recently argued must be integrated into psychohistory.[2] It is difficult to know how to respond to such an argument. Piaget's thought, fascinating though it be, analyzes the birth and development of categories of human understanding in a way that does not allow one to go from the general demonstration to the kind of concrete application that interests the historian. But as a general system, genetic epistemology confirms on certain points the notions of psychoanalysis, notions that by definition are applicable to specific cases.[3]

Turning to the various theories of the personality, one is faced with yet another choice; in making his choice, the historian must logically rely on the following criteria:

1. In its fundamental concepts, the theory must be compatible with the basic modes of historical investigation, and must be in harmony with the historian's project. The evolutionary—and therefore historical—character of the theory is particularly important.

2. The theory must be applicable to problems of human behavior that are sufficiently complex and many-faceted to permit the investigation of the major psychological questions encountered by the historian.

3. The theory must form a sufficiently consistent and structurally coherent whole to be utilizable.[4]

Now an acceptance of these criteria just about excludes the choice of one of the theories of personality based on experimental psychology—both for the aforementioned reasons and because such theories are fundamentally ahistorical. This is particularly true of the method of factorial analysis developed by Eysenck and Cattel; in addition, the questionnaires and other measures that this type of research requires are not applicable to the study of people who are no longer alive. Similarly, it is their ahistorical, nonevolutionary character that disqualifies, from our point of view, the theories of Kurt Lewin or that of Gordon Allport: Lewin's principle of "contemporaneity" and Allport's principle of "functional autonomy" exclude the application of their conceptions of the individual to a domain where the emphasis must be placed precisely on the different stages in the development of the personality and on the origins of diverse kinds of motivation. The theory proposed by Sheldon, based on the correlation between physical characteristics and personality traits, satisfies neither the first criterion (it is ahistorical) nor the second (its simple, not to say simplistic, categories allow one to deal only with elementary traits, and that in a totally static manner); the same can be said, on the whole, of the theories of La Senne.[5]

A very different criticism applies, on the other hand, to the theories of Murphy and Murray, two researchers who come in fact quite close to psychoanalysis: their conceptions of the personality contain so many heterogeneous elements and are so lacking in structural coherence that the historian will most probably find them unusable in practice.

Our summary rejection of theories of the personality not based on psychoanalysis must not be misunderstood, however; our purpose is to "do history," and according to our chosen criteria these theories do not lend themselves to the work of the historian. That does not mean that they cannot be used on occasion in an auxiliary way, or that they are in themselves unimportant: we have shown the contrary to be true in the case of Sheldon (see note 5), and could have done likewise for Murphy and Murray. In fact, psychohistorical investigation must be constantly on the lookout for new explanations, whether they occur in the field of psychological theory or in those of genetics or neuropsychology.[6] Nevertheless, it would seem in the last analysis that only the psychoanalytic (or psychoanalytically influenced) theories can furnish psychohistory with an adequate general framework, for these theories are the only ones that satisfy the criteria which *for the historian* are fundamental.

Psychoanalysis itself and the theories influenced by it also constitute a vast domain whose limits, furthermore, are difficult to trace exactly. One finds within it the different variants of Freudian thought, the theories of Adler and of Jung, the conceptions of existential psychologists such as Rollo May and Binswanger, as well as—at the outer limit—existentialist theories that have only one point in common with psychoanalysis: their name. Sartre's thought is a case in point.

We ourselves have opted for Freudian thought in its broadest sense, for subjective reasons no doubt and also because an absolute eclecticism would give rise to total confusion. But even though, taken as a whole, the obscure and often mystical character of Jung's notions makes them unappealing, and even though an existential psychology like Sartre's, which rejects the notion of the unconscious, seems unacceptable,[7] a certain eclecticism will be nonetheless necessary—especially on the level of applied psychoanalysis—as long as psychoanalytic theory proper remains lacunary and incomplete.

It has often been pointed out that the fundamental aim of history and that of psychoanalysis are identical: to discover human motivations, whether in the individual or in a group.[8] In fact, the process is similar in the two cases, for the psychoanalytic method is, by its very essence, historical. The notions of "time," "development," and "memory" play a primary role in it. Is not the fundamental principle of analytic therapy that one understands a patient by gradually getting to know his past? It is impossible to separate psychoanalytic theory from the "case history" and psychoanalytic concepts have, for the most part, a temporal dimension: they seek to describe either the development of a process or a crucial stage in human existence.[9]

For a historian, the situation and the interaction of events in time constitute the very content of his discipline; for the psychoanalyst, the situation and the interaction of events in the course of the evolution of the personality through its various stages constitute the essential basis of his investigation. For the one as for the other, the evolution of man is determined by the past. It has often been noted how much Freud was fascinated by the weight of the past in the evolution of the personality, by the unalterable impact of a memory buried in the deepest unconscious: "Our hysterical patients suffer from reminiscences. . . ." Freud italicized this passage, notes Philip Rieff, and he adds: "He intended the model of time to become of central importance to his readers. The emphasis is all on reminiscence. History, the memory of existence in time, is the flaw. Neurosis is the failure to escape the past, the burden of one's history. Neurotics 'cannot escape from the past.' . . . Freud was fascinated and horrified by the power of the past. The whole uniqueness of man, the cause of his agony, his anxiety, is that man is a historical person, the mask of his history."[10]

The parallel between the aims and procedures of the historian and those of the psychoanalyst was worth emphasizing; it seems superfluous, on the other hand, to demonstrate here the validity of our other two criteria: certainly no reader is unaware that psychoanalysis represents a theory concerned with extremely complex aspects of human motivation that are likely to interest the historian, and that it is a structurally coherent theory, whatever its conceptual shortcomings may be.[11]

If it is not difficult to justify the choice of psychoanalysis as a theory suited to the historian, it must still be shown that the theory in question can claim a convincing scientific status, or rather that it is capable of furnishing acceptable explanations for the phenomena that belong to its domain. No one would suggest that psychoanalysis can arrive at the precision of physics or even of econometrics; accepting that as a given, can we say that psychoanalytic explanations are, despite their lacunae, the most satisfying psychological interpretation we have of the most complex human behavior?

The controversies concerning the scientific status of psychoanalysis have dogged Freudian doctrine since its beginnings, and the polemic remains to this day extremely sharp. Critics have noted that Freud drew his conclusions without having recourse to the most elementary criteria of empirical control. For the philosopher of science Karl Popper, psychoanalytic theory is as solidly grounded as Homer's mythology.[12] The mathematician and theorist of science Anatol Rapoport, on the other hand, considers Freud's theory as the richest of all the contributions to the science of human behavior.[13] In the face of such starkly opposing judgments, can one hope to reach a few reasoned conclusions?[14]

Certain empirical arguments are frequently mentioned in discussions on the subject. The controversy centers on the conclusions one can draw, as far as the status of psychoanalysis is concerned, from the latter's therapeutic results, from the validity of the clinical material, from psychoanalytic prediction, and finally from the independent experimental confirmation of psychoanalytic concepts and hypotheses.

Let us begin by considering the therapeutic criterion. Can it be proved that psychoanalysis or techniques related to it have cured more neurotic or psychotic patients than totally different methods? The survey conducted in 1952 by the British psychologist H. J. Eysenck, involving several thousand patients, indicates that the number of cures obtained by psychoanalysis is no greater than those obtained by other methods, or by no treatment at all.[15] It is true that, as Hilgard has noted, statistics on the order of Eysenck's are very hard to interpret, for one would need to establish a consensus on the seriousness of all the cases studied, as well as on what one means by "cure."[16] Despite Hilgard's arguments against Eysenck's approach or other research of the same type, the latter serve at least to show that there is no convincing statistical proof establishing the superiority of psychoanalytic therapy over other methods; this criterion does not, therefore, allow one to prove the validity of psychoanalytic theory itself.[17]

As concerns the second criterion, how can one evaluate the confirmation of the theory by means of the "clinical material" furnished by patients during the treatment? The principal objection to such an attempt is obvious: the conflicting hypotheses of Freud, Jung, Adler, Horney, and Fromm all draw their confirmations from the "material" brought by patients in treatment with a therapist belonging to one of the schools in question. The explanation that immediately comes to mind is that psychoanalysts unwittingly elicit from their patients the proofs that will confirm their theory.[18] More exactly, the analytic situation perhaps provokes the reinforcement or the elimination of certain responses by the patient, according to the best behaviorist tradition; the correspondence between the therapist's theory and the clinical material would thus be, in a sense, produced by means of suggestion.[19]

The arguments used by psychoanalysts against the theory of suggestion are not lacking; they maintain, notably, that when an interpretation is confirmed by a convergence of various dynamic manifestations in the patient, one can assume that it is objectively valid.[20] In addition, it is argued, the evolution of psychoanalytic theory has produced a considerable diversity of control methods available to the analyst, thus excluding more and more the possibility of tautological reasoning.[21] Despite all this, however, and just as in the case of the therapeutic criterion, one cannot accord an overriding importance to the role of the clinical material.

The value of psychoanalysis as a method for predicting the development of the personality—and especially of its neurotic characteristics—is equally uncertain, and Meehl's comparative studies on the accuracy of clinical prognoses versus statistical prediction show that the latter have a slight edge over the former.[22] Here too, a whole range of possible counterarguments exists.[23] But, once again, we do not have a decisive criterion for the verification of psychoanalytic theories. That leaves only the fourth possibility: independent experimental confirmation.

The reader will not be surprised to learn that, in this instance as in the previous ones, the results are not unequivocal. Certain psychoanalytic concepts and hypotheses have been confirmed by independent experiments; others are not verifiable experimentally; still others seem to be contradicted by the experimental results.[24] In reality, the question is whether a system such as that of psychoanalytic theory can be translated into behaviorist terms and tested by independent experimentation. One can very much doubt it, both because of the nature of psychoanalytic concepts, which are not identifiable with the observable facts of behavior and of experience, and because of the inherent complexity of the interactions in any specific case.[25] As Robert Waelder has noted:

> A middle-aged person may suffer from depressions. We may approach this study with ideas gained in prescientific experience, viz., the idea that depressions may hang together with severe frustrations and disappointments, and we

may look for them in this person's life. There may be many—in his marriage and family life; disappointments with his children or with their attitude towards him; disappointments in extramarital love relationships; a decrease of sexual prowess or of attractiveness; illnesses or a general feeling of aging; disappointments in work, career, or social recognition; or financial worries. All this may be complicated by organic, perhaps involutionary processes. Then there are the factors suggested by psychoanalytic theories that would have to be considered, such as, e.g., the loss of an object, abnormal forms of object relationships in terms of introjection and expulsion, loss of love from the superego, aggression turned against oneself, or a feeling of discouragement, fatigue, and defeat. . . . Several of these factors will probably be present in any one case, and many of them can be found in people of the same age group without depressions. In our search for the etiological importance of any one of these factors, or any other factor that may be suggested, we are not able to isolate it, while keeping all others unchanged, and so to study its consequences alone. We will always have many more unknowns than we have equations, so to say, so that no conclusion can be made without the exercise of judgment which may be considered arbitrary.[26]

The range and importance of the conclusions one can draw from these various empirical arguments appear very limited: the experimental criterion, as we have just seen, is not really applicable to the situations with which psychoanalysis deals; the therapeutic criterion is not considered significant even by psychoanalysts; the ability to predict is as spotty in psychoanalysis as in the other social sciences, due to the interaction of many different factors; finally, the divergences in clinical confirmations are no different from the divergences in interpretation that one finds in sociology, political science, or even in economics and demography. The discussions concerning the logical framework of psychoanalysis and the nature of its concepts seem, on the other hand, to be more significant from the start.

The logical—and at first glance decisive—argument directed against the scientific nature of psychoanalytic theory and of its concepts was first formulated by Karl R. Popper and has often been repeated since in a great many different forms. The inherent weakness of psychoanalysis consists, according to Popper, in the fact that its concepts allow one to justify any hypothesis whatsoever, and that no event seems capable of refuting a single one of its propositions: "Every 'good' scientific theory is one which forbids certain things to happen; the more a theory forbids, the better it is."[27]

Although it is cited everywhere in relation to psychoanalysis, this argument is false on certain specific points and is logically flawed. As far as the specifics are concerned, one can empirically define a whole series of psychoanalytic concepts that obviously forbid certain things to happen. More generally, as Abraham Kaplan has convincingly shown, Popper confuses "contrary" things with "contradictory" ones. The contrary of black is white, but some objects are neither black nor white; the "contradictory" of black is "non-black." If psychoanalysis could in every instance prove both a fact and its "contradictory," then its nonscientific character would be clear—but in reality the nature of its reasoning only allows it occasionally to prove both a fact and its "contrary"; that means that a third *datum* might prove both hypotheses false in a given situation, and that is precisely the criterion that Popper cites as the *sine qua non* of a scientific theory. The attachment of a child to his mother, for example, attests to the reality of the Oedipus complex; the manifest hatred of a child toward his mother is sometimes explained as a reaction formation against a love that the child feels for many reasons to be dangerous, and the Oedipus complex is again confirmed. But these two contrary hypotheses do not exclude a third possibility which would be total indifference, the absence of any emotional relation of a child to his mother; this third situation would disprove the theory of the Oedipus complex,[28] or at least dispute its universal character.

Kaplan's reply eliminates Popper's formal objection. As for the fact that psychoanalytic theory sometimes permits the affirmation both of one thing and its contrary, that is merely a reflection of certain obvious psychological realities: every reader of Dostoevsky knows that Rogozhin hated Prince Myshkin but loved him too, and that every one of his actions could be interpreted as a sign of his love or of his hatred. We are no longer unaware of the fact that most feelings are ambivalent. The question is whether we must blame psychoanalysis for its lack of logic, or whether it is human behavior that is loaded with paradoxes. In other words, which is the logic that must prevail?[29]

Granted all this, it is still true that psychoanalytic formulations are at times so metaphorical and vague that it is a practical impossibility to decide whether an explanation really follows from the theory or whether it is linked to the theory only because someone made a haphazard association between one element and another.[30] This lack of precision is only partly a result of the nature of the phenomena being analyzed, and there is no doubt that an evolution of the theory in the direction of greater conceptual refinement is possible.

What are we to conclude?

The empirical arguments for or against the scientific status of psychoanalysis are not decisive in either one sense or another, and, as we have seen, their pertinence is in the last analysis quite limited. As for the logical arguments of the opponents of psychoanalysis, they are refutable. It is undeniable, however, that even the most farfetched and absurd theories can point to "facts" that confirm them; and that a religious shrine may boast of as many cures (if not more) as the couch of the psychoanalyst. For a strict positivist, there can be no difference, in logical terms, between psychoanalysis and any kind of religious belief.

So be it. What nevertheless leads us to adopt the psychoanalytic theories as working hypotheses is a series of observations—or, if one likes, of convictions. It seems to us, first of all, as it does to many others, that an exclusively experimental psychology is, and will be, necessarily restricted to the explanation of only the simplest kinds of human behavior. We have already alluded to the reason for this: the existential situation of man excludes, by definition, the possibility of controlled and significant psychological experimentation, except in some very limited areas. But—and here is where a second observation comes into play—as soon as one leaves the area of the strictest experimentation, psychoanalysis alone allows one to explain some extremely complex forms of behavior and to apprehend man "in situation," even while maintaining an empirical basis accessible to observation. Furthermore, psychoanalytic theory is founded on a series of hypotheses and concepts that permit a progression toward greater precision and rigor: the theory can evolve in the light of new empirical observations.[31] Finally, Freudian theory is applicable, "as if" it were true.

We do not, and cannot, know whether all of the somewhat "mechanical" system used by Freud to explain human behavior has an objective reality. The relations between the ego and the id are not experimentally demonstrable, and neither are sublimation or reaction formation. On this point at least, could Karl Popper be right (at least for the sake of argument)? We are perhaps dealing with a mythology—but with a mythology that functions as a valid paradigm. Human beings behave "as if" Freud's theories were on the whole correct. The Freudian paradigm, whatever its objective validity, is—to date— the most complete explicative paradigm we have of human behavior, and, *up to the present,* no important fact or clearly definable anomaly has challenged it. Of all the arguments concerning Freudian theory, this one, it seems to me, is the only really significant one, after the refutation of Popper's thesis that psychoanalysis proved both a thing *and* its opposite.

These general remarks obviously concern the utilization of psychoanalysis in history. A recourse to Freudian theories in this domain opens up perspectives, forces us to ask questions and gives rise to inquiries that, in themselves, considerably enlarge the "territory of the historian." (We shall return to these themes later.)

At this point in our discussion, we must ask ourselves which branch of Freudian thought is the most adaptable to psychohistorical investigation. Without undue hesitation, we can opt for what has been called, over the past few years, the domain of "ego psychology." In the context of orthodox Freudian thought, ego psychology[32]—whose foundations were laid by Freud himself as early as the 1920's—is less concerned with the vicissitudes of the instincts than with the adaptive and structuring function of the ego. This shift in emphasis allows for the integration of most of the culturalist theses; generally speaking, the attention it focuses on the mechanisms of interaction between the ego and the surrounding reality and between the ego and others, allows one to integrate the structure of the personality and the social structure into a unified context. This kind of integration is a necessary condition for any psychohistorical investigation that seeks to avoid an extreme reductionism.

The choice of ego psychology is justified by the needs of our object of study, and is in no way indicative of a polemical position as regards the theoretical validity or the therapeutic effectiveness of various contemporary Freudian schools. Although the contribution of Jacques Lacan, for example, is of considerable importance, I would argue that psychohistory requires other methods of investigation.

On the other hand, let us recall that the historian can allow himself an eclecticism that the therapist or the strict theoretician would doubtless reject:

thus, even though Jungian theory and existential psychoanalysis appear on the whole unacceptable, each of them can shed light, for the historian, on problems that Freudian theory has not, up to the present, been able to treat in a satisfactory manner.

Due to its own development in a relatively uniform and stable social context, Freudian theory is unable, for example, to explain the effect of sudden upheavals in the environment on the adult personality, especially in the case of extreme situations such as imprisonment, emigration, etc.[33] Ego psychology offers perhaps an adequate conceptual framework, but its application remains, for the moment, doubtful. By looking at the problem from another angle, existential psychoanalysis sheds light on this kind of situation. A phenomenological observation of individual behavior makes clear the fundamental need of every human being to safeguard his "self." But this is a fact that cannot be explained in terms of narcissim or of ego ideal, nor even in terms of Erikson's notion of identity, which relies too heavily on instinctual or cultural components; it is a phenomenon that existential psychoanalysis describes without attempting to reduce it to elements devoid of meaning. Now one characteristic of extreme situations is precisely that the external circumstances tend to make the human being lose that feeling of the integrity of his "self"—sometimes to such a point that the subject loses all sense of his individual existence. We know that such psychic frustration can accelerate the process of physical debilitation and lead to illness and death. The existentialist notions allow us to come close to a phenomenon from which the analytical reasoning of Freudian theory might risk cutting us off.[34]

The same is true of certain kinds of psychosis, notably of schizophrenia. Applied to this kind of disturbance, Freudian psychoanalysis can appear too schematic and seems at times to mask the abyssal fall into madness; existential analysis, especially that of Ludwig Binswanger, allows us—thanks to a phenomenological approach using very broad and polyvalent concepts—to "feel" and to "understand" the case, both in its irreducible complexity and in its poignant simplicity.[35]

Freudian theory is equally inadequate in its approach to the psychic processes that appear in the latter part of life, at a time when the adult, in our Western context, has more or less resolved his material problems and begins to search for the meaning of his existence—a search he undertakes with all the more anguish the closer he gets to the reality of death. In Erikson's schema these last phases are not forgotten, but they remain empty spaces: when applied to the stages after adolescence, Erikson's thought loses all substance and fails to be convincing. On the other hand, the second half of a man's life was a subject that particularly interested Jung, and his "process of individualization" is not incompatible with Freudian psychoanalysis, especially not with ego psychology.[36]

It is the historian's task to contribute to the refinement of certain psychoanalytic hypotheses by contributing elements he finds in his own domain. He can also make use of his knowledge to answer certain questions on which psychoanalysis remains astonishingly vague. But this qualified optimism does not yet allow us—far from it!—to resolve the second major problem confronting psychohistory: what are the foundations and the limits of psychohistorical explanation?

Psychohistorical Explanation

Does psychohistorical research lead us to something other than the fantasies provoked in the historian by what he is describing or interpreting? This is not a discussion of the problem of the historian's subjectivity, for in the case of a social or political historian, even if one allows for selectivity and subjectivity, certain "objective" relations are evident in the field under study, relations that are independent of personal interpretation: the relations between demography and the economy in the French rural world of the seventeenth century, or between the Dantzig question and the German attack on Poland in 1939, are objective relations that have little to do with the historian's subjectivity.[37] In psychohistory, the situation is different.

In order to understand the unconscious meaning of a phenomenon, the historian can only proceed like a psychoanalyst: he must exclude nothing and overlook nothing. A "floating attention" will allow him to be on the lookout for the slightest detail until certain significant relations became apparent, which are subsequently confirmed by a growing number of elements. This receptivity of the observer, his openness to all the possible meanings of a text or an event, necessarily implies a countertransference effect according to the model of the actual analytic situation: the historical text or event will provoke some more or less perceptible unconscious reactions in the historian himself. But this fact itself can lead to two conclusions, which appear at first glance contradictory.

One can conclude, in fact, that all "applied psychoanalysis"—and psychohistory in particular—is but a more or less interesting testimony relating to the unconscious tendencies of the observer, in this instance the historian. We would have, in that case, a kind of closed system not unlike the philosophical system of Bishop Berkeley. Indeed, is it not along these lines—but in a wholly positive way—that Jacques Hassoun interprets Theodor Reik's writings on Jewish religious rites? Hassoun writes: "The pleasure that Reik seeks to communicate to us comes, therefore, from his allowing himself to let others know what the practice of couvade, the puberty rites of primitives, the Kol Nidre, or the Shofar were able to arouse as echoes in his own discourse, recognized and provoked by that familiar 'elsewhere.' "[38] Presented in this way, applied psychoanalysis refers to no reality other than the mind of the observer himself.

For Alain Besançon, on the other hand, "the fantasy induced in the psyche of the historian is in a direct relation—one that can go as far as imitation or duplication—with the one that underlies the reality being studied."[39] Thus, the fantasy provoked in Michelet by the contemplation of Valentine de Birague's tomb "was [probably] never consciously formulated by anyone in the 16th century, but the fact that it appeared in Michelet's mind shows that it existed unconsciously, combined with an infinite number of others that might reappear, if the occasion presented itself, in the framework of a fantasy system other than Michelet's. We are therefore led to suppose that every man possesses, in virtuality, a complete register of the imagination, and that it is this which allows him to establish with the imagination of others a communication operating through the correspondence of fantasy to fantasy."[40]

In reality, there is no difference between Alain Besançon's position and that of Hassoun; if one adopts Besançon's thesis, then Reik's way of interpreting the Kol Nidre, for example, corresponds to one of the fantasies provoked by that prayer in the distant past when it was first formulated. Consequently, Reik's interpretation uncovers for us certain aspects of an unconscious objective reality, as would any other interpretation. This relativism of psychohistorical interpretation risks putting its very foundation into question. Granted that the tomb of Valentine de Birague provoked certain fantasies in the historian Michelet; these fantasies throw light on Michelet, not on the 16th century. But then, how are we to grasp certain unconscious problems of French society in the 16th century? Not by using countertransference fantasies as our guide, *but by attempting to place them between parentheses.*[41] We must pay careful attention to the signs transmitted by the individual, the society or the culture we are observing, under the assumption that these signs have a decipherable meaning, subject, in an absolute sense, to innumerable variations, but whose specific sense can be objectively understood if they are replaced in their precise historical context. There are as many different versions of Oedipus as there are individuals; everyone goes through this decisive phase of his evolution in his own way, and regardless of the nature of the countertransference, it is *this* idiosyncratic experience, as it was lived, that the analyst must discover.

Another question: are the psychic processes identified by the psychoanalyst invariable, not only from one culture to another but from one period to another—in the midst of what can be called a single culture? Here we are confronted with the famous debate that theoretically divides the orthodox Freudians and the neo-Freudians.

In the beginning, the "orthodox" Freudians emphasized the universal and determined character (as far as the development of the personality was concerned) of the instinctual traits in human beings and of certain stages in their evolution, as well as of certain psychic conflicts from which no one was exempt; the neo-Freudians or "culturalists," on the other hand, affirmed the relativity of unconscious psychic formations and of the modes of individual development, according to the form and orientation of various human cultures.

Today, this debate is at least in part outdated: few psychoanalysts, no matter how orthodox, would deny the crucial influence of sociocultural factors on the elaboration of the family practices that determine the development of the child as he goes through the stages of instinctual maturation. The orthodox and the culturalist theses have been brought closer together as a result both of psychoanalytic practice and of a double scientific evolution: on the one hand, the emphasis placed in contemporary anthropology on certain characteristics common to all human beings, as opposed to the cultural differences that were emphasized during the preceding decades;[42] on the other hand, the acceptance by "orthodox" psychoanalysts of more abstract—and more polysemic—formulations of certain basic concepts such as the Oedipus complex.[43] Finally, the development of ego psychology reinforces even more the points of convergence between Freudian "orthodoxy" and its one-time opponents, the culturalists. The differences between the two camps have not entirely disappeared, but henceforth certain syntheses are possible; indeed, they are essential for the psychohistorical investigation of collective phenomena, for they make possible, in the study of what we designate as homogeneous groups, the utilization of a schema that establishes a direct relation between culture and personality, while at the same time preserving what is essential from a Freudian point of view—namely, the existence of developmental stages and instinctual conflicts that are universally valid. These stages are lived through in different ways, according to the influence of a given social structure or cultural *milieu.*

These remarks allow one to envisage the possibility of psychohistorical explanations based on general psychic elements that can ostensibly be found, *in various forms,* in all cultures and all periods. But the road is long from the principle to its concrete application. In fact, cultural variations in relation to the theoretical or abstract norm are little known to the historian.

In his famous study of the mores of the Trobrianders, Bronislaw Malinowski discovered a definite variation on the Oedipal constellation that Freud had found in Western societies: according to Malinowski, the biological father plays an effaced role in the Trobriander family; since it is the maternal uncle who plays the central male role, it is toward him that the emotional ambivalence of the Trobriander child is directed.[44] Nevertheless, despite the sound and fury aroused by the controversies on the subject, there is not the slightest doubt that Malinowski's findings do not put into question the universality of the Oedipus complex as such, but only the universality of the specific Oedipal relations that exist in the Western family. A broader definition of the ternary structure that characterizes the Oedipal situation allows one to include the Trobriander phenomenon as a possible variation on a fundamentally stable type of relationship. But in order to arrive at this conclusion, one must know the meaning of the Oedipal problem from a theoretical point of view, be familiar with its manifestations in the West *and with its "deviant" manifestations among the Trobrianders.*

Posed in these terms, the problem does not exclude the psychohistorical study of societies far removed from ours, on condition that the mores and institutions of these societies be known in sufficient detail; that way, one can be in a position to discover "deviations" such as the one we have just mentioned.

Finally, however, the problem of psychohistorical explanation as such can be formulated as follows: how can one make sure that the psychohistorian does not end up by explaining anything and everything—thanks to concepts that are sometimes vague and polyvalent, and despite the apparent impossibility of identifying with certainty the nature of unconscious processes outside the therapeutic framework—in terms of a code that is wholly arbitrary?

Psychohistorical explanation is constantly exposed to the danger of the double "as if." Let us consider the classic example, the paradigm of psychohistorical explanation (without taking into account, for now, the factual errors that have been discovered in it, nor the specific problems of psychoanalytic biography): Freud's essay "Leonardo da Vinci and a Memory of His Childhood."[45]

Simply summarized, Freud's hypothesis consists of two distinct yet interrelated propositions: as an illegitimate child raised without a father during the first years of his life, Leonardo was coddled by a mother on whom all of his precocious sexuality would be fixated; the result was a passive homosexuality, but also various inhibitions in his artistic career. On the other hand, his scientific curiosity could develop unhampered, since as a child he was never exposed to the repressive rigor of paternal authority.

We need not linger over the remarks concerning Leonardo's inhibitions in the domain of painting, remarks based on the observation that some of his paintings remained unfinished. The same was true of many other masters of the period.[46] But how about the relation between the fixation on the mother and homosexuality, or between the absence of the father and Leonardo's adventurousness in the most varied kinds of research? On these two points, psychohistorical explanation proceeds in two complementary stages: (1) the formulation of a general principle, in this instance the relation between a fixation on the mother and homosexuality, or between the absence of the father and the development of scientific curiosity; 2) the application of these general principles to the particular case of Leonardo da Vinci. This manner of proceeding is characteristic of all scientific explanation, but in the case of psychohistory we find ourselves up against a double approximation: the general rule is often neither clear nor certain, and furthermore the historian lacks the means that would allow him to affirm that the known elements of the particular case coincide exactly with the necessary conditions of the general rule.

That the general rule is often not certain is demonstrated by Freud's second hypothesis: no clinical experience has confirmed the relation established by Freud between the absence of paternal authority and intellectual audacity. On the other hand, one could argue, the first hypothesis is amply confirmed by clinical experience: the relation between homosexuality and fixation on the mother has often been noted. That is true, but formulated in this way, the general rule is not sufficiently clear. First of all, this type of fixation is qualitative and it is only through the analysis of a concrete case that one can decide whether the fixation was powerful enough to prevent any possibility of heterosexual ties; one therefore runs a strong risk of begging the question. Secondly and above all, it is generally admitted that it is at the stage of the resolution of the Oedipal conflict that such a fixation can have a disruptive effect. In Leonardo's case, however, the story of his early y ars is extremely vague. We know that he left his mother between the ages of three and five years and went to live with his father (remarried in the meantime), who in a sense readopted him. In all probability, therefore, he entered on the Oedipal stage far from his mother, in a new family environment. One may well suppose that the attachment to the lost mother was more intense than the attachment to a mother who was present would have been, but that is only a conjecture. In fact, in a case such as this one only the clinical context could furnish the necessary details; and we are far from that. The indeterminacy of the particular context is thus added to the imprecision of the general rule, whence the existence of a double "as if."

Having arrived at this point in the discussion, the historian may decide to go no further. And yet, the difficulties are surmountable—both through a growing precision in the formulation of psychoanalytic hypotheses and through the elaboration of criteria that would endow with greater validity the application of the general rule to the particular context. The margin of indeterminacy would persist, but it would perhaps be possible to reduce it to acceptable proportions.

Four principal criteria seem to be necessary:

First, the criterion of *convergence,* which is one of the fundamental criteria of any scientific explanation. As Kaplan writes: "What counts in the validation of a theory, so far as fitting the facts is concerned, is the convergence of the data brought to bear upon it, the concatenation of the evidence. . . ."[47]

This criterion obviously implies, in psychohistory, the principle of documentary noncontradiction, or more exactly of a convincing degree of noncontradiction (on this latter point, only the intuitive judgment of the historian can provide an answer); it also corresponds to a fundamental psychoanalytic notion, that of *overdetermination.*

Overdetermination, according to the authors of *The Language of Psychoanalysis,* means that "formations of the unconscious (symptoms, dreams, etc.) can be attributed to a plurality of determining factors. This can be understood in two different ways: a) The formation in question is the result of several causes, since one alone is not sufficient to account for it; b) The formation is related to a multiplicity of unconscious elements which may be organized in different meaningful sequences, each having its own specific coherence at a particular level of interpretation. This second reading is the most generally accepted one."[48]

For the psychohistorian, the concept of overdetermination is essential: "Overdetermination does not mean," write Laplanche and Pontalis, "that the dream or symptom may be interpreted in an infinite number of ways. Freud compares dreams to certain languages of antiquity in which words and sentences appear to have various possible interpretations: in such languages ambiguity is dispelled by the context, by intonation or by extra signs. . . . Nor does overdetermination imply the independence or the parallelism of the different meanings of a single phenomenon. The various chains of meanings intersect at more than one 'nodal point,' as is borne out by the associations; the symptom bears the traces of the interaction of the diverse meanings out of which it produces a *compromise.*"[49]

We are clearly dealing here with a concept familiar to the historian: from his point of view, the outbreak of the World War in August 1914 is an over-determined phenomenon, the end point of various causal series, each of which unfolds at its own level but not independently of the others. The causal sequence constituted by the economic factors of the war is not independent of the one formed by the arms race or even by the rise of nationalisms. Their points of intersection are identifiable.

This additional parallelism between history and psychoanalysis gives the criterion of convergence a privileged position in the verification of psycho-historical explanations; it forms in a sense the basis of verification.

The second criterion is not unrelated to the first, even though it derives essentially from psychoanalytic theory itself. (This fact does not make our argument tautological, for we are supposing that the fundamental notions of psychoanalysis are generally accepted and can consequently be used to support certain verification criteria of psychohistorical explanation.) Clinical experience shows that ultimately there are only a limited number of plausible forms, or *Gestalten,* which can account in a coherent manner for the manifest elements of a given individual or collective behavior, for the unconscious impulses behind it, and, sometimes, for the identifiable facts or fantasies from which it originates.

For certain psychoanalysts, the manifestation of a formal pattern, in which all the elements of a case fall into place like the pieces of a puzzle, represents in itself a definitive proof of the only correct solution.[50] Some have even chosen this single criterion as a basis on which to found the possibility of the application of psychoanalytic theories to history: a particular structure of manifest data and their repetition, be it on the individual or collective level, is taken to indicate *the* underlying unconscious constellation, thus allowing for a precise psychohistorical explanation.[51]

Now the fact is, as we shall see when we discuss the problem of psycho-analytic biography, *that a single plausible pattern exists only very rarely.* It is, however, true that the number of coherent explanatory structures in a particular case is always limited, and this limitation is in itself a verification criterion from the psychohistorical point of view.

Let me cite a concrete example of *Gestalt* in the sense in which I am using it here. In this instance it is perhaps even possible to speak of a single pattern; I am referring to the case of Woodrow Wilson as it was analyzed by Alexander and Juliette George.[52]

We need not consider here the characteristics of Wilson's behavior in his "search for power." Once he acquired power, on the other hand, whether as president of Princeton, as governor of New York State or as president of the United States, he repeated, after a certain time, the identical pattern of self-destructive behavior: as soon as he encountered opposition on a subject that seemed to him important, he became rigid, lost all capacity for negotiation, endowed his own action with the character of a moral crusade and refused, in the name of absolute principles, any compromise with the enemy, which he soon identified with a specific individual. A strategy of flexibility and compromise would have allowed Wilson to get out of the impasse and eventually achieve his aims, but he insisted on maintaining his aggressive intransigence, wishing for only one thing: the absolute submission of his enemies. He ended up by guaranteeing his own defeat and provoking the ruin of his ambitions.

This pattern of repetitive behavior was so clear that even Wilson's "traditional" biographers noticed it; Arthur S. Link, for example, who is the most eminent contemporary specialist in this field, writes about Wilson's attitude while he was president of Princeton:

> The years of the Princeton presidency were among the most important in Wilson's life. The Princeton period was the microcosm of a later macrocosm, and a political observer, had he studied carefully Wilson's career as president of Princeton University, might have forecast accurately the shape of things to come during the period when Wilson was president of the United States. What striking similarities there are between the Princeton and national periods! During the first years of both administrations, Wilson drove forward with terrific energy and momentum to carry through a magnificent reform program, and his accomplishments both at Princeton and Washington were great and enduring. Yet in both cases he drove so hard, so flatly refused to delegate authority, and broke with so many friends that when the inevitable reaction set in he was unable to cope with the situation. His refusal to compromise in the graduate school controversy was almost Princeton's undoing; his refusal to compromise in the fight in the Senate over the League of Nations was the nation's undoing. Both controversies assume the character and proportions of a Greek tragedy. . . .[53]

A repetitive structure of behavior like the one we have been discussing clearly indicates an unconscious ambivalence toward the exercise of power: on the one hand, a practically limitless thirst for power, refusing the slightest concession that might appear as a limitation of power; on the other hand, a self-destructive attitude that lays bare the presence of strong guilt feelings as far as the possession of power is concerned—feelings that can only result in ruin (my own interpretation here is slightly different from the one proposed by the Georges). An interpretation of this kind is itself supported by certain conspicuous facts in the development of Wilson's personality, notably by the nature of his feelings toward his father: respect, devotion and unlimited love on the surface, but also, no doubt, a repressed hostility toward a man who, more than once during the crucial years of childhood, humiliated the future president.

The facts concerning Wilson's childhood are, in this instance, merely a supporting hypothesis, and we will have occasion later to see just how uncertain the biographical reconstruction is. The important thing is the convincing nature of the repetitive form of behavior that is observed, and, from the point of view of psychoanalytic theory, the practically obligatory character of the explanation that comes to mind.[54]

It is in relation to the third criterion, that of *comparability,* that the preceding criterion takes on a new dimension: when, in an individual, a para-doxical attitude toward others manifests itself in the same form at different periods in his life, as is the case with Wilson, this *Gestalt* suggests the existence of an unconscious psychic constellation that psychoanalytic theory allows us to identify. But this criterion will take on added significance if the historian observes a manifestation of the same form in a whole category of personalities linked to each other by other univocal common denominators (revolutionary personalities, religious reformers, etc.). This double compari-son can be considered as a practically empirical demonstration of the validity of the proposed explanation; in effect, if for a single personality the possi-bilities of comparison are limited, they are less so in a larger category, and one can always consider an additional case that will confirm (or weaken) the hypothesis.

The three criteria we have enumerated so far pertain either to the exhaustive study of a single case or to the comparative method, both of which are methods that the historian practices frequently and almost exclusively, and which the specialist in the "hard" social sciences will not reject either. The fourth criterion allows us to establish an even closer link with the current metho-dology of the social sciences: it is the criterion of *quantitative analysis,* which allows one to confirm psychohistorical hypotheses with the help of statistical analyses whose conceptual framework is more or less independent of psycho-analytic theory. This type of verification is not always possible or significant, and it requires in any case a separate investigation, one that is extremely precise and detailed. It can be applied to biographical studies as well as to the study of collective phenomena; one can use the content analysis that Alfred Baldwin was among the first to apply to the study of personality,[55] or have recourse to Schneidman's recent work on the logical idiosyncrasies present in all individual speech; finally, one can take as a model McClelland's statistical studies of certain collective motivations. It is the quantitative method as such that matters in this instance, rather than certain of its technical aspects, which are subject to change.[56]

The diverse verification criteria of psychohistorical explanation apply to biographical studies as well as to the analysis of collective phenomena; in both cases, one must look for the convergence of proofs, for significant structures, for comparability and for quantitative confirmation. But even an integral and simultaneous application of these four criteria leaves a greater margin of indeterminacy than the one confronting the traditional historian.

There has been a great deal of discussion about the problematic and sub-jective nature of historical explanation in general, but there is no historian (and here I am not including the philosophers of history) who is unaware that, in most fields of history, the discovery of new facts or of "missing links" gradually leads to a more precise understanding of the causes of a phenome-non, whether it be the fall of the Roman Empire, the Puritan revolution or the First World War. Our understanding of the fall of the Roman Empire is different from Gibbon's, but it is not a question of two equally valid interpre-tations: today we are better informed than Gibbon was. Now this cumulative process, this narrowing of the margin of error, will less easily find a place in psychohistory, even if psychoanalytic concepts are made more precise and the theory is further refined; for research concerning unconscious processes, whether individual or collective, outside a clinical context, *can never—by definition—be anything but indirect.* Typological comparisons and statistical investigations may indicate various plausible correlations, but *the explanation of these correlations* will still not be definitely established. Thus, paradoxically, to a greater extent than the other kinds of historical investigation, psychohistory will have not only to make systematic use of *Erklären—* explanation as it is envisaged in the social sciences—but will also, and simultaneously, have to continue relying on *Verstehen—*intuitive comprehension. To repeat what we have said before: by itself, intuitive comprehension can lead to absurdities; combined with explanation, it is not only justifiable, but is essential in a domain such as this one.

The Document

For the psychohistorian, a document is whatever reveals the psychic processes of the individual or group under study. That is a broad definition, but one that traditional historians would doubtless not reject. It was Henri Marrou who wrote that any source of information that the historian can use in order to know the past represents a document; consequently, a restrictive definition of the historical document is impossible.[57] A conception so broad, matched by the method of psychoanalysis itself, which seeks a meaning in the most massive symptoms as well as in the slightest word or deed, should, at least in principle, make psychohistory an excessively rich domain, teeming with possibilities.

But the line between excessive richness and confusion is a narrow one, especially if one takes account of a fact emphasized by Alphonse Dupront— namely, that psychoanalytic history, like psychoanalysis, is as interested in what is not said as in what is said, in what is not done as in what is done. What Dupront says about history in general is true above all of psychohistory: "We now know that silence itself speaks, if to no other effect than to make us aware of what has been destroyed and thus to oblige us to diversify our approaches in order to attain the lived reality of a period."[58] The meaning of a text's silence, or of an individual's or group's inertia, can only be judged in relation to certain words or certain actions whose obviousness and necessity strike us only afterward. But how much place that leaves for purely subjective interpretation!

We must also note the opposite difficulty: in biography as in the study of collective phenomena, a crucial piece of documentary evidence is often missing, concerning the childhood of the individual or a particular kind of family life, or else the mothering and child-raising practices of a whole group. Biographers fall prey to the temptations of generalization and analogy, and as Dominique Fernandez has noted, their interpretation is speedily reduced to an art of conjecture.[59] One can cite, in this context—even if it belongs only marginally to the domain of psychobiography—Sartre's attempt at a purely imaginary reconstruction in his biography of Flaubert, due to a lack of sufficient documents concerning the young Gustave's family life.[60] Above all, one can cite the "model" psychobiography, with its arbitrary inferences founded on manifestly insufficient documentation. In his study of the young Luther, Erikson literally invents little Martin's relation to his mother, using as a basis (as a "document") the behavior of Luther the man. Erikson writes:

> It has been surmised that [Luther's] mother suffered under the father's personality, and gradually became embittered; and there is also a suggestion that a certain sad isolation which characterized young Luther was to be found also in his mother, who is said to have sung to him a ditty: "For me and you nobody cares. That is our common fault."
>
> A big gap exists here, which only conjecture could fill. But instead of conjecturing half-heartedly, I will state, as a clinician's judgment, that nobody could speak and sing as Luther did if his mother's voice had not sung to him of some heaven; that nobody could be as torn between his masculine and feminine sides, nor have such a range of both, who did not at one time feel that he was like his mother; but also, that nobody could discuss women and marriage in the way he often did who had not been deeply disappointed by his mother—and had become loath to succumb the way she did to the father, to fate. And if the soul is man's most bisexual part, there we will be prepared to find in Luther both some horror of mystic succumbing and some spiritual search for it, and to recognize in this alternative some emotional and spiritual derivative of little Martin's "prehistoric" relation to his mother.[61]

This is enough to make the most well-disposed historian shudder. . . .

Erikson, one could argue, merely reconstructed a possible *Gestalt* on the basis of elements available to him, and the example in question shows the weakness of the verification criteria of psychohistorical explanation. In fact, that is not the case. Erikson does not interpret a repetitive behavior on young Luther's part in terms of an unconscious dynamic; he jumps from a presumed characteristic of the Reformer to the inferential reconstruction of essential data about the latter's family environment. We have here, instead of the legitimate confirmation of an outline whose essential shape is already traced, the creation of a quasi-arbitrary drawing. The virtuosity of the artist does not make the proceeding more acceptable.

If the absence or the paucity of documents is, in the last analysis, only a practical problem which at the very worst can force the historian to abandon his project, the ambiguity and polysemy of documents that do exist is, on the contrary, a complex problem inherent to psychohistory. Admittedly, even political texts, economic statistics, and workers' demands are subject to the most diverse interpretations; what are we then to say of a myth, a dream, an *acte manqué*, a convulsion or some other crisis in behavior, whether on the individual or the collective level? What are we to say of a fantasy? Let us take as an example a famous passage in Dostoevsky—Raskolnikov's dream in *Crime and Punishment,* in which the novel's hero sees himself as a child watching a drunken *muzhik* torture and finally kill a mare by forcing her to pull an overloaded cart. The mare is not able to go forward, the *muzhik* whips her all the harder: he whips her on the eyes, then exchanges the whip for a wooden shaft and the shaft for an iron crowbar, with which he finally finishes off the animal.[62]

For an interpretation of Dostoevsky's work and personality, Raskolnikov's dream seems to have a crucial importance. In *A Writer's Diary,* Dostoevsky recalls having witnessed, at the age of fifteen, a somewhat similar scene on the road to St. Petersburg: a drunken ministerial courier struck his coachman, and the coachman took vengeance on the animal.

> This disgusting scene [writes Dostoevsky] has remained in my memory all my life. Never was I able to forget it, or that courier, and many an infamous and cruel thing observed in the Russian people, willy-nilly, I was inclined for a long time thereafter to explain obviously in a too one-sided sense. . . . This little scene appeared to me, so to speak, as an emblem, as something which very graphically demonstrated the link between cause and effect. Here every blow dealt at the animal leaped out of each blow dealt at the man. In the late Forties, during the period of my most unrestrained and fervent dreams, it suddenly occurred to me that should I ever happen to found a philanthropic society, I would by all means engrave this courier's troika on the seal of the society, as an emblem and warning sign.[63]

May we then interpret Raskolnikov's dream as a kind of summary of the way Dostoevsky perceives Russian society in its entirety? Certainly, but this text can also be the expression of deeper obsessions. Thus, again in the *Writer's Diary,* Dostoevsky reports the same scene with a slight modification, but that modification is crucially significant. In Raskolnikov's dream, three figures give the scene its whole meaning: the drunken *muzhik*, the nag, and the terrified child looking on. In the other scene, Dostoevsky replaces the mare by the *muzhik*'s wife, retaining the other elements unchanged:

> He [the *muzhik*] is getting excited; he begins to savor the thing. Presently he becomes wild and this he realizes with pleasure. The animal shrieks of the woman go to his head as liquor. . . . At length she grows quiet; she shrieks no longer; now she merely groans wildly. . . . Suddenly, he throws away the strap; like a madman, he seizes a stick, a bough, anything, and breaks it over her back with three last, terrific blows.—No more. . . .The little girl . . . trembling on the oven in the corner tries to hide: she hears her mother shrieking.[64]

Here again, Dostoevsky recounts an event that really took place and which he read about in the newspapers, for the *muzhik*'s wife hanged herself. But the details of this scene and those of Raskolnikov's dream are practically identical: the use of the whip, then of the piece of wood, the terror of the child. One is tempted to seek, beneath the social meaning of this description, a more personal meaning, or perhaps an even deeper link to identical themes in dreams described by other Russian writers, thus moving from unconscious individual structures toward certain fundamental themes of a collective unconscious. This latter transposition is precisely what Alain Besançon accomplishes in his excellent essay, "The Function of Dreams in the Russian Novel."[65]

As for the personal meaning of this scene, it seems evident by its obvious sexual symbolism, by what we know of Dostoevsky's hatred of his father—the man the *muzhiks* called "the wild beast," and whom they eventually murdered—and by the circumstances of the child Fiodor's first epileptic seizure: "We know that when he was seven years old," writes Dominique Arban, "Fedia was woken up one night by cries and shouting, and ran to his parents' room. What spectacle met his eyes? He fell down, unconscious. We know no more about it, but isn't that sufficient?"[66]

The interpretation of Raskolnikov's dream is thus fraught with uncertainty.[67] But perhaps we are dealing here with an example of the process of overdetermination. In effect, the basic personal conflicts of the writer, his way of experiencing a problematic Russian reality, as well as the reactions that these attitudes provoked in the face of more immediate social problems, all seem to be imbricated in this dream. Understood in this way and submitted to a much more detailed exegesis—notably by comparing it to other dreams described in Dostoevsky's novels—such a document, however imprecise its meaning appears at first, could become a key piece of evidence for the understanding of the writer and of the fundamental themes of his work.

Paradigms of Psychohistory

There is no such thing as *one* generally accepted paradigm for the application of psychoanalytic theory to historical research. If, as far as biography is concerned, a generally acceptable model can be easily formulated, the study of collective behavior presents immediate difficulties. On this level, the "reductionist" paradigm used by Freud himself and by numerous psychoanalysts after him is unacceptable. We shall briefly discuss its shortcomings and then present three partial schemata, each of which is applicable only to some of the phenomena that interest the psychohistorian: the paradigm of psychoanalytic structuralism, the paradigm of culture and personality, and the paradigm of the internalization of social norms.

One can infer the general framework of psychobiography—in other words, the application of psychoanalytic concepts to biography—from the basic hypotheses of psychoanalysis: on the one hand, every personality forms a whole whose elements are linked to each other, and the observation of one aspect of the personality leads the way to an understanding of the dynamics of the whole; on the other hand, the individual speaks a series of languages (the language of words, that of nonverbal behavior, that of somatic reactions, etc.) whose manifest content masks a latent content. The manifest content of these languages generally provides enough perceptible indices to inform us of the nature of the latent content. As for this latent content, it is in large part determined both by the typical and the idiosyncratic development of the individual, especially by the unconscious intrapsychic conflicts that characterized that development. The aim of the biographer, like that of the therapist, is to discover—when such an investigation is possible—the key to the latent content of the various languages, by relating the manifest elements to each other and by studying the knowable aspects of the individual's evolution.

The therapeutic context is not essential to the decoding of the manifest content of an individual language. The historian, working at a distance—on defunct beings—can obviously not count on the verification of his hypotheses through the analytic dialogue, but he has other advantages that the analyst lacks: an overview of the subject's life, the availability of testimony by others,[68] as well as, possibly, the content analysis of texts or other quantitative means of verification.

The simplicity of the psychobiographical model should not mislead us, however; we shall see in the next chapter how difficult and uncertain its concrete application can be.

If one wishes to apply psychoanalysis to the historical investigation of collective behavior, one must first of all reject the Durkheimian argument according to which social behavior is exclusively the province of sociology. The opposition thus established, although it must be mentioned, is hardly convincing. In fact, when in his study of suicide Durkheim sought to demonstrate the uselessness of a recourse to psychology, he was not able, without that very psychology, to explain his sociological diagnosis.[69] And how are we to explain without psychology the relation between a Calvinist upbringing and a high degree of individual aggressivity, or between the system of the concentration camps and the victims' imitation of their tormentors, or again between a slave society and the infantile behavior of slaves? How can we explain without psychology the relation between the social structure of the Third Reich and the "final solution"?

The strict Durkheimian tradition was never followed (and for good reason) by Durkheim himself. According to Marcel Mauss, Durkheim was "always ready to accept the progress of psychology;" Mauss notes, furthermore, that in *Suicide* Durkheim was forced to refer to the rudimentary notions of "sthenia and asthenia, courage and weakness in the face of life."[70] For Marcel Mauss himself, a recourse to psychology in the explanation of "facts of collective consciousness" was essential;[71] but how can one dissociate the facts of collective behavior from facts of consciousness? Claude Lévi-Strauss[72] emphasizes this tendency in the thought of his teacher, and although he himself reacts against the excessive psychologizing of a certain kind of American social anthropology, he nevertheless recognizes the necessary complementarity of the two disciplines.

Turning to the domain of "pure" sociology, one notes that Talcott Parsons is attempting to discover the connections between social structure and the structure of the personality;[73] one also notes that Neal Smelser, after having been tempted by the purely sociological explanation of collective behavior,[74] is becoming one of the most convincing theoreticians arguing for the necessity of integrating sociology and psychology in order to arrive at a satisfactory explanation of the behavior of human groups.[75] "An adequate psychological theory is not possible unless it is, at the same time, social; and an adequate social theory is not possible unless it is, at the same time, psychological," writes Smelser.[76] Now for Parsons and for Smelser (and also for Mauss, considering the time when he was writing), the term "psychology" refers not to some vague discipline, but, quite clearly, to psychoanalysis. What sociology is tending to admit in this domain, the historian must also, *a fortiori*, admit: no historical explanation of collective behavior is possible, unless history assimilates psychology.

Having said this, we must still ask what model of application we can use. The situation here is not as clear as in the case of biography. We may mention, first of all, Freud's own way of proceeding, which we shall call "reductionist," using that term in its etymological sense rather than in a pejorative sense. Reduced to its simplest expression,[77] Freud's analysis implies the direct transposition to the collective level of mechanisms observed on the individual level, as well as the hypothesis, implicit or explicit, that these mechanisms allow one to explain the behavior of the group as of the individual, without the necessity of distinguishing between different levels of analysis. Freud is quite clear on this point: "No one can have failed to observe," he writes at the end of *Totem and Taboo,* "that I have taken as the basis of my whole position the existence of a collective mind, in which mental processes occur just as they do in the mind of an individual."[78] More emphatically and more specifically, he writes in *Moses and Monotheism*: "Early trauma—defence—latency—outbreak of neurotic illness—partial return of the repressed. Such is the formula which we have laid down for the development of a neurosis. The reader is now invited to take the step of supposing that something occurred in the life of the human species similar to what occurs in the life of individuals: of supposing, that is, that here too events occurred of a sexually aggressive nature, which left behind them permanent consequences but were for the most part fended off and forgotten, and which after a long latency came into effect and created phenomena similar to symptoms in their structure and purpose."[79] The same sweeping transposition occurs in *The Future of an Illusion,* where religion is identified as a collective obsessional neurosis,[80] and in *Civilization and Its Discontents,* where sublimation seems to function on the level of humanity as a whole according to the same rules one can discern on the individual level.

Freud arrives at this type of transposition by means of an inductive reasoning oriented toward the observation of individual phenomena. He reaches the conclusion that certain aspects of individual behavior can be explained by the hereditary effect of an ineradicable collective experience, whence the possibility of going from one level to another, from the collective to the individual and vice versa: "The behaviour of neurotic children towards their parents in the Oedipus and castration complexes abounds in such reactions," he writes, "which seem unjustified in the individual case and only become intelligible phylogenetically—by their connection with the experience of earlier generations."[81] Phylogenesis thus determines and explains ontogenesis.

As we know, this conception implies the hypothesis of an actual traumatic event occurring in the archaic past (the murder of the father of the primitive horde by his sons united against him) and the hereditary transmission of acquired characteristics—a kind of unconscious biological memory of the human species.

We need not repeat here the quasi-unanimous objections that have been raised against these hypotheses. Many psychoanalysts reject these hypotheses as well, for they are superfluous. It has been pointed out, for example, that the transmission of unconscious psychic material from generation to generation is conceivable without the necessity of postulating a biological memory, given the effect of a whole array of sociocultural institutions, whose possibilities include much more than the oral tradition mentioned by Freud.[82] As for the intensity of the Oedipal hostility and of the castration complex, which has often been demonstrated clinically and which is often inexplicable in terms of the objective relations between father and son, one can suggest that the beginnings of sexual maturation in the child, the intensity of his unconscious incestuous desires and the obvious difference in strength between father and son, are in themselves sufficient to account for it on the ontogenetic level. The explanation becomes even more convincing if one accepts the theory according to which the child's fear of castration is but the projection of his desire to castrate the father.[83] In either case, a recourse to phylogenesis is useless.

The reductionism of many psychoanalysts who have attempted to interpret collective phenomena of the past does not, therefore, necessarily follow from an acceptance of Freud's notions in this domain, but is due rather to the overall procedure that consists of explaining complex social and cultural phenomena by projecting on the large screen of society a few psychic mechanisms observed on the individual level, without distinguishing the two levels of analysis: the social and the psychological. Thus Géza Roheim gives us an explanation of the origins of monarchy based on the libidinal circulation between the phallus and the rest of the human body,[84] and he interprets the birth of agriculture in terms of Oedipal attitudes and castration anxiety.[85] As for Wilhelm Reich, he, like Freud, reduces religious feelings to a neurotic symptom: more exactly, he attributes it to guilt feeings caused by masturbation. In this context, the belief in God is but a "sexual excitation that has exchanged its goals and content."[86] In the same vein, Norman O. Brown[87] offers us an excremental theory of capitalism—and so on.

Roheim's extrapolations are harmless, compared to Hanns Sachs' thesis concerning the nondevelopment of a machine culture in the Roman Empire,[88] or to Kurt Eissler's delirious idea that the birth of the State of Israel was a direct consequence of the (unconscious) psychological effect of Freud's *Moses and Monotheism.*[89] This last example is an aberration, even from a "reductionist" point of view.

The reductionist thesis was stated unequivocally by Raymond de Saussure, when he wrote that in every civilization the relation between the individual and the society is identifiable with the relation between the individual and the father, according to a kind of measurable index one could call the "libidinal index of a civilization." This index would ostensibly allow one to evaluate the force of the superego in a given cultural entity, and deduce from that the specific manifestations of the libido. Thus, for example, the greater the severity of paternal authority, the greater will be the homosexual tendencies in the society in question.[90]

Obviously, one cannot absolutely prove that the reductionist position is false, but every historian knows that a social phenomenon must above all be analyzed in its own terms of reference, as a social phenomenon, not as the resultant of individual actions or as the projection of psychic conflicts observable only on the individual level. Such is the argument of the "two levels of analysis," formulated in particularly lucid terms by Talcott Parsons.

Parsons emphasizes that our present state of knowledge concerning social systems does not allow us to consider them as the resultant of individual motivations, especially given the fact that there is no simple correspondence between the structure of personality and the structure of institutions. Because of this, the problems of motivation must be treated in the framework of their relation to the overall social structure, taking into account the forces that tend to maintain or to transform the latter.[91]

In other words, the study of a social phenomenon, in any perspective whatsoever—including the perspective of psychological analysis—requires, first of all, that one examine the sociological factors in order to arrive at an explanation of the phenomenon according to its "natural" rules of interpretation. Only after that can one undertake the psychological investigation which, in the majority of cases, is an indispensable complement to the sociological study.

The distinction between the two levels of analysis is essential, with one exception (and here is where the second paradigm of the psychohistorical explanation of collective phenomena comes into play)—that of "psychoanalytic structuralism," which in principle is conceivable only on the level of psychological analysis, since its domain is that of symbolic relations.[92]

According to psychoanalytic structuralism (as I propose to call it), a cultural and social phenomenon can express, through its symbolic manifestations, a singular pattern, a specific structure that can also be found in the symbolic expression of other phenomena belonging to the same sociocultural entity. These structures reveal a specific unconscious model of the sociocultural entity in question.

The "genetic" explanation of these structures is impossible, and one can therefore not reduce their origin to a particular type of family or to certain primary institutions of the group. Consequently, psychoanalytic history cannot claim to provide causal explanations, since even the exact sequence of events is not available to it; it must first of all identify the patternings and the transformations of constant psychic elements in a specific historical context, and, above all, interpret the meaning of these symbolic patterns, be it in a culture, a religion, or an ideological system.[93] These symbolic patterns can in principle correspond to the most varied unconscious constellations, but one particular pattern occupies "a dominant strategic position": it is the Oedipus complex. Only the resolution of the Oedipal conflict makes possible the socialization of the individual, the passage from the family triangle to the society; it is in the universal context of Oedipus that the historian's unconscious will encounter that of the men he is studying; finally, Oedipus provides the model for the relation between man and authority, whatever its nature—religious, ideological, or political.[94]

Psychoanalytic structuralism differs radically from the reductionism of the preceding paradigm; its justification is the same as that of any structuralist analysis. One must note, however, that its field of application is quite specific, for the analysis of symbolic networks is possible only when it is applied to a culture considered in its totality, or else to a limited phenomenon envisaged in its relation to the surrounding culture and to its most general mode of expression.

We are thus dealing here with a paradigm of macrohistorical explanation. It can be used for the analysis of collective mentalities, for the study of a culture as a total phenomenon, or possibly in studies seeking to discover in a national character certain underlying characteristics. It can be used, but prudently, for—as we hardly need point out—psychoanalytic structuralism is faced with the same theoretical and methodological problems that confront any structuralist undertaking.

We shall not attempt here a discussion of structuralism in general; it is beyond doubt, however, that in order to be convincing, any structuralism must be absolutely rigorous.[95] Now the fact is that, from this point of view, the concrete applications are sometimes aleatory. Lévi-Strauss has been criticized for the often approximate character of his demonstrations, as well as for his rather arbitrary handling of examples (not to mention his choice of examples itself).[96] Yet, due to the fact that he concentrates on purely formal relations between elements rather than on interpretations of content,[97] Lévi-Strauss's structuralism is probably more rigorous than psychoanalytic structuralism. It is perhaps dangerous to use in psychohistory a method of analysis that would reinforce the indeterminate character of psychohistorical explanation. Nevertheless, the attractiveness of this kind of approach is undeniable.

Those who reject Freud's "reductionism" and recognize that the application of psychoanalytic structuralism is at best limited might turn to two other paradigms, which in fact are those we shall refer to most often in this book: the paradigm of culture and personality, and the paradigm of "continuous internalization."

In a very simplified way, one can say that society influences the development and the behavior of the individual personality in four principal ways: through the influence of "primary institutions" on the child; through the constant adaptation of the ego to its environment; through the internalization—throughout the existence of the individual, on the level of the superego as well as on that of the ego—of the basic social norms; finally, through the reactions that are provoked on the level of the individual unconscious by the symbolic systems adopted by the society.[98]

Conversely, in the interaction between the society and the individual, the latter exerts an influence on his environment through his emotional investment or disinvestment in the existing norms and institutions, through the creation of new symbolic systems (cf. the influence of religious or artistic expression on social evolution, and vice versa) and through the creation of new norms (cf. the influence of charismatic personalities in politics or in religion).

The schemata I shall present in the pages that follow are but the elaboration of these basic kinds of interaction. I shall concentrate only on the socialization of the child through the mediation of the primary institutions and on the models of internalization, for the other types of interaction are in a sense obvious. But it is important to emphasize that these diverse kinds of interactions function simultaneously, in stable or temporary homogeneous groups as in heterogeneous ones. *There exist only differences in degree.* I shall merely outline here in a very general way a type of analysis whose specific aspects and variations I shall treat in detail in chapter 3.

What do we mean by "homogeneous" and "heterogeneous" groups? The homogeneous group is characterized by a relative absence of social differentiation, by a high degree of isolation from the outside world, or else by the unifying role of an ideology, a collective obsession, a "total institution"[99] or a personality. If the homogeneous group has control over unified primary institutions (mothering and child-raising practices, etc.), it can be considered stable; if not, then such a group is generally temporary. As for the heterogeneous group, it is socially diversified, in permanent contact with other groups, and its primary institutions are not unified.

The paradigm of interaction between culture and personality—the one, in other words, that places the greatest emphasis on the socialization of the child by means of the primary institutions—applies essentially to stable homogeneous groups as the dominant paradigm.[100] It goes without saying, however, that, except for the temporary homogeneous groups in which primary institutions seem to play no role whatsoever, this same paradigm functions, in a more diffuse but nevertheless real way, in heterogeneous groups as well. We may summarize the paradigm as follows:

The culture and the social structure of a group determine in a specific manner the evolution of the personality of the members of the group, on the level of conscious attitudes but above all on the unconscious level. This unconscious development derives from *the manner in which the ego of the members of the group integrates the elements of the surrounding culture and society into each stage of the development of the personality*—the various stages of childhood as well as the ulterior phases, notably that of adolescence.[101]

The personality thus shaped by the specific interaction between the culture of a group and the attitude toward the world of its members at the various stages of their development will in turn influence the social structure of the group through the way in which the roles assigned to each of its members are fulfilled; the individual personality will also influence the culture of the group through various practices as well as through the works of members of the group. This interaction, which appears circular, does not at all exclude the diachronic dimension, as we shall see.

Given the fact that in adolescence the crucial phases of the individual's evolution are already completed, it is obvious that it is the family structure characteristic of a group, its various mothering, toilet-training, and general disciplinary practices (its "primary institutions") that determine the formation of certain typical unconscious aspects of the personality of the members of the group—their "basic personality." "The basic personality," writes Mikel Dufrenne, "designates a particular psychological configuration characteristic of the members of a given society and manifesting itself in a certain style of life on which individuals imprint their own particular variations. The combination of traits that compose this configuration (for example, a certain aggressivity combined with certain beliefs, with a certain suspiciousness toward others, with a certain weakness of the superego) may be called the basic personality—not because it constitutes, strictly speaking, a personality, but because it constitutes the basis of the personality for the members of the group, the "matrix" in which character traits are developed."[102]

For Kardiner and Linton, as for Erikson, the typical unconscious traits of the members of a sociocultural entity are reflected on the level of the group's "secondary institutions" (according to Kardiner's terminology): thus the religious rites, the matrimonial practices or the behavior in war of the Alorese, the Comanches, the Sioux, or the Yuroks are the result of the specific shaping of the individual by the primary institutions of the group, which influence his unconscious development. Formed by the primary institutions, the group's basic personality determines certain essential characteristics of the secondary institutions.[103]

Let us take the example of the Alorese studied by Kardiner and Linton (and especially by their collaborator, Cora DuBois).[104] One of the dominant characteristics of Alorese society consists in the fact that most of the agricultural work necessary for the subsistence of the community is done by women. One important result of this is that the mother cannot take care of the newborn child: around two weeks after giving birth, she goes back to work. The child is left to the "care" of his brothers and sisters, who feed him irregularly, tease him, maltreat him, and on the whole behave toward him in the most arbitrary manner. There is no discipline, no systematic upbringing, not even a coherent mode of punishments and rewards. The child grows up with an attitude of generalized distrust, doubt, and shame.

The basic personality of the Alorese will be characterized by passivity, the absence of curiosity, the absence of initiative and of any capacity for organization, but also by a profound distrust of others and by sudden, sporadic, and violent outbreaks of aggressivity. The secondary institutions bear the trace of this typical personality.

The Alorese male has perfected an extremely complex but totally unproductive financial system, and his life is spent in exchanges and barters whose sole objective is to acquire, by means of a totally fictitious wealth, a certain prestige that will compensate for his fundamental feeling of frustration and inferiority. The initial hostility toward the mother is reflected in the relation between the sexes: it is the women who do the courting in Alorese society, and the divorce (or infidelity) rate is particularly high. Finally, the Alorese religion also bears the traces of distrust: nothing is expected from a rather ill-defined, supreme divinity, and "the spirits of the dead are but impatient creditors who must be nourished through sacrifices that are brought to them with a great deal of reluctance: so poor is the balance between frustration and reward, so great is the distrust. Naturally, there is no question of assuring the favor of the gods through moral behavior: in fact, the Alorese do not possess a moral conscience."[105]

The notion of basic personality has not been confirmed beyond a doubt empirically,[106] but the reason for this could be our lack of sufficient knowledge concerning certain crucial aspects of the first stages of human development, whence the diversity of interpretations regarding the interaction between the individual and society through these stages. Thus, despite the generalization of the Eriksonian "model" relative to the first stage of the relations between the child and his environment, a more orthodox Freudian conception is also possible, and so is a Kleinian conception of the same stage. But whatever option one chooses, the conclusions will be too general not to affect the empirical studies; it is actually about "the nature of the child's tie to its mother"[107] that we must seek to arrive at a firm and unanimous judgment, one that will allow us to analyze with precision the interaction between a certain type of maternal care and a certain type of evolution in the child. The current lack of precision in this domain does not affect the value of the "culture and personality" paradigm as an ideal type, nor its possibilities of general or partial application. One must simply keep in mind that one is dealing in this instance with a heuristic schema, rather than with a model whose various elements are all empirically confirmed.

One can go a step further, and introduce a diachronic dimension into this apparently static context. A significant change in the social structure, due to endogenous and exogenous factors, will doubtless provoke changes in the family structure and eventually in the primary institutions; consequently, certain characteristics of the basic personality will be modified, and so on.

We thus dispose of a quite simple model of change, adaptable to crisis situations—those involving sudden changes—by considering the following alternatives: either a sudden change in the family structure is accompanied by the adaptation of individual development to the new context (in that case we have a return to gradual evolution), or else there is a continued inadaptation between the relations existing inside the family group and the changes occurring in the environmental structure. In the latter case, individual development remains arrested at the previous stage and a serious long-term crisis occurs; it will be resolved either by the belated adaptation of the family and the individual to the new social structure, or by a social restructuring that will signal a kind of return to the *status quo ante*.

This model of evolution is obviously very rudimentary, and there exists in fact a large number of variations on it. The major difficulty on the concrete level comes from the differences in rhythm that one finds between the evolution of the social structure, the evolution of the basic elements of the culture of the group and the evolution of the family structure. It would seem that basic cultural elements and family structure evolve more slowly than the other components of the social structure; the result is a series of syncopations whose influence on the development and on the socialization of the individual is difficult to determine. But here again, the paradigmatic value of the proposed model is evident, despite the technical difficulties in its application.

The primary institutions are the key element in the model we have been discussing. The model is dominant in the study of stable homogeneous groups, inapplicable to the study of temporary homogeneous groups (in which the primary institution plays no role), and has only a supporting explicative role in the case of heterogeneous groups where the primary institutions are diversified and where it is difficult to determine their common characteristics. This is why the study of heterogenous groups requires that one have recourse to a different explicative model, one in which the socialization of the child by means of the primary institutions is secondary and where the individual's internalization of the norms of the group becomes essential. One can observe, in fact, that the individual internalizes certain social norms throughout his existence, not only through the channel of the superego but also through that of the ego, given the interaction between the total personality and the social environment.

Freud already glimpsed this possibility, but —to be perfectly frank—there is no thesis one cannot prove by invoking a few chance remarks he let fall. . . . It is Talcott Parsons who stated the most convincing case for an enlargement of the areas of interaction between the social structure and the structure of the personality (including, incidentally, the id among the components of the personality subject to the direct influence of the social structure—a hypothesis difficult to accept in theory and impossible to demonstrate empirically, given the nature of the id).[108] Parson's theses were adopted and elaborated on the basis of ample psychoanalytic material by Fred Weinstein and Gerald M. Platt,[109] who demonstrated that certain essential aspects of the psychoanalytic study of collective phenomena were otherwise impossible.

On the static level, this model requires no other explanation than the one implicit in the very definition of internalization, namely: "all those processes by which the subject transforms real or imagined regulatory interactions with his environment, and real or imagined characteristics of his environment, into inner regulations and characteristics."[110] On the other hand, *an interpretation of social change* based, on the psychological level, on the notion of internalization, is not as self-evident as the processes of change that occur in homogeneous groups. In this regard, one can propose the following points:[111]

In a heterogenous group, certain fundamental norms essential to the existence of the group as such are internalized by the majority of the members of the group, by means of a constant interaction between the social structure and the structure of the individual personality, on the levels of the superego and of the ego. The emotional investment linked to this internalization is transposed, and is integrated into the symbolic system that expresses the norms in question. The fact that one symbolic system is adopted rather than another is due to its conformity with the social context, but also with the affective needs[112] of the members of the group.

A transformation of the symbolic system without any change in norms represents a *reordering,* not a transformation, of the social system. In order to be adopted, a new symbolic system must conform to the new social situation, but it must also satisfy the affective needs of the majority of the members of the group. A transformation of the fundamental norms themselves represents a *transformation* of the entire social system. The new norms, emerging from the old system or from one coexisting with it, will impose themselves according to the evolution of the social system and according to the ease with which they are internalized by the members of the group, depending on their fundamental affective needs.

According to this model, the essential causes of the reordering or the transformation of a social system are social, not psychological, in nature. However, the integration of a new symbolic system (in the case of reordering) or of new norms (in the case of transformation) into the society in question depends not only on social factors, but also on the affective reactions of a majority of the members of that society—facts that are interpretable only in psychological terms.

Determinism and Individual Freedom in Psychoanalysis

Psychoanalytic theory is compatible with the notion of individual freedom.

Why should we, in concluding this outline of the theoretical framework of psychohistorical investigation, insist on this particular point, when on the whole we have left it up to the reader to become acquainted with the fundamental aspects of Freudian thought? First of all, because this subject is fraught with confusion, but also because the "traditionalist" historians conceive of psychoanalysis as inexorably deterministic, and for that reason reject its utilization in a context which, according to them, still implies the active presence of free choice.

The imprecision that surrounds the concept of a free ego in psychoanalytic theory is due in large part to explicit or implicit "ideological" premises, according to which no discipline can be considered scientific unless its field of study is subject to the laws of a strict determinism. For the representatives of experimental psychology, the necessity of reducing the totality of the field of human behavior to quantitative sequences is not open to doubt; according to them, it is only by this means that psychology can escape from metaphysics and become one of the exact sciences.[113]

The preponderant influence of Fechner's and Brücke's deterministic theories on Freud's thought has often been mentioned, and it was only after 1923, with the publication of *The Ego and the Id,* that Freud seems to make some allowance for an autonomous ego. On the whole, however, the position of the founder of psychoanalysis may be defined as deterministic in the fullest sense of the term; and the great majority of psychoanalysts follow in his path. Ernest Jones, for example, admits the possibility that "the irruptions of spontaneous and unrelated phenomena supposedly emanating from 'free will' would make nonsense of its [psychoanalysis'] scientific pretentions."[114] Consequently, for many psychoanalysts "the autonomy of the ego is strictly relative,"[115] and in the last analysis the human being's sense of free will does not correspond to any objective reality.[116] Even Erik H. Erikson's use of these terms lends itself to confusion, and one has the impression—at least in the theoretical part of his work—that free will is nothing but a purely subjective experience on the part of the individual. Thus, in discussing the various aspects of the second stage of the development of the personality, Erikson states that it is at this time that a "sense of self-control without loss of self-esteem is the ontogenetic source of a sense of free-will."[117]

The same is not true of the works of Heinz Hartmann and especially of David Rapaport, the two outstanding theorists of "ego psychology." Heinz Hartmann describes the autonomy of the ego in the following terms:

> Not every adaptation to the environment, or every learning and maturation process, is a conflict. I refer to the development "outside of conflict" of perception, intention, object comprehension, thinking, language, recall-phenomena, productivity, to the well-known phases of motor development, grasping, crawling, walking, and to the maturation and learning processes implicit in all these and many others.... I propose that we adopt the provisional term "conflict-free ego sphere" for that ensemble of functions which at any given time exert their effects outside the region of mental conflicts.[118]

Later, Hartmann qualified these functions as "autonomous functions of the ego."

The enumeration of the autonomous functions of the ego offered by Hartmann does not indicate whether, outside the cognitive, mnesic, and other processes, the ego can also escape from the determinism of the unconscious in the use of its selective and creative functions—in other words, whether an autonomous will is conceivable. In fact, an examination of Hartmann's work as a whole confirms the impression that in his conception of the ego there is a place for the exercise of will as an autonomous function, even though the term "free" is never used, chiefly for semantic reasons.

It was above all David Rapaport, however, who undertook to integrate the notion of a free ego into the framework of psychoanalytic theory. "The behavior of man is determined by the instincts he harbors within him, but he is not entirely at their mercy; he possesses a certain independence in relation to them," writes Rapaport, and he goes on:

> We refer to this independence as *the autonomy of the ego from the id.* The most common observation which necessitated this conception was the responsiveness and relevance of behavior to external reality. But this dependence of behavior on the external world and on experience is not complete either. Man can interpose delay and thought not only between instinctual promptings and action, modifying and even indefinitely postponing drive discharge, he can likewise modify and postpone his reaction to external stimulation. This independence of behavior from external stimulation we will refer to as *the autonomy of the ego from external reality.* Since the ego is never completely independent from the id nor from external reality, we always speak about *relative* autonomy. [And Rapaport concludes:] While the *ultimate guarantees of the ego's autonomy from the id* are man's constitutionally given apparatuses of reality relatedness, the *ultimate guarantees of the ego's autonomy from the environment* are man's constitutionally given drives.[119]

Rapaport's conception does not actually exclude the acceptance of psychic determinism in a very general sense: *a free act, in effect, is not an unexplainable act without a cause; it is a voluntary act that implies the existence of choice; ex post facto, however, this choice can be explained, and its cause can be found. Free acts are not imposed on one by a psychic compulsion, but that does not mean that they have no cause.*[120]

Interpreting Rapaport's theses a bit, one can consider the elements of unconscious determinism studied by psychoanalysis as *limits* imposed on the activity of a creative ego which, within the framework of its limits, remains a sovereign entity, even though it is subject to causality. It follows that the more "neurotic" a personality is, the more restricted is the field available to the free ego. In the case of psychosis this field disappears altogether, and the human being is wholly under the sway of unconscious forces over which he has no control. The opposite situation, one in which the impact of unconscious determinism would be reduced to zero and where the whole person would exist in a state of unlimited possibilities where his creative freedom could exercise itself with no obstacles, is inconceivable. One can suggest, however, that in extreme situations, in experiences of total possibility—the "peak experiences" that Abraham Maslow speaks about[121]—the individual approaches a state of this kind. It matters little to us where the free ego originates—indeed, all speculation on this subject is useless—but we postulate that it is not a subjective illusion without any corresponding reality.

Such a conception is in fact easily integrated into the developmental model proposed by Erikson and into his hypotheses on the formation of identity, notably in the course of adolescence—this despite the ambiguity of some of Erikson's statements concerning the reality of individual freedom.

For the author of *Childhood and Society,* the identity of the self corresponds to an internal feeling of continuity and cohesion, which the individual also hopes to make perceptible to others. Now in their quest for identity, adolescents elaborate what Erikson calls their "internal life design."[122] That is a key term. In effect, even if Erikson's writings are ambiguous, so that one can, if one wishes, conceive of individual identity as a simple resultant of solutions elaborated in the previous stages of development, is it not more convincing to think of the "internal life design" as a free project, a necessary axis of individual identity, without which identity itself cannot be achieved? Nevertheless, this internal life design, this choice, will not find its most mature and most meaningful formulation unless the individual has succeeded in resolving the problems that marked the previous stages of his development, and in integrating the positive solutions with the unconscious options available in the course of each of these stages.

2. Is Psychoanalytic Biography Possible?

Of all the fields of historical research, that of biography seems at first glance to be best suited to the utilization of psychoanalysis. It is here that psychoanalytic theories are most often applied, and here that psychohistory has claimed its most far-reaching results—but it is also here that the aspirations of psychohistory have most often been questioned.

From the very beginnings of the psychoanalytic movement, the lives of "great men" have provoked considerable interest. The "Wednesday seminars" conducted by Freud and his closest collaborators were often devoted to the biographical analysis of famous writers: Lenau, Wedekind, Jean-Paul, Konrad Ferdinand Meyer, Grillparzer, and Kleist, to mention the best known ones.[1] It was at one of these seminars, in 1909, that Freud presented his interpretation of the personality of Leonardo da Vinci; his paper, published the following year,[2] constitutes his major contribution to psychobiography (save for his later biography of Woodrow Wilson, written in collaboration with William Bullitt[3]).

The naive self-assurance of the first psychoanalysts, the apparent ease with which they could, on the basis of a few key pieces of evidence and a few key theoretical concepts, arrive at original "discoveries" concerning the people studied, as well as the total absence of historical training on the part of the analysts—all these factors made the psychobiographies of the heroic period (and many later psychobiographies as well) no more than dilettantish studies, superficial at best.[4] As for Freud himself, his remarks on "Dostoevsky and parricide" are too short and too casual to warrant criticism; his interpretation of a childhood dream of Leonardo, on the other hand, is for the most part based on an error: a wrong translation of the name of a bird, which plays a major role in the interpretation.[5]

Recently, controversies have again come to the fore with the publication of the Freud-Bullitt biography of Wilson and various studies devoted to King George III of England; these controversies, moreover, concern more than just the studies in question. In the case of George III, for example, it is not only

Guttmacher's psychobiography[6] or some other psychoanalytic interpretation of the king's illness that has been challenged; rather, once again, it is psychoanalysis as a whole that is being rejected.[7] The debate, then, goes on.

Psychobiography, its critics might argue, eliminates the social dimension and has all the pitfalls, comic and otherwise, of the "stories of great men." That, of course, is not true. Anyone who has followed our discussion until now will realize that there can be no explanation of individual behavior without a constant integration of the latter into a social context, one that marks the individual not only in childhood (through the socialization of the child in the framework of the primary institutions), but that molds the personality throughout one's lifetime—both during the crucial period that determines the formation of the individual personality, and in later periods through the permanent internalization of social norms. Conversely, the individual influences the society, especially if he creates new symbols or new norms. He then plays a major historical role. One cannot study Luther without investigating the social and religious context that produced him—but can one study Protestantism without studying Luther, or Bolshevism without Lenin, or Nazism without Hitler?

Still, why can't one simply study the work itself, whether it be an artistic creation, a political decision or a set of new social norms? What is the importance of biography as the study of a life? The answer is simple: the work is not comprehensible independently of the personality that created it. The personality is a single entity: the study of the work and of the personality forms a single whole. The work, which reflects the society and the personality, is at the same time the expression of something that transcends both the one and the other.

The aim of the biographer will be to discover the link between the personality and the work, to rediscover the coherence that characterizes any personality and its creation—and to do this not only on the synchronic level but also through time, in the genuinely historical dimension. The demonstration of the cohesion of the personality is essential to the demonstration of the coherence of the work.

The conception of the personality as an identifiable, coherent whole is, in itself, not open to doubt. Personal experience or introspection demonstrates its validity and psychoanalytic theory confirms it, as does experimental psychology. Experimental studies on child behavior, for example, bear out the astonishingly permanent character of an individual personality "style," even during the phase of development where everything is transformed: "As one notes behavioral alterations from infancy to . . . later pre-school ages," write Heider and Escalona, "one knows that not a single behavior has remained the same, yet one is struck with the inherent continuity of behavioral style and of the child's pattern of adaptation."[8] Psychoanalysts discovered, quite early, this unity of style or of type in the neurotic personality,[9] but in so doing they were simply restating a very old theory concerning the "styles" or "types" of personality in general. A report in the *British Journal of Psychology* shows that recent experimental and statistical studies have led to a classification of individuals into types that correspond exactly—leaving aside the differences in terminology—to Galen's medieval classification.[10]

We shall come back, at the end of this chapter, to the problems raised by typological studies; for the moment, it is the question of the relation between the typical and the idiosyncratic that must be considered. Here again, one might ask, should biography not yield to a different kind of study, one that seeks to discover "styles" or "types" as such? The answer, as one might suspect, is negative. A style and a type are probably determined by certain similarities in hereditary traits and in environment. But every individual represents a variation in relation to the type, and if the latter provides a general pattern, the idiosyncratic variation denotes a specific one. Even if the individual life project cannot ignore certain limits imposed on it by the social framework and by the typical elements (in our present sense of the term), it nevertheless remains unique, even while assimilating certain social and typical constraints. The biographer studies the interaction between the free, individual life project and the determinisms that shape it.

These general remarks do not, however, indicate the difficulties encountered by psychobiography on the concrete, practical level.

Some Problems and Pitfalls of Psychobiography

Let us take the case of Adolf Hitler. The biographer will have no difficulty sketching in the relevant social context. A typical pattern will also appear, even though certain of its elements will be contradictory. The "paranoid" style generally attributed to Hitler is in fact selective: if, toward the Jews, his attitude reveals the presence of psychosis, his paranoid tendencies diminish considerably in the face of a concrete political or military situation, and are replaced either by a flexible and realistic evaluation of the situation or by an obsessional impulse to action, a feeling that time is short and that one lightning strike has to follow another if the decrees of Providence are to be fulfilled. The internal coherence of behavior is there and can be identified, but the usual typologies risk leading one astray, due to their too facile schematization.

The real difficulty, however, lies elsewhere: the biographer will not be able to avoid interpreting one of the dominant elements in Hitler's mental universe, namely his anti-Semitism. The biographer will describe it but will also attempt to explain it, and, according to the usual way of proceeding in psychobiography, he will try to indicate its origin by referring to certain known elements in the development of Hitler's personality. The case of Hitler is a particularly good example, because it allows us to compare the results of a series of interpretations of a single phenomenon.

Erikson's explanation is an indirect one: in the chapter of *Childhood and Society* entitled "The Myth of Hitler's Youth," he explains Nazi anti-Semitism in terms of the identity crisis, without, however, referring to the Führer's personal motivations.[11] According to Gertrud M. Kurth, on the other hand, Hitler's murderous anti-Semitism was an unconscious reaction to powerful incestuous impulses which were themselves obviously repressed but which provoked an intolerable feeling of guilt and were projected onto an external figure: the Jew. Hitler's life manifests some notable quasi-incestuous relations; in his writings, the Jew is associated with incest; during his adolescence, the Jewish doctor Bloch took the place of the father next to his beloved mother, thus establishing, according to Gertrud M. Kurth, the link between Hitler's incestuous tendencies and the figure of the Jew. She writes: "The connection I am bold enough to believe I have established is the paradoxical conclusion that the torrent of apocalyptic horrors that engulfed six million Jews was unleashed in the futile endeavor to exterminate that incestuous, black-haired little monster that was Adolf Hitler's Mr. Hyde."[12]

Georges Devereux, in turn, presents a quasi-rational theory to account for Hitler's exterminating orders: "Let us recall," he writes, "the way Genghis Khan and Hitler recruited some of their cadres. Their absolute loyalty, like that of the Mau-Maus, was guaranteed precisely by the fact that their initiation involved such hideous crimes that in executing them they 'burned their bridges' behind them, thus making it impossible for them to re-enter society except as absolute victors."[13] Admittedly, this "political" exploitation of the murder of the Jews does not exclude the possibility of profoundly irrational motives. It is the latter that are emphasized by Gustav Bychowski, according to whom Hitler's pathological anti-Semitism was related to a deep psychosexual conflict and probably represented the effect of a projection of frustrated sexual desires on the part of the dictator.[14]

We may mention briefly the study by Rudolph Binion in which Binion concludes that Hitler identified his mother's fate (in his mind she was poisoned by the Jewish doctor's harmful injections) with his own poisoning by gas in 1918. His aim therefore became to avenge that double poisoning, with which the Jews were directly associated.[15]

With Walter Langer, whose study was written during the war for the American Secret Service but was only recently published, we return to a very general explanation in which Hitler's hatred of the Jews is interpreted broadly in terms of projection: all of Hitler's undesirable characteristics were projected onto the Jews—among these characteristics, Langer mentions in particular a tendency toward feminine passivity and sexual perversion. Through the effect of projection it was the Jew who came to symbolize sexual perversion, and if Hitler felt poisoned by his perverse self, it was the Jew who became the poison. "In his treatment of the Jews we see the 'Identification with the Aggressor' mechanism at work," writes Langer. Hitler, in other words, applied to the Jews in reality the treatment he feared he would receive from his victors in fantasy. This brought him several kinds of gratification. First, he could appear in the eyes of the world as the pitiless brute he imagined himself to be; second, it was a way of proving to himself that he was as brutal and merciless as he wanted to be; third, by eliminating the Jews he felt unconsciously that he was ridding himself, and Germany, of the poison that lay at the source of all their troubles; fourth, as the masochist he was in reality, he obtained a "vicarious" pleasure from the suffering of others, with whom he identified himself; fifth, he could express his deep hatred and scorn for the world in general by using the Jews as scapegoats; finally, his action brought him considerable material benefits, as well as serving him greatly in terms of propaganda.[16]

Robert G. L. Waite finds in Hitler all the general traits of the anti-Semite, but he adds to these a series of specific traits: first of all, Hitler's hatred of the Jews was a projection of his intense self-hatred, as well as of his guilt feelings. For Waite, in effect, as for Gertrud Kurth, Hitler projected on the Jews his violent incestuous impulses as well as his tendencies toward sexual perversion (of which Waite, like Walter Langer, offers us a detailed description). Furthermore, Hitler's morbid attachment to his mother, his hostility toward his father, the identification of the latter with the Jewish doctor who took care of the mother during her last illness, notably by administering numerous injections—all this indicates the "Oedipal" character of Hitler's anti-Semitism and brings us back both to the theme of incest and to that of poison. Waite also emphasizes the compensatory character that the extermination of the Jews had for Hitler—it acted as a compensation for his own physical inadequacies, for his feelings of doubt, as well as for his conviction that the war could not be won, a conviction that became virtually a certainty for him around the beginning of 1942; it is at that time, according to Waite, that Hitler made the final decision to exterminate all the Jews.[17] Finally, Waite invokes the plausible hypothesis that Hitler believed he had Jewish blood in his veins; considering all the other factors, that belief was enough to provoke in him the most extreme destructive fury, whereby he sought to deny any possibility of being himself infected in some way by Jewish blood.[18]

In my own study of Nazi anti-Semitism I devoted a chapter to the anti-Semitism of Adolf Hitler, the conclusions of which can be summarized in three essential points. The general aspects of Hitler's hatred of the Jews are linked to a deep psychosexual conflict whose Oedipal character appears obvious: the Jew is identified with the hated father, all the more so since Hitler seems to have been informed relatively early of the latter's possible Jewish origin; the psychosexual conflict was in this case intimately linked to a violent identity conflict: was Hitler "German" or "Jewish?" In order to extirpate the Jew he bore within him, Hitler undertook to eliminate the Jews around him, pursuing them to the ends of the earth; as for his fantasy identifying the Jew with an element of pollution of the blood, of sexual pollution linked to bio-logical infection—*notably to syphilis*—it can be explained both in terms of the Oedipal conflict and its analogical corollaries implying a pollution of the blood, and in terms of a more specific hypothesis based on the young Hitler's strange sexual abstinence, reported by all those who knew him during his Viennese years. It is plausible to infer that a fear of the father inhibited the development of a normal sex life, but that the humiliating inhibition was rationalized and attributed to the fear of syphilis, which Hitler often men-tioned. Now since the father was himself identified with the Jews, it was the Jews who, through syphilis, threatened the health and the life of non-Jews.

The Jews and syphilis, or infection in general, soon became one and the same thing.[19]

The various interpretations we have mentioned agree, for the most part, on one essential fact: the psychosexual origin of Hitler's anti-Semitism. For anyone who has studied the subject, there can be no doubt on that score. But the statement as such is too general to be meaningful. Once one admits the psychosexual origin of Hitler's anti-Semitism, one must necessarily look for specific causes in the childhood or the young manhood of the future dictator. All of the studies did in fact search in that direction, and that is where the divergences began. Why? Because of the absence of significant biographical information, certainly (this despite Hitler's own recollections, as well as those of his supposed childhood friends—Kubizek, Greiner, Hanisch—and despite the few more or less exact reconstructions attempted by postwar historians); but above all because the facts we do possess can be related to each other and to subsequent events in various ways. *What we cannot know is how Hitler experienced the events we know, and what fantasies they evoked in him.* We have seen, for example, that most interpreters accord a great importance to the fact that after the death of Hitler's father, during the mother's last illness, it was a Jewish doctor, Dr. Bloch, who in a sense took the father's place; great importance has also been attributed to Bloch's method of treatment, which seems to have consisted in injections of morphine. On the surface, Hitler felt nothing but gratefulness toward Bloch: he wrote to him several times, and much later, after the annexation of Austria he authorized him to leave for the United States. But how can we ever know the unconscious fantasies that became associated with Bloch's role and with his status as a Jew?

Whatever hypothesis one chooses, one can find a way to integrate it into a total context that will appear coherent, for the possible variations are extremely numerous. For each hypothesis, one can find sufficient proof in the huge mass of Hitler's writings, speeches, and conversations, the texts of which have been preserved. One could conclude that this is precisely the problem of the verification of psychohistorical explanation and that all of the criteria we discussed in the preceding chapter prove to be inapplicable to a concrete biographical case: in this instance several *Gestalten* are possible, each one no less plausible than the others; any explanation one chooses will be confirmed by convergent elements, so that the overdetermination effect will appear. An objective criterion for selecting the correct interpretation thus becomes difficult to find.

It is not psychobiography that is at fault here, and the example chosen is an extreme one because of the plurality of possible explanations to which it gives rise. But we should nevertheless beware of this danger: certain cases present limits that the biographer cannot hope to go beyond. One can define an unconscious structure, both in its typical and its specific characteristics, *but its genesis is sometimes inaccessible to historical study.*

The interpretation of childhood events represents therefore the most uncertain aspect of biographical investigation, due to the idiosyncratic forms of individual fantasy as well as to the obvious lack of sufficient documentation.

In adolescence, on the other hand, when the identity is formed, when the various conflicts crystallize and when a crucial choice of cultural models takes place, the psychic structure appears much more clearly. Often, in the case of writers or artists, the first works—the *Juvenilia* that Mauron talks about—are produced at this time.[20] But in fact it is at the end of this crucial phase that the complex relation between the personality and the work (in the broadest sense of that term) develops, according to a dynamic whose mechanism we shall discuss in detail but which, in any case, excludes univocal correlations. Whatever the nature of the work, it obeys an autonomous logic that introduces into the biographical context a complementary element of indeterminacy.[21]

Paradoxically, the biographer cannot escape from the opposite difficulty either—that of a case where a manifest determinism exists, but whose implications cannot be exactly evaluated: the determinism of heredity or physiological determinism in general. The pathological heredity of Van Gogh, for example, is certainly recognized: Vincent's sister spent thirty-eight years in a mental institution, and his brother Theo was himself the victim of nervous disorders that hastened his death.[22] But only in rare cases is the genetic influence as clear as this, and in most instances the biographer will not know how to interpret elements that are less clearly marked but that nevertheless play a preponderant role. One finds a sporadic instability in the Stephen family, for example, but was it this instability—which never reached the stage of madness—that accounted for the psychotic outbreaks of the most famous descendant of the line, Virginia Woolf? Or were the perturbing events of her childhood sufficient cause to explain her illness?[23] We cannot go wrong by affirming that there was a convergence of the two factors, but that is simply an elegant way of masking our ignorance.

The degree of repercussion of physiological disorders on behavior is not easy to determine. We may recall that McAlpine and Hunter attributed to porphyria the behavior King George III of England, while others explain it in terms of psychotic attacks. It seems impossible to settle the controversy, and there are many cases of a similar kind. To cite Hitler again, up to 1940 we can exclude the possibility of a pathological disorder as a decisive influence on his personality, since detailed medical reports are available to us.[24] After that date, however, it is not impossible that the medications prescribed by Dr. Morell influenced the evolution of the Führer's fantasies and behavior.[25]

Lord Moran's indiscretions have confirmed the role of illness in Churchill's behavior.[26] The repercussions of cerebral palsy on the last years of Roosevelt, Lenin, and Wilson are evident, but we cannot say in what way exactly or to what degree. As concerns Wilson, for example, a study by Edwin Weinstein seems to suggest that one can explain part of the behavior that Alexander and Juliette George attributed to the president's psyche as the result, rather, of the deterioration of the cerebrovascular system, the first signs of which were supposedly discovered while Wilson was at Princeton, *before* the outbreak of the controversy that eventually provoked his resignation as president of the university.[27] As Weinstein himself notes, the facts concerning Wilson's neurological illness do not exclude the possibility of a psychodynamic explanation of his public behavior, but to ignore the organic factor is to risk arriving at "unacceptable simplifications."[28]

But in that case, can we still speak of psychobiography? Yes, but in the conditional mode. The "yes" has just been demonstrated, in a sense, by a *reductio ad absurdum,* for the enumeration of imprecise and divergent factors which all influence behavior in no way alters our initial statement: the personality possesses a perceptible coherence which continues to exist despite the most diverse influences, and it is this coherence that forms the theoretical basis and justification of psychobiography. As for the "conditional mode," it is directly linked to the difficulties we have discussed, and it is clear that in certain cases a psychoanalytic biography is impossible. In fact, if a successful psychobiography finds its theoretical justification in the "principle of coherence," its success will nevertheless be due as much to fortuitous circumstances (as concerns, notably, the documentary sources) as to the keenness of the methodology. The limits of the field are therefore visible, but the field is there. We shall try to explore it by way of three distinct approaches: the relation between the personality and the work of art (the psychoanalytic biography of artists); between the personality and political behavior (the biography of political figures); and between the personality and a change in collective identity (the biography of charismatic leaders).

Personality and the Work of Art

The problem of the relation between the personality of the artist or writer and his work has been at least as hotly debated as that of the nature of history, and here too the opposing positions are categorical and often unreconcilable. Thus, for T. S. Eliot, the attempt to correlate the artist's personality with his work is anathema: "Poetry," he writes, "is not a turning loose of emotion, but an escape from emotion; it is not the expression of personality, but an escape from personality . . . significant emotion . . . has its life in the poem and not in the history of the poet."[29] If we look for other expressions of the same view, we think immediately of Paul Valéry, of American New Criticism or of the Russian Formalists. But opposite Eliot, we find Edmund Wilson and Lionel Trilling; opposite Valéry, we find Gide.

We might recall the famous polemic that broke out in France during the 1960's, concerning the so-called "nouvelle critique." A virulent pamphlet by Raymond Picard posed the problem with perfect clarity, if not with perfect fairness: the "new critics," claimed Picard, did not believe in the "specificity of literature"; they smashed the traditional framework of literary works in order to arrive at an anthropology or a psychoanalysis of the author, and they did so by means of the most arbitrary comparisons and analogies. Yet, these comparisons are necessary, as Serge Doubrovsky very justly pointed out in his response to Picard: "There is no way of preventing meanings from drawing other meanings to them, from proliferating: Raymond Picard's criticism is a Malthusianism struggling in vain to combat a semantic explosion."[31]

At the same time, the French new criticism in no way implies a necessary linking of the work to the personality of its author. On the contrary—in addition to the psychobiographical approach one finds various other approaches, all of which place the artist's personality between parentheses: Lucien Goldmann's Marxist or para-Marxist method, for example, or the various kinds of contemporary structuralism (which include, as we know, a psychoanalytic structuralism). Once again, we shall limit ourselves to defining our position concerning the two principal "anti-biographical" approaches,[32] without going into the details of a controversy that is still in full swing.

Lucien Goldmann, reiterating in *Pour une sociologie du roman* the themes already present in his earlier book, *Le Dieu caché (The Hidden God)*, affirmed categorically that only a social group is capable of elaborating that coherent "vision of the world" without which the work of art is inconceivable. Sociology can discover the necessary link between a work and its social context, but no psychology can possibly "account for the fact that Racine wrote precisely the corpus of his dramas and tragedies, and explain why he could in no case have written the plays of Corneille or those of Molière".[33]

Without launching a full-scale critique of Goldmann's methods as a whole, we can raise certain inevitable objections to it.

As concerns the monopoly presumably exercised by the group in the formulation of a coherent vision of the world, how does one explain the fact that so many creative personalities are "out of phase" with their society, and that so many works of art have no discernible relation to the social context in which they were produced?[34] We can, as a matter of fact, borrow an example from Lucien Goldmann himself: in *The Hidden God,* Goldmann gives us the definition of a "tragic vision" found in Pascal and Racine, a vision whose social bases he analyzes at length as a specific relationship between the *noblesse de robe* and the monarchy. Now if there is a single other authentic exponent of the same "tragic vision," it is certainly Kierkegaard. Yet, the social context in which Kierkegaard's work and personality existed bears no relation whatsoever to the one that Goldmann considered as the basis for the "tragic vision."

Would it not be more convincing to postulate the partial influence of the social context, even though it is not always evident, together with the equally partial influence of personality factors and of autonomous formal elements inherent to a given artistic domain? The specificity of the individual personality (more or less strong, depending on the artist in question) can give rise to an "out of phase" relationship between the artist and his group, but since the work itself will influence the sensibility of the group, it will be integrated into the collective vision after a gestation period whose length will vary with the circumstances. As for the possibility of psychology's identifying and explaining the particular character of the work of Racine, Corneille, or Molière, we shall see a bit further on that it does exist, provided that certain essential elements be present. But Goldmann, in a work subsequent to *The Hidden*

God, directs a more specific attack against the psychoanalytic method as a means of explaining the work of art. He bases his critique on two main arguments:

> a) There exists almost no psychoanalytic interpretation of a great literary text which embraces that text in its entirety. Yet the unity of the text as a whole constitutes an essential element of its literary significance.
> b) Since the libidinal significance of any behavior is, according to Freud himself, always consistent with the individual's biography and situation, we do not see how a psychoanalytic interpretation can—*in its own terms*—distinguish between a work of genius and the delirious production of a madman.[35]

The word "almost" in Goldmann's first proposition might allow us to suppose that it is simply a question of perfecting the technique of psychoanalytic interpretation of texts, and that analysts have occasionally succeeded in furnishing total interpretation. I don't believe that for a moment, but it would be easy to demonstrate that sociological interpretation has had no more success in understanding a text in its unity and its totality—indeed, that the search for a total interpretation *by a single method* is a delusion, and that only a reading on several levels will allow one to grasp the multiple meanings of a single text.

As for the supposed impossibility of distinguishing, in a psychoanalytic reading, between a work of genius and the delirious production of a madman, given the necessary coherence of the relation between work and personality according to the criteria of psychoanalysis, that impossibility disappears as soon as one grants a central position to the various functions of the ego in one's conception of the personality. These functions manifest themselves very differently in the case of the madman, where the field of creative freedom is reduced to zero by the afflux of libido, and the case of the genius, where the ego shapes the libidinal material in order to give rise to a constellation of totally new esthetic elements. As Ernst Kris points out, the productions of the madman take on for him a wholly personal meaning that rapidly becomes incomprehensible to others: "By his word the insane artist commands the demons, and by his image he exercises magic control. Art has deteriorated from communication to sorcery."[36]

This brief critique of some of Goldmann's positions in no way implies a denial of the influence of the social context on the artistic or literary work. But one must recognize both the influence of the social context and that of the artist's or writer's prsonality.

Structuralist analysis also concentrates essentially on the work and places the biographical element between parentheses. Yet, we shall see that even Lévi-Strauss occasionally attempts a synthesis between the structuralist approach and the genetic one. For the moment, we shall consider only the question raised by psychoanalytic structuralism, in relation to the problem of the biography of the creative personality.

Psychoanalytic structuralism finds its inspiration in Freud. In the works of art that he interpreted, Freud looked for variations on universal themes whose intelligibility was based on their repetitive structure.[37] Thus, it has been noted, in his comparison of *Oedipus Rex, Hamlet,* and *The Brothers Karamazov,* Freud found in each work the theme of parricide motivated by sexual competition for a woman.

This kind of structuralist analysis proceeds in two stages: first of all, it seeks to discover in the work a particular organization of certain "psychic forms" common to all human beings; this organization can be grasped independently of any reference to the personality of the artist, to his social situation, etc. In the next stage, the object is to determine the particular form or the style of this organization, by considering once again only the elements intrinsic to the work; this procedure is similar to that of the therapist, who—moving from the examination of the libidinal content of a case to the patient's particular way of relating to the world, his immediate object relations—can understand a "life style" without having recourse to a detailed anamnesis.[38]

Due to the theoretical development of ego psychology and the importance attached to object relations, analysts of individual works are naturally led to shift their attention from the thematic content to the mode of expression. On this particular point, therefore, the structuralist approach has nothing unique about it. On the other hand, as concerns the bracketing of elements extrinsic to the work, one runs up against a general difficulty that structuralism is incapable of surmounting: namely, the absence of any verification criteria, other than an element of internal cohesion. In fact, only a correlation between the psychic structure expressed in the work and the psychic structure discoverable in the artist allows for a certain degree of verification. Freud himself clearly showed the way: most of his analyses apply both the structural method and the genetic method. A common structure certainly appears in *Oedipus Rex,* in *Hamlet,* and in *The Brothers Karamazov,* but "in these three works the Oedipal structure is manifested in different variants due to the differences in historical periods, in the author's biographies and in the variation of repression. Thus, according to Freud, there exists an undeniable link between the murder of the father in *The Brothers Karamazov* and the fate of Dostoevsky's own father, just as there exists a link between Shakespeare's life and the personality of Hamlet."[39] In any case, even the most convinced supporters of psychoanalytic structuralism end up by admitting that "intrinsic analysis [of the work] can be enriched and confirmed by the use of historical data, whether relating to the author's biography or to the esthetic movement to which the work belongs."[40] Such a synthesis leads us quite naturally to the biography of the artist, as we conceive of it in this book.

According to the paradigm of psychobiography which we discussed in the last chapter, the problem here is that of the *individual* bases of the artist's language of symbolic transformation: can the historian interpret this language not only in terms of the manifest characteristics of the work, but also in terms of the known elements of the artist's life? (We shall leave aside for now the problem of scientific creation, which many people believe can be assimilated to artistic creation—despite the absence of proof to that effect—and which is often explained as the consequence, on the emotional level, of a basic inability to establish interpersonal relations.[41]) We must, in fact, attempt to answer four essential questions:

1) What, generally speaking, is the relation between creativity and the unconscious?

2) What is the relation between the personality of the artist and the content of the work (the subject, the musical theme, the choice of pictorial objects, etc.)?

3) What is the relation between the personality of the artist and the form of the work?

4) Finally, what is the relation between society and personality in the elaboration of the work?

As concerns the first of these problematic relations—the one between creativity and the individual unconscious—Freud's own position is clear: the language of the artist replaces another one, which is the language of neurosis. On the level of individual creation, the work of art is therefore a reelaboration of the artist's infantile fantasies. The forces whose convergence and/or opposition lead to artistic creation "are the same conflicts which drive other people into neurosis."[42] The work of art is a substitute for neurosis: the artist escapes the paralyzing effects of neurosis thanks to his capacity for sublimation and to the weakness of his repressions. For Freud, the work of art is thus the expression of a psychic conflict which in most people would lead only to neurosis, but which, in a few rare individuals endowed with a particular capacity for sublimation, leads to creativity. At the same time, Freudian theory maintains that a trace of the original conflict, in other words some element of neurosis, remains in the artist's personality; often, therefore, traditional psychobiography looks for the meaning of the work by studying this "nonsublimated" aspect of the artist's behavior.

Most psychoanalysts accept Freud's basic notions on this point, even if they reformulate them in a more refined way: the creative act corresponds, in their eyes, to the solution of a conflict-laden intrapsychic situation. Thus, Jean Delay speaks of the search for a new equilibrium provoked by the lack of fulfillment that is the neurotic conflict;[43] Melanie Klein evokes the need for "repairing the damaged object," a need provoked by the feeling of guilt resulting from the destructive rage of the small child's depressive position, as well as by the need for a sense of wholeness on the part of the subject; this theme is also developed by Janine Chasseguet-Smirgel;[44] Anthony Storr emphasizes the adaptive function of the creative act, whose aim is to reestablish an internal order, to overcome the conflict-laden oppositions and dissociations and to establish a solid identity.[45]

We may note that for these authors, the creative act is, in one form or another, an attempt to restore a lack provoked in the artist's personality by an initial intrapsychic conflict (the conflict itself obviously being the result of the relations between the individual and others at certain initial stages of the development of the personality). One can certainly accept this explanation, just as one can accept Anthony Storr's data concerning the types of personality disorders frequently encountered in creative individuals. But is all this sufficient?

First of all, the nature of the initial lack is not comparable, it would seem, in all artists. To come back to the notions advanced by Melanie Klein and Janine Chasseguet-Smirgel, it is not necessary to attempt to unify these various hypotheses, as Janine Chasseguet-Smirgel tried to do: one can easily imagine that, in some artists, the creative act aims to fill in the gaps of their maturation at every stage of development in order to arrive at "narcissistic completion,"[46] while in others its aim is to arrive at the "reparation of the object" that Melanie Klein evokes in most of her writings. In each case, the historian must attempt to determine the specific kind of lack, as well as the particular mode adopted by the artist in order to make up for it. But (and this is where traditional psychoanalytic theory seems to me insufficient) neither the idiosyncratic restoration of a lack, nor the ability—described by Storr—to integrate the discordant elements of a personality, to submit to the impulses of the unconscious and to assimilate them without neurotic collapse,[47] is identifiable with the very essence of creativity or with the creative act in its entirety.

The existence of an unconscious relationship between intrapsychic conflict, an initial lack, and the creative act is conceivable, but it is only *one* element of explanation. It would be dangerous to search in the themes or the form of a work only for a direct and univocal reflection of the psychic conflicts one may have identified in its author. This impossibility of reducing the work to an exclusively biographical explanation (or, indeed, to an exclusively sociological or cultural explanation) is very well stated by Jean Starobinski: "The work is dependent both on a lived experience and an imagined future. To choose only the dimension of the past (childhood, etc.) as an explanatory principle is to treat the work as a result, whereas in fact it is often a means whereby the writer anticipates himself. Far from being simply the product of previous experience or of an original passion, the work must itself be considered as an original act, a *point of cleavage* where the self, no longer subject to its past, undertakes to invent both its past and a mythical future, a configuration outside of time."[48]

Can we define even more precisely this relation between the personality and the work, this "dependence" of the work on the "lived experience" of the creative personality? Once again, we can look to Jean Starobinski for a possible answer:

> If the documents are numerous enough to allow one to reconstruct a "probable" image of the author's empirical personality, then it becomes possible to evaluate another distance: the one whereby the work transmutes and transcends the immediate facts of experience. In considering the distance between the work and the life of the psyche we are no longer guided by the principle of emanation or of reflection, but rather by the principle of original invention, of creative desire, of successful metamorphosis. One must know the *man* and his empirical existence in order to know what the work is opposed to, what constitutes its coefficient of negativity. It follows from this that psychology will not directly elucidate the work itself: *it will allow us to understand the movement toward the work,* and if it remains incapable of explaining the work in terms of its sufficient causes, it gives us at least a glimpse of its necessary causes. . . .[49]

The dialectical relation between the personality and the work, as envisaged by Starobinski, *does not exclude the "reflection" aspect of the work, but rather transcends it.* Some studies, which we shall cite later, evoke on the whole the "reflection" stage of the work; as far as I am aware, there exist no studies to date which show the interaction between the element of necessary dependence and the element of creative transcendence; but the direction, at least, is clearly indicated.

In good logical order, the first task of the biographer will be to identify the repetitive elements in what constitutes the manifest structure of a work and of a life. This is precisely what Roland Barthes has in mind when he states, in the first lines of his book on Michelet: "... there is an order to follow. We must first give this man his coherence." For Barthes, this means looking for a thematics, an "organized network of obsessions."[50]

This search for the unconscious coherence, for the "organized network" of obsessions, will be more or less easy depending on the degree of subjectivity of the creative personality. At the end of her study on Poe, Marie Bonaparte proposed the idea of classifying writers according to their degree of subjectivity—a naive formulation for a correct view. In effect, in creative personalities whose subjectivity is extreme, certain dominant themes of the unconscious are reproduced almost literally, and one can risk various hypotheses concerning the origin of the psychic constellation which influences their life and their work. In the case of others, the unconscious material is more or less completely reworked and is much more difficult to arrive at.[51]

Let us take the case of Edgar Allan Poe. The obsession with the "dead mother" dominated the work of the writer, through a series of obvious symbols, just as it dominated his life: his marriage, his impotence, his alcoholism, his final escapade. Even though it is often too schematic, Marie Bonaparte's analysis is on the whole correct—which does not exclude, of course, the possibility of a more detailed interpretation, dealing perhaps with biographical elements that she did not perceive, or with more general unconscious problems revealed in Poe's work.

For the biographer, the death of the mother becomes the fundamental absence, the narcissistic wound that Poe's life and work attempted to *overcome.* The extreme subjectivity of this *auteur maudit* designates this central theme in a convincing manner. But the insufficiency of the usual psychobiographical method becomes apparent as soon as one compares the case of Poe with that of another writer, who was just as subjective, just as "explicit" about the psychological bases of his creative quest, just as deeply hurt by a maternal absence which, although benign and temporary—thus not at all comparable to death—nevertheless provoked an emptiness that the work sought to fill: I am referring, of course, to Proust. The bedtime kiss, once it was refused, became a wound perhaps as intolerable as the one suffered by little Edgar, whose mother abandoned him by dying. From that moment on, writes George Painter, "[Proust] sought everywhere for the infinite, unconditional love which he had lost. . . ."[52]

The demonstration offered by Painter in his two fine volumes is impressive; the proofs provided by Marie Bonaparte are convincing. In both cases, the extreme subjectivity of the writers in question makes the central theme of their quest evident—and yet, what a difference between the two men, the course of their lives and every aspect of their work! In the two cases, the fundamental absence of the mother was experienced in a different "key," fantasized in a different way and transposed into different symbols and forms. In this kind of analysis, it is the particular setting up of relations, the specific structures, the individual nuances, and only they, that count: the historian must be able to rely both on systematic explanation, which leads from the discovery of a fundamental lack to its transmutations, and on his intuition, which alone allows him to evaluate the importance of each element; at the same time, he must not attempt to establish an exclusive and univocal causal relation between the psychic structure he has identified and the nature of the specific symbolic transformation.[53]

On the level of the search for an unconscious coherence of themes in the work and their correlation with the biographical context, the historian can study the life of artists by the same method as the life of writers. Thus, in his study of Michelangelo, Dominique Fernandez interprets certain major themes in the work as the obsessive echoes of fantasies provoked in the artist by the death of his mother when he was six years old, by his conflict with his father, and by a homosexuality whose roots are to be found in conflict and in absence.

When Michelangelo treats the subject of the Holy Family or the Madonna and Child, it is always the same strange relation between the mother and the child that appears: no bond, no tenderness, no mutual moving toward each other. In *The Holy Family of Doni,* for example, there is a kind of acrobatics on the part of the Virgin, who throws the child backward toward the father; in the *Madonna of la Scala,* there is a movement thrusting the child away from her, "as if she wanted to put him out of her sight."[54] The repetition is significant. According to Fernandez, Michelangelo treated this subject a half dozen times: in the *Madonna of Bruges,* "the Virgin, seated on the right with her son standing between her knees, stares straight in front of her, without the slighest bend of her head, without seeing him or paying the least attention to him, except for the fact that the fingers of her left hand are linked with the fingers of the child's right hand. . . ."[55] One finds the same stare, "fixed, empty and absent," in the Virgin of the reliefs known as *Tondo Taddei* and *Tondo Pitti.* Finally, in the *Virgin and Child* of the Medici Chapel, the "tragic fixity of the mother's stare is made all the more apparent by the fact that the child, seated on her lap, twists himself violently backward, as if he wanted not only to catch hold of the breast but to attract to his little self the attention of that indifferent, impenetrable and distant face."[56] Still other examples confirm this obsession with the "dead mother" or the "absent mother," and Fernandez shows that in Michelangelo this absence was experienced and expressed as a fantasy of abandonment of the child by the Mother and, perhaps once, in *Venus and Two Cupids,* in the form of a reaction-formation: the abandonment of the mother by the child.[57]

We need not repeat here Fernandez' detailed discussion concerning the relation between Michelangelo's work and the conflict with the father; it will be enough to mention that Fernandez establishes a correlation between the internal discord that this conflict entailed (the desire to attack the father versus the prohibition against doing so) and the unfinished state of works representing paternal figures. After citing a long series of examples of different works in which the feminine or young figures are finished whereas the male paternal figures are not, Fernandez adds: "The contrast is even more striking if one compares the statues of a single series or a single group. Opposed to the old and bearded *Slaves* of the Academy, which are unfinished, are the young, finished *Slaves* of the Louvre. Opposed to the bearded, unfinished figures of *Day* and *Twilight* in the Medici Chapel are the beardless, finished figures of *Julius* and *Lorenzo*. Finally, it may happen that in a single group, such as *Victory*, which includes two men, the young one has the polish of a finished work, whereas the old one has the tremor of the *non finito*. So many examples, spanning the whole career of the artist, cannot be simple coincidences; whence the following law, which seems to govern Michelangelo's unconscious: each time he *goes to work* on a figure whose age or attributes make him appear as a figure of paternal authority, he *goes at it* with incredible violence, a sacrilegious temerity atoned for by the sudden interruption of the work. . . ."[58]

Michelangelo's homosexuality need no more be documented, as such, than his conflict with his father; it is a fact that all his biographers have noted, and Michelangelo himself admitted it. But what one looks for in his work is the expression of the hidden fantasies that this homosexuality engenders. Now it seems to be the case that Michelangelo was dominated, because of his tendencies, by a feeling of intense guilt which made him imagine the most terrible punishments—a fact that would perhaps explain the persistently self-punitive behavior that the artist inflicted on himself in his everyday life. Dominique Fernandez illustrates this hidden dialectic between homosexuality and fantasies of punishment by means of a comparative analysis of three drawings: Ganymede carried off by an eagle, Tityus endlessly devoured by the vulture, and Phaeton falling with his chariot.

The Ganymede/Tityus/Phaeton series offers three successive images of the naked adolescent body, first upright, then lying on the back, then in a backward swoon. According to Vasari, the three drawings were given in that order to Tommaso [Tommaso Cavalieri, a young man with whom Michelangelo was in love—S.F.]: Ganymede, then Tityus, finally Phaeton. The meaning of this progression is easily deciphered. The rape of Ganymede, executed in an ascending movement from bottom to top, symbolizes the stage of hope, of illusion; the punishment of Tityus corresponds to the immobile continuity of endless torture; the fall of Phaeton indicates the final catastrophe. The three nudes are all endowed with intense sensuality, like three images of the most shameless abandonment and self-exhibition. At the same time, however, these three poses constitute the punishment itself, according to the secret law which makes Michelangelo condemn himself for the very thing that arouses his passion. Ganymede with his legs spread apart represents an invitation to love, the excitation of the first step, a provocative enticement, but also, *at the same time*, the body pulled apart, imprisoned in the claws of the predatory bird, mortally paralyzed. Tityus lying on his back represents the imminence of pleasure, but also, *at the same time*, the eternity of punishment. Phaeton, in his backward swoon, represents the climax of voluptuous ecstasy but also, *at the same time*, the irrevocable engulfment by the waves.[59]

Although it is widely practiced, the analysis of the thematic content of the work is perhaps of secondary importance. As Jean-François Lyotard writes in his preface to the French translation of Anton Ehrenzweig's important study, *The Hidden Order of Art,* "Applied psychoanalysis has most often neglected the choice or organization, whether conscious or unconscious, of the formal constituents of artistic works, even though everyone knows that it is there, rather than in the 'subject' (when there is one) that the artist's efforts are concentrated."[60] That is true, but the essential relation between the individual unconscious and the form or style of the work requires a method of analysis that it has not been possible, until now, to elucidate. We have seen that the structural analysis of works of art attaches particular importance to the discovery of a relation between the form of the work and certain general structures of the unconscious evoked by the artist, without considering it necessary to refer to the latter's biography. Other attempts, equally general in nature, have been made to relate certain forms of artistic expression (poetic rhythm[61] or kinesthesia, for example)[62] to certain unconscious processes. But as far as specific relations on the level of psychoanalytic biography are concerned, there has been nothing. The fascinating study by Anton Ehrenzweig—which attempts to show that the primary processes, far from being the domain of formlessness and chaos, are a structured field from which all genuine artistic creation derives, thus constituting a substratum that encloses the "hidden order" of art—contributes very little to the questions that concern the biographer. When Ehrenzweig evokes the particular form of certain works by Beethoven or Mozart, it is in the framework of a general demonstration, just as when he analyzes works by Picasso, Jackson Pollock, or Bridget Riley. His specific remark about Brahms' music ("this intransigent music pleased me because of its virility. It seemed to harmonize with the forbidding and solitary personality of Brahms"[63]) is merely an aside. It is only in the last part of the book, where Ehrenzweig takes up the great themes of the "dying god" or of the "white goddess," that we find an attempt to relate these to specific works—but at that point we are back to thematic analysis.[64]

We might end by quoting Dominique Fernandez' concluding remarks in his study of Michelangelo: "The contradictory alliance of opposing stylistic traits in Michelangelo's work, his 'movement without locomotion' (Panofsky), his 'withheld leap of a dog' (Stevenson), the number and variety of 'compromises' he opted for, his 'baroque' innovations (brutal distortion, serpentine S-shaped line, *contrapposto,* contrast through symmetry), which art critics explain by invoking either the culture . . . or the artist's temperament . . . all point perhaps to a historical childhood situation, to the problems of the stepson obliged to please both his father and his stepmother. Anything one can say on this subject is purely hypothetical. . . ."[65] In this particular case, we must agree. Yet, is this not a particular aspect of the psychoanalytic biography of artists whose analysis will have to be attempted? Is this not what William Langer would call "the next assignment?"

In his *Art and Illusion,*[66] the art historian E. H. Gombrich shows that the artist does not copy an "objective" reality, but represents a stylized vision of the world in the famework of conventional schemata current in the period and in the culture in which he lives. This seems undeniable. But in that case, could we not say that it is the social context which in large part determines the conventional schemata that the artist relies on, whereas the individual variations in relation to this "norm" are determined by the artist's personality, and especially by the play of unconscious processes? We have here a possible model of the interaction between society and personality as regards the creation of works of art. An example borrowed not from Gombrich but from Lucien Goldmann will make this hypothesis more concrete.

According to Goldmann, the economic and social structure resulting from a *laissez-faire* economy produced, in literature, a certain type of novel: the novel with a problematic hero. Since Malraux's novels were written toward the end of this period,[67] he still used, necessarily as it were, the typical schema. Goldmann stops there, but one can go a step further: if Malraux internalized the conventional novelistic schema imposed by the social structure in which he lived, his interpretation of this schema was very different from the interpretation one finds in Roger Martin du Gard, Jules Romains, or Thomas Mann. It is in the particular interpretation of the conventional schema, both on the thematic and on the formal levels, that one can situate the influence of the personality.[68]

One can also come back to a variant of the classical model of culture and personality, in which society influences the personality, notably in the framework of the family. The family is both the mirror of a typical social reality and a particular way of experiencing this typical context. In the *Critique of Dialectical Reason,* Sartre shows this double aspect of the family milieu, as well as the link—obvious, as far as we are concerned—that the family represents between the general social structure and the formation of the artistic personality:

> The Flaubert family was of the semi-domestic type; it was a little behind the industrial families which the father Flaubert cared for or visited. The father Flaubert, who felt that he was "wronged" by his patron Dupuytren, terrorized everyone with his own worth and ability, his Voltairian irony, his terrible angers and fits of melancholy. We will also easily understand that the bond between the small Gustave and his mother was never determining; she was only a reflection of the terrible doctor. Thus we have before us an almost tangible cleavage which will often separate Flaubert from his contemporaries; in a century when the conjugal family is the type current among the wealthy bourgeoisie, when Du Camp and Le Poittevin represent children freed from the patria potestas,

Flaubert is characterized by a "fixation" on his father. Baudelaire, on the other hand, born the same year, will be fixed all his life on his mother. And this difference is explained by the difference in their respective environments. Flaubert's bourgeoisie is harsh, new. (His mother, vaguely connected with the nobility, represents a class of landowners in process of liquidation; the father comes straight out of a village and wears strange, peasant clothing even at Rouen—a goatskin in winter.) This bourgeoisie comes from the country; and it returns there, too, since it uses its gradually won wealth to buy land. Baudelaire's family, bourgeois, urban for many years already, considers itself in some small way belonging to the new nobility (la noblesse de robe); it owns stocks and bonds. Sometimes between two masters, the mother appeared all alone in the glory of her independence. Later it was all in vain for Aupick to play at being the "boss"; Mme. Aupick, stupid and rather vain, but charming and favored by her period, never ceased to exist *in her own right.*[69]

We need not be concerned here with the fact that Sartre establishes only a "surface" relation between the particular family constellation and the writer's personality; what matters, once again, is the encounter of the typical with the idiosyncratic. In effect, the schema inspired by Gombrich's notion and the one we have just illustrated by an example from Sartre dovetail with each other—and they do so, furthermore, in the theoretical context of the modes of socialization of the individual, which we presented in the preceding chapter. The example given by Sartre illustrates the socialization process of the child; Gombrich's notion illustrates the internalization of norms which takes place throughout one's lifetime. But that is not all.

In his admirable reading of the "Dinner in Turin" episode told by Rousseau in his *Confessions,* Jean Starobinski notes that ". . . the three phases of Mademoiselle de Breil's story correspond . . . to an affective archetype of Rousseau's, one that is present in everything that bears the stamp of his imagination: the actors' roles are distributed, furthermore, according to the structural constellation of the myth of the 'forbidden princess.' (We may recall here the story of Turandot, and the role played in it by the riddle that must be solved.) We have the impression of encountering here the personal interpretation of an immemorial legendary situation. . . ."[70]

First, Rousseau's *Confessions* and the "Dinner in Turin" episode in particular could easily be placed into their sociological context. Next, the ternary movement of the narrative allows one to develop an independent structural analysis. Furthermore—and here we find a third level of analysis— Jean Starobinski shows that this triple movement can be found in Rousseau's other works, which suggests that one can "recognize in it one of the privileged 'structures' through which Rousseau interprets himself, interprets the world and his own situation in the world."[71] This provides us with an essential key to psychobiographical interpretation. Finally, the work in question also embodies a deeper model: a particular archetypal constellation, that of the "forbidden princess."

The work thus bears within itself its own structural coherence, the imprint of the society around it and the imprint of the author's personality, as well as, sometimes, the traces of fundamental archetypes whose source is in the deepest unconscious. It is in the work itself that one can locate the integration which will point the way toward a veritable total history.

The possibilities opened up by the interpretation of the work as an essential part of the biography, and the richness of the correlations one can thereby establish, would appear to make the psychobiography of writers and artists a privileged field of investigation. But, at least in principle, the biography of political figures or charismatic personalities offers the same possibilities. What the work is to the artist, the political decision is to the statesman and the formulation of a new norm is to the charismatic personality. In discussing these two categories of biography, we shall not enter into the same detail but shall simply point out the particular problems posed by each. The possibilities of a global context should, however, be kept in mind.

Personality and Political Behavior

If the language of artistic creation is fraught with a degree of irreducibility, the language of politics, oriented as it is toward immediate communication and action, is more accessible to analysis. Nevertheless, the historian must confront here, besides the general difficulties of psychobiography, a series of specific obstacles, not the least of which is the classical problem of the relation between role and personality.[72]

In effect, if the work of the writer and of the artist can be considered from a subjective standpoint, as the expression of a social situation to be sure, but *not* as the fulfilling of a role strictly determined by social expectations, the same is not true of the behavior of political figures: by definition the politician must act, at least in part, in response to the demands, expectations, and needs of the group. Is it therefore necessary, in order to understand a behavior of this type, to have recourse to psychological explanations founded on a theory of the personality, or is it sufficient to analyze the role played by a political figure in terms of social function, according to certain norms defined by the group?

Examples drawn from everyday life may give, at first, the impression that the public role and the function create a new identity which it would be useless, indeed impossible, to interpret in terms of personality: in order to understand the gesture of the person in uniform who stretches his hand out to you as you board a train, you don't need to look for personal motives, remarks Raymond Aron.[73] That is true, but the example he cites is a special case which allows one to explain only a limited sector of human activity, the sector in which "the person wholly disappears behind the function."[74] This kind of case offers no particular interest to the biographer. But the moment one attempts to deal with more complex and more ramified functions which contain elements of uncertainty and choice, one inevitably observes the relevance of personal motives.

Thus, in the case of political figures, the circumstances surrounding the choice of a career are often crucial, for they contain a first concrete manifestation of the personality: Hitler, as we know, first planned to become an architect, and Trotsky had trouble choosing between mathematics and revolutionary agitation.

Even more than the choice of a role, it is the creation of a new political role that is determined by the personality in the case of the most famous political leaders: Napoleon crowned himself emperor, Hitler proclaimed himself Führer at the death of Hindenburg, and of De Gaulle it has been written that "it is as if he had chosen to tailor himself to his role in history from the very beginning of his childhood, as if he had carefully selected from his heritage and his personality those elements which would allow him to play the role to perfection."[75] Every leader can alter the model of a preconceived role, refuse to submit to it, shatter the old system, and establish a wholly new system of norms and expectations.[76]

The moment that a role has a certain degree of complexity, there exist as many ways of accomplishing it as there are individuals. Every politician often finds himself grappling with role conflicts or with conflicts provoked by the contradictions inherent in a single role. The personality determines the kind of solution one brings to the conflict, just as it determines the choices one makes when the role is ambiguous and—as is frequent in great national crises—when the options available to those holding the top political posts are contradictory and apparently of equal value. It is clear that British policy in 1938 would not have been the same if Churchill had been prime minister, and that, on June 18, 1940, the politics of France would not have been what it was if De Gaulle, and not Pétain, had been chosen to head the government in place of Paul Reynaud. . . .

It seems evident, therefore, that just as one cannot wholly deny the influence of the role on the personality, one cannot ignore the opposite influence, that of the personality on the role. This obvious interaction, even while it eliminates a first objection, leads straight to another problem: how can the biographer distinguish the specific influence of the role from that of the personality, in studying a particular decision for example? How is he to find, beneath the mask imposed by the role, the idiosyncratic elements of the personality?[77]

The answer can be briefly stated: by comparing the behavior of the same individual in several different roles, one can attribute the characteristics that change to the influence of the various roles, and the permanent characteristics to the influence of the personality.

The rate of success is no higher in the domain of political psychobiography than it is in that of psychobiography in general. Simplistic interpretations are found side by side with traditional biographies, which may themselves use a few psychoanalytic concepts, thus adding very little to an understanding of the personality studied.[78] Even more than in the case of writers and artists, there is obviously a great temptation to analyze according to the criteria of psychohistory the behavior of political figures who are still active. In such instances, the objective difficulties are compounded by the hazards of highly incomplete documentation, the latter being further distorted by the more or less conscious attitudes of the author toward his living subject.

Yet, in the field of political biography as well, certain works succeed in presenting a coherent and complex psychobiographical explanation.[79] Among the latter, we have chosen to examine in some detail Alexander and Juliette George's biography of Wilson, using this example to show how various verification criteria can be applied, as well as to indicate certain gaps and difficulties.

It is when one compares the Georges' work with the psychoanalytic biography of Wilson by Freud and Bullitt that one sees, once again, to what a great degree psychobiography—and psychohistory in general—remains an art. Bullitt and Freud were not lacking in documentation, and in his preface Bullitt cites an imposing list of sources they consulted. In fact, he notes that Freud "was dissatisfied by his studies of Leonardo da Vinci and of the Moses statue by Michelangelo because he had been obliged to draw large conclusions from few facts, and he had long wished to make a psychological study of a contemporary with regard to whom thousands of facts could be ascertained."[80] The simplistic character of the result, the quasi-mechanical application of the least elaborated analytic concepts, give one the impression that most of the work is attributable to the American ambassador rather than to the father of psychoanalysis. Yet, for our purposes this study is not lacking in interest, for despite all its faults, it confirms on the essential points the hypotheses at which the Georges arrived independently. (Their book was published in the early 1950's; the manuscript of the Freud-Bullitt book was completed in the 1930's, but was not published until 1966.) In certain instances, the Freud-Bullitt work even furnishes added elements to complete an explanation by the Georges.

Let us begin by recalling the main characteristics of the unconscious repetitive structure in Wilson's behavior as outlined in the Georges' work, a structure that they discern at every decisive stage in Wilson's public life. The structure in question can be reduced to three distinct propositions.

First proposition: It is necessary to distinguish Wilson's behavior at the time he was a "power-seeker" from the time he was a "power-holder." In the first instance, Wilson was able to act with sufficient flexibility; it was in the second situation that the difficulties appeared. When he was in a position of power, Wilson manifested an aggressive behavior tending to force others into the most total submission. Whenever he came up against significant opposition, he was unable to act with enough flexibility to overcome the obstacle. On the contrary, he would formulate the conflict in terms of absolute principles and, in their name, adopt an attitude of total intransigence; the result was inevitably disaster, whereas any willingness to compromise would have assured his success.

Second proposition: Wilson's hunger for success was limitless. As soon as he had realized one ambition he launched himself into a new task, without granting himself so much as a moment of rest to savor the success already attained.

Third proposition: One of the most disastrous consequences of Wilson's personal insecurity was his inability to ask for other people's advice concerning problems which for him were charged with emotional significance, unless he was sure that his advisers were not in a position to oblige him to change his mind.

For the Georges, the origin of this behavior is to be found in Wilson's childhood: "It is our thesis that underlying Wilson's quest for political power and his manner of exercising it was the compelling need to counter the crushing feelings of inadequacy which had been branded into his spirit as a child. . . . His interest in power, in political leadership, was based, we submit, on the need to compensate for damaged self-esteem. The urgent inner need constantly to struggle against these mischievous self-depreciating legacies from his early years crippled his capacity to react objectively to matters at hand."[81]

We may briefly summarize the Georges' hypothesis as follows: Wilson's father was excessively strict, and manifested an ironic attitude toward him which had disastrous effects. The child, however, reacted to this only in a very indirect way: he learned to read considerably late, and this inaptitude represented a symbolic affront to the ambitions and demands of the father. On the other hand—and it is here that one can, by inference, propose the thesis of repressed and displaced hostility—in his adult life the young Wilson manifested toward his father a deference, a devotion, and a love that immediately strike one as "reaction formations" because of their excessive and unusual character. The result was a displacement of hostility such that Woodrow Wilson never allowed any other person to exercise power over him. He constantly took revenge on others for the humiliation inflicted on him by his father, since he could not express his hostility toward the father himself. As the Georges put it: "Throughout his life his relationships with others seemed shaped by an inner command never again to bend his will to another man's. He seems to have experienced men who were determined to make their viewpoints prevail against his own—men like Dean West at Princeton or, later, Senator Lodge—as an unbearable threat. They seem to have stirred in him ancient memories of his capitulation to his father and he resisted with ferocity. *He* must dominate, out of fear of being dominated. It was a need so strong that nothing—except, on occasion, the lure of achieving higher office—could overcome his determination to bring his opponents to heel. Not the pleas of his friends, not even the recognition, deep within himself, that sometimes it is necessary to compromise with one's adversaries to achieve desirable goals."[82]

The Georges thus identify in Wilson a particular psychic structure whose unconscious dynamic provoked a clearly discernible repetitive behavior. Their book abounds in documentary evidence, and the *Gestalt* they define seems incontrovertible. Let us, however, try to verify the scheme they suggest by using as many supplementary sources as possible,[83] in order to see whether there is any documentary counterevidence and whether the choices made by the Georges were not arbitrary.

We may begin by recalling that the most competent and most recent of Wilson's "traditional" biographers, Arthur S. Link, also perceived the repetitive characteristics of the behavior on which the Georges based their study. That in itself is a significant confirmation. But let us examine the Georges' three propositions, going from the minor to the major one.

According to the second proposition, an insatiable hunger for success constantly propelled Wilson forward, without respite or rest. The entire career of the president is witness to this fact, and all the biographies agree on it. Among the documents I have consulted there is nothing that would contradict it, except perhaps that there was a certain falling off of Wilson's drive after the death of his wife, and again during the first months of his relationship with the woman who was to become his second wife, in 1916. Yet, in Wilson's entourage this trait of his character was hardly mentioned, except by the president's closest adviser and friend, Colonel House. House's remarks, to which the Georges allude without quoting them, are worth reproducing: "One thing the president said," he noted in his diary entry for October 16, 1913, "was that he always lacked any feeling of elation when a particular object was accomplished. When he signed the Tariff Bill he could not feel the joy that was properly his, for it seemed to him that the thing was over and another great work was calling for his attention, and he thought of this rather than the present victory."[84]

Freud and Bullitt noted this same characteristic in Wilson and cited many examples of it: his lack of joy at the success of his first courses at Bryn Mawr, the depression that followed the realization of his fondest wish at the time, the acceptance of his first book, *Congressional Government,* for publication, his morbid reaction in 1906 when Harvey, one of the key men in the Democratic Party machine, mentioned him as a possible candidate for the presidency.[85] We shall see that the explanation given by Freud and Bullitt fits perfectly into the general schema proposed by the Georges.

Let us next consider the third proposition, the one concerning Wilson's hostile attitude toward any advice that did not confirm his own ideas. The documents attesting to this characteristic are numerous and convincing, the only possible exception being Wilson's attitude toward Colonel House. It is clear that the president had no doubt about House's profound loyalty (at least not until 1919, when his doubts were unjustified); the colonel's suggestions seemed to him, therefore, to emanate in a sense from himself: "Mr. House is my second personality. He is my independent self. His thoughts and mine are one. . . ."[86]

No one else, it is true, could claim to have a genuine influence on the president—who, the moment he thought he had discovered a flaw in House's absolute loyalty, broke with him. Wilson himself sincerely thought he could accept advice, but as House remarks, he really took the advice of no one: "At another time in our conversation, he [Wilson] remarked that he always sought advice. I almost laughed at this statement, for McAdoo had just been telling me to-day that he was at White Sulphur with the president and his family when the despatch arrived from Admiral Mayo concerning his demand of Huerta to salute our flag, and he said the president never even mentioned the matter to him."[87] Link's exhaustive study of the archives shows that, as a matter of fact, even House's influence remained secondary.[88] It is also Link who provides conclusive evidence of the tremendous self-assurance which made Wilson scorn any advice or idea different from his own. According to Lansing, Wilson's secretary of state, he did not accept reasonable advice when it did not correspond to his own intuition. For Link, Lansing's testimony is confirmed by Wilson's secretary of defense, Garrison, by his most intimate adviser in New Jersey, La Monte, as well as by his White House physician, Carry T. Grayson, and others.[89]

Thus, even if the Georges' thesis can use some minor qualification as concerns the position of Colonel House, its general content seems to be confirmed.

Obviously, it is the Georges' first proposition, concerning Wilson's emotional investment in certain conflict situations and the self-destructive rigidity of his behavior in such instances, which represents the essential basis of their thesis and reasoning. Among the documents one can consult, nothing contradicts this thesis and many elements confirm it.

We may note, first of all, that Wilson was not unaware of his own intransigence and that at times he must have vaguely realized its self-destructive character: "I can only do what I believe to be just, whether public opinion is for or against the judgment of my conscience," he declared at a meeting of the Big Four,[90] and, even more revealingly, at another meeting: "There is nothing more honorable than to be thrown out of power because one was right."[91] Even more significant perhaps is the conversation recorded by House several years earlier, in December 1913: "I spoke of his success, and he said his Princeton experience hung over him sometimes like a nightmare; that he had wonderful success there, and all at once conditions changed and the troubles, of which everyone knew, were brought about. He seemed to fear that such a dénouement might occur again."[92]

This repetitive behavior did not escape Link, as we have already noted. In the preface to the first volume of his biography, Link discusses the problem in general but unequivocal terms: "There was something about Woodrow Wilson that inevitably engendered controversy when he occupied positions of power and influence. Wilson was a headstrong and determined man who was usually able to rationalize his actions in terms of the moral law and to identify his position with the divine will. This combination of strong, almost imperious will and intense conviction operated to great advantage when Wilson had support among the trustees at Princeton, the legislators at Trenton, or the congressmen in Washington, because it gave him great power and an impelling drive. The time came at Princeton, Trenton, and Washington when Wilson did not command the support of the groups to whom he was responsible.

Naturally, he was not able to change his character even had he wanted to change it, with the result that controversy and disastrous defeat occurred in varying degrees in all three cases."[93]

The documents I have been able to examine confirm, almost without exception, the hypotheses of the Georges. Freud and Bullitt arrived at very similar conclusions: according to them, it was the unconscious conflict with the father that explained, in large part, Wilson's rigid attitude (a genetic explanation that the Georges also propose), and it was also the weight of the superego imposed by the father which incited Wilson to incessant effort so that success never brought him any rest. Despite all this, however, the Georges' study shows once again how even the most successful psychobiographies present certain problems that cannot be overlooked.

In the Georges' biography, Wilson's repetitive behavior, determined by his unconscious conflicts, occupies all of the foreground, whereas the projects of the president, of the man responsible for formulating a basic conception of international order, appear only incidentally and are practically submerged by the force of his unconscious conflicts. In Link's biography, on the other hand, even if the outline of Wilson's repetitive behavior is sketched in, its unconscious character, its conflictive origin and the influence of the unconscious tendencies in question on the other aspects of Wilson's behavior are not indicated: we have, instead, the evolution of a conscious will enriched by an increasingly varied and complex experience, aiming for the conquest of power but also for the realization of political principles belonging to the American progressive tradition. A complete biography of Wilson should in fact be a synthesis of the two studies, Link's and the Georges'. Such a study would allow us to follow the growth of Wilson's project stage by stage, *but within the limits imposed by the unconscious structure of the President's pesonality; it would show us—in the realization of this project—the tragic interaction between a conscious will pursuing its goal and the unconscious impulses that divert it and eventually lead it to arouse opposition to its own desired ends.* Can such a double gaze be united into a single vision, one that avoids mere artificial juxtaposition? One may well doubt it.

Furthermore, the Georges did not at all consider the possible influence of organic illness on Wilson's behavior. Freud and Bullitt, on the other hand, were aware of the possibility and posed the question repeatedly, but in the absence of documentation they could not provide an answer.[94] In the intervening years, we have acquired further information. Thus, as we noted earlier, Edwin Weinstein indicates that Wilson probably suffered from a cerebrovascular illness as early as 1896, and that in 1906 in any case, a definite deterioration was noticeable. His aggressivity and intolerance at the time of the Princeton controversy could therefore be attributed, at least in part, to an organic cause.[95] An examination of Wilson's behavior from the end of the war on leaves no doubt about this point; the clinical and documentary evidence provided by Weinstein is massive, and the behavior that the Georges explain exclusively in psychodynamic terms was very probably due to the effect of a serious deterioration in the cerebrovascular system.[96] Thus, if one does not take the physiological processes into account, one ends up with an over-simplified uni-causal explanation; if one does take them into account, one necessarily adds yet another element of indeterminacy to the overall picture of the relation between Wilson's real personality and his public behavior. As Lucien Febvre would say, however, "What matter? The historian does not have the right to desert. . . ."

Finally, Wilson's political behavior was certainly influenced by the traditions and the conscious and unconscious beliefs of the group to which he belonged. One can in fact ask oneself to what degree the American "collective mentality" was responsible for the obstinacy, but also the idealism, of the president. The psychoanalytic history of collective phenomena meets up at this point with psychobiography and gives it its veritable import: the collective identity of the group contributes to the formation of individual identity, and the study of individual identity cannot, because of that very fact, be separated from the study of the group. Could we not say that one of the objectives of the psychobiography of a political figure is to teach us something about the profound beliefs of the group to which he belongs and whose leadership he has assumed? *Even more important, could we not say that major political decisions, like great works of art, result from the convergence of a social structure, the evolution of a personality, the profound beliefs of a collective identity and perhaps, in the case of choices with universal implications, a set of archetypal configurations buried in the deepest regions of human experience? Political decisions, like works of art, are situated at the point where a total history converges.* The fundamental norms of a group, those that the charismatic personality reinforces or transforms, represent the third element of these zones of convergence.

Personality and Collective Identity

Charisma is a particular type of "grace." In Max Weber's words, it is "a certain quality of an individual personality by virtue of which he is set apart from ordinary men and treated as endowed with supernatural, superhuman, or at least specifically exceptional qualities."[97] Because the group recognizes this particular grace or charisma in an individual, it accepts to be dependent on, if not totally obedient to, the charismatic personality: the charismatic leader dominates his group.

The recognition of a charismatic personality and the desire for his domination occur in certain circumstances, most often in situations of extreme hardship which lead people to call for a savior. According to Erikson, these hardship situations can be reduced, on the psychological level, to three principal forms: fear in the face of a grave danger which poses a physical threat to the community; anxiety provoked by the disintegration of a group identity; finally, the existential anguish experienced by people for whom the usual rituals of existence have lost their meaning.[98] Up to this point one can hardly disagree, but two questions immediately present themselves: how can the charismatic personality, who generally addresses himself to a very large group, transcend the limited sociocultural milieu which shapes every individual? What are the psychological foundations of charisma?

Weinstein and Platt[99] have very justly noted that in order to be able to answer the first question, one has to admit the possibility of a direct relation between social structure and personality, and invoke the process of internalization. The charismatic personality would then be defined as a personality able to internalize and make explicit new norms pertinent to all, or to internalize and revive old norms, whereas the society around him, in its crisis state, was able to perceive neither the new norms nor the old ones. (Obviously, the primary institutions play no role at all in such a process.) But in that case, what are the psychological qualities that allow for this unusual kind of internalization and "explicitation?" In other words, what is the nature of charisma?

It has often been suggested that what characterizes all charismatic personalities is their absolute confidence in themselves, their unshakable faith in their personal mission.[100] The charismatic leader always considers himself as the chosen instrument of some superior force, whether God or History, or God acting through History. Classical psychoanalytic theory allows us to interpret charisma in terms of an extreme narcissistic withdrawal in the personality of the subject, followed by a quasi-megalomaniac action in relation to the group.[101] This is an explanation (or rather, a description) which, without being incorrect, remains extremely narrow.

On the contrary, if one distinguishes between the language of the artist, essentially oriented toward symbolic elaborations, and the language of the political personality, directed toward the manipulation of real objects and situations, could one not suggest that the charismatic personality is able to use these two languages at the same time, being both an artist and a politician, or—to quote the title of the Hoffmans' study on De Gaulle—a "political artist" in the literal sense of both these terms? Like the artist, the charismatic personality projects and compensates for certain internal lacks (those of the group, in this instance) by means of a symbolic transposition of the problem to a general existential level where the "true" answer seems to appear; at the same time, like the politician, he knows how to manipulate reality so that the solution he offers will be accepted and, above all, so that it becomes the basis for collective action. It is in this very general explanatory context that the biographer can look for a more exact relation between the personal conflict of the charismatic leader and the new system of values that he proposes.

Erikson has shown that, in the case of Luther as in that of Gandhi, the conflict between the son and the father was the emotional source of the new system. The Reformer transformed Catholic theology and changed God's attitudes in order to give himself an image of the Father that allowed him to bear the rejection and the anger of his earthly father, while at the same time accepting the paternal role of God and submitting to it: "Luther crowns his attempt to cure the wounds of this wrath [his father's] by changing God's attributes: instead of being like an earthly father whose mood-swings are incomprehensible to his small son, God is given the attribute of IRA MISER-ACORDIAE—a wrath which is really compassion. With this concept, Luther was at last able to forgive God for being a Father, and grant Him justification."[102]

In his biography of Gandhi, Erikson raises the individual conflict between father and son to the level of a nuclear conflict in the charismatic personality in general.[103] This hypothesis is not enough to replace the larger framework we evoked above, but it can allow us to define some of its aspects more precisely. Concerning the relation between the charismatic leader and his followers, for example: the conflict with the father, which is reflected in the leader's relation with the sons, allows him not only to formulate the bases of a new identity and a new ideology, but also to establish with his disciples and the masses a relation of love, one that does not, however, exclude hostile authority; such a relation is in fact the only kind that will satisfy the needs of the masses, who hunger for emotional bonds but also for submission.

Corresponding to the typical conflict of the charismatic leader, there seems to be a typical emotional need in those who become his disciples. Let us take the men around Gandhi: "These young people," writes Erikson, "highly gifted in a variety of ways, seem to have been united in one personality 'trait,' namely, an early and anxious concern for the abandoned and persecuted, at first within their families, and later in a widening circle of intensified concern. At the same time, they were loyal rebels: loyal in their sorrow, determined in their rebellion. All this they offered Gandhi, displaying a wish to serve, which was determined as much by personality as by tradition. Gandhi's capacity both to arouse and to squelch ambivalence [in his disciples] must have been formidable; but he put these men and women to work, giving direction to their capacity to care, and multiplying miraculously both their practical gifts and their sense of participation."[104]

Despite the nebulousness of the style, Erikson presents a simple hypothesis: the disciples of charismatic leaders are men who find a satisfying solution for their personal problems and achieve a sense of personal equilibrium by submitting to a leader who provoked ambivalence, even while he channels the energies of his followers toward practical tasks that reinforce each one's sense of participation.

The real gap in Erikson's analyses appears when he tries to explain the role played by the personality of the charismatic leader in the *restructuring of a collective identity* on the level of the larger group. In his *Gandhi,* Erikson tries to resolve the problem by what amounts in fact to begging the question: ". . . when Gandhi listened to his inner voice, he often thought he heard what the masses were ready to listen to. That, of course, is the secret of all charismatic leadership. . . ."[105] This is a correspondence that every traditional history book duly notes, but it does not in itself constitute an explanation. The explanation Erikson offers in *Young Man Luther* is hardly more convincing; he repeats the classical themes concerning the evolution of Christian thought from its beginnings to the 16th century, without making clear, for all that, the nature of Luther's own ascendancy.

The supplementary notion of "ideology" which Erikson introduces at this stage offers no more of a solution. According to Coles, Erikson succeeds, thanks to this concept, in transforming "the clinical question of 'identity-formation' into a universal and historical issue. . . ."[106] The intermediate concept is defined as a collective need for restructuring the image of the world. This is no more than a repetition, with the term "unconscious" tacked on, of a notion one finds in the most traditional historians.

In fact, by going beyond the general explanatory framework used until now, we can suggest certain elements of a reply to the following two questions:

1) What are the conditions favoring the internalization, by the charismatic personality, of the norms of a new system (the bases of a new collective identity), when in general it is the old system which is still being expressed by the primary institutions that shaped that same personality?

2) How does the charismatic personality succeed in provoking a restructuring of fundamental values in the midst of a heterogeneous, often very large group?

A charismatic personality will tend to define himself, not in relation to the values of his immediate limited group but in relation to those of a new system whose norms are, by definition, integrative or totalizing, if the particular circumstances of his individual development were such that they interfered with the process of assimilating the values of the immediate limited group (e.g., an unresolved conflict with the father, who is the natural mediator of the values of the immediate group, the absence of a normal family framework, etc.); if the immediate group is undergoing such rapid transformations that a coherent assimilation of old and new values becomes impossible; finally, if social, political or cultural circumstances violently impose the absolute priority of general values, as totalizing as possible. Sometimes these various conditions come together and mutually reinforce each other. Thus, in Adolf Hitler one finds at the same time the conflict with the father, mediator of the values of the Austrian Catholic petite-bourgeoisie; a rapid transformation in the living conditions of the Austro-German middle class during the second half of the nineteenth century; and the sudden and imperative imposition of Germanic national values by the war, and by the threat of disintegration that followed the defeat of 1918. Given all these conditions, the relation between such a personality and vast heterogeneous groups becomes easier to understand.

In a society undergoing rapid transformation, the old values appear inadequte to deal with the global changes; the collective identities of small groups crumble and make way for a synthesis operating on a level of abstraction sufficiently vague not to be immediately destroyed by the consequences of social change, and, in certain cases, capable of meeting the most general needs created by the changes taking place. Now since the charismatic personality has formulated the synthesis in question for idiosyncratic reasons, he has an answer all ready at the moment when the community's urgent need finds expression.

We must still explain, however, why the masses turn toward a particular personality and not toward another, even though the new synthesis may have been formulated by a certain number of people belonging to the same socio-cultural milieu, sometimes acting together in the same religious or political arena. Why did the masses turn toward Hitler and not toward a whole series of other German right-wing agitators of the same period, most of whom had arrived at the same basic reformulation of German identity in general racial terms?

Here we encounter the artist's particular talent for symbolic reformulation, which nothing allows us to identify or explain with precision. The conditions favorable to the domination of a charismatic personality, the mode of domination of that personality at various levels, the particular circumstances which allow him to reformulate the values of a group—all this is open to psycho-historical investigation, as it is to more traditional modes of inquiry. The fundamental nature of charisma resembles the symbolic language of the artist, applied to the reality of the political or social world. Further than this, we cannot go.

Psychohistorical Typology

At the beginning of this chapter, we showed the intimate connection that exists between the "type" and the individual. Biography, admittedly, is the search for a particular style, for the idiosyncratic variation in relation to a typical norm, but it is nevertheless true that typology is important in its own right as an autonomous field of study, as a verification criterion for psychohistorical explanation in general,[107] and as a specific verification criterion in the analysis of stable homogeneous groups.[108] I shall discuss it here as an autonomous field of study.

The typologies inspired by psychoanalysis have long ago gone beyond the limits of clinical classification, in search of significant categories in the domain of politics or ideology,[109] in that of intelligence or cognition,[110] or else in that of moral behavior: we may recall, for example, the fascinating perspectives for research opened up by the few remarks Stefan Possony devotes, at the end of his biography of Lenin, to the psychological type of the traitor.[111]

Any typology is first of all a matter of definition, and a given social or political category does not necessarily have a psychological equivalent; conversely, certain identifiable psychological types are not easy to incorporate within the known frameworks of a given sociocultural system. The revolutionary personality or the fascist (authoritarian) personality, for example, have been studied more than once. But, to take only the latter example, is there in fact a type of personality that corresponds to the label of "fascist?" There is reason to doubt it. Edward Shils showed that the authoritarianism defined by Adorno and his collaborators was as much a phenomenon of the left as of the right,[112] a fact that in itself would have caused problems if the "fascist" label had remained attached to the authoritarian personality. Nor is that all. One can show convincingly that neither right-wing authoritarianism nor left-wing authoritarianism, neither fascism nor communism, corresponds to a single psychological type, and that in each of these recognized groups one can discern personalities similar to personalities of the same type in the opposing camp and opposed to very different personalities in the same camp. Harold Lasswell was aware of the problem when, in his psychoanalytic studies devoted to various kinds of political behavior, he chose to examine the "propagandist" or the "bureaucrat," rather than the communist or the fascist.[113] On a different level, Roger Stéphane seized on the same problem when he brought together Malraux and Ernst von Salomon in the unifying context of the "adventurer" type,[114] without worrying about either one's political choices. An "operative" definition of a type is, as we can see, less easy to formulate than it first appears, but it is obviously the *sine qua non* of any study in this domain.

In what follows, I shall present two methodological exercises, as it were: first, showing how an apparently solid typology can be invalidated by the mere study of a few historical cases belonging to the same category; second, offering an example of psychohistorical typology that seems to satisfy our verification criteria.

It is not Adorno's or Rokeach's typology that I shall try to invalidate even though both of them need considerable modification. Nor will I consider Wolfenstein's "revolutionary personality," for in addition to the weaknesses inherent in the study itself, the author's choice of his three "revolution- aries" does not satisfy the elementary criteria of precision: to endow Lenin and Trotsky with a "revolutionary personality" is conceivable, but to com- pare them to Gandhi implies an extension of the term "revolutionary" which excludes the possibility of a precise typology. I have chosen to discuss a lesser-known work, one that is apparently rigorous since it is based on a long series of experimental studies: the typology established by David McClelland for the "creative physical scientist."[115] By drawing to- gether the convergent conclusions of experiments concerning the charac- teristics of creative physical scientists and linking them to certain aspects of classical psychoanalytic theory, McClelland arrived at the definition of a genuine type, characterized by his personality traits and by the specific characteristics of his evolution. According to the author, one can distinguish eight principal characteristics:

1) Men are more inclined than women to be scientifically creative; 2) physical scientists come more often than mere chance would account for from a radical Protestant milieu, but are themselves irreligious; 3) creative scien- tists are such hard workers that they appear to be obsessed by their work; 4) scientists avoid complex emotions which make them feel uneasy; 5) aggres- sivity strikes them as particularly painful; 6) physical scientists love music and appreciate neither poetry nor the plastic arts; 7) physical scientists are exces- sively masculine; 8) physical scientists develop, very early in life, a powerful interest in analysis, in the structure of things.

The dynamic explanation that McClelland offers for these personality traits is based on the following common denominator: the future scientist encounters particular difficulties in his interpersonal relations during child-hood. These difficulties manifest themselves especially on the level of feelings of love toward the mother, feelings that the child tends to repress. Such an attitude leads to a general regression in the emotional sphere, and in parti-cular to the impossibility of finding a normal mode of expression for aggres-sivity, due to an excessive identification with the father: the aggressivity is thus displaced toward inanimate objects, and this displacement contributes to a constant investigation of the structure of the material world.

We need not stop to discuss either the predominance of men in the scientific domain, or the Protestant origin of a large number of physical scientists. It is obvious that these are specific sociological and historical conditions, subject to change: thus, if the data concerning women are still partially correct, those concerning Protestants are totally out of date.[116] As for McClelland's other hypotheses, we shall examine them by considering the biographies of three of the greatest English scientists: Newton, Faraday, and Rutherford.

It turns out, first of all, that the thesis according to which scientists become irreligious is invalid, even if one considers only the period during which the correlation between science and Protestantism could be confirmed. Newton and Faraday, for example, both remained profoundly religious; religion occu-pied as great a place in their lives as science.[117]

The thesis according to which scientists tend to avoid overly intimate interpersonal relations is not determined by sociohistorical circumstances. Perhaps true in the case of Newton,[118] this thesis is partially false in the case of Faraday, who had many childhood friends and whose marriage seems to have been happy and harmonious,[119] and is totally false as concerns Rutherford. According to one of his biographers, "If he had not been a scientist, Ruther-ford would have proved an ideal negotiator in modern international politics." Or again: "The great gift Rutherford possessed for friendship was exercised all through his life."[120] We could accumulate a whole pile of quotations to support this view.

Newton, Faraday, and Rutherford were all hard workers in their field, but it is only in the case of Newton that one could speak of a veritable obsession.[121] Faraday had numerous duties as a councillor of the realm in various domains, and part of his time was devoted to visiting the sick as well as to his activities as an elder in the sect to which he belonged, the Sandemanians.[122] As for Rutherford, the range of his various social activities was a natural conse-quence of his warm and "extroverted" personality.

As concerns the avoidance of complex emotions and especially of all inter-personal aggressivity, McClelland's thesis is no more valid than on the other points. Admittedly, one could explain Newton's intense aggressivity toward Leibniz or Hook as an "ideological" corollary to his strict Protestantism, but what can one say—as far as complex emotions are concerned—of his rela-tionship with the young Swiss Fatio de Duillier, and of the depression that followed their break?[123] In Faraday the aggressive element is not evident, but on the other hand we know how intensely he courted the woman who was to become his wife, Sarah.[124] As for Rutherford, his aggressivity, amply documented throughout his career, manifested itself already in his student days;[125] and in the course of his life he was intensely involved in the most diverse causes.

McClelland's hypothesis concerning the artistic preferences of scientists is secondary, but is as false as the others: Faraday was an avid reader and received a prize in English literature in secondary school; he loved poetry and painting, had close ties with the Royal Association of Artists, Poets and Painters, and in his youth did not fail to "visit works of art . . . the works of Hogarth or other graphic arts."[126] We do not know how Newton felt about music, but he is the only one of our three scientists who apparently had no penchant for poetry or belles lettres.[127]

The hypothesis concerning masculinity is too vague to be verifiable, and in any case masculinity is a concept particularly subject to cultural variations. That leaves only the last of the eight characteristics, the one concerning the development of an interest in analysis, in investigating the structure of things, very early in life. This tendency is confirmed by the biographies of the three scientists, but what it indicates in fact is a powerful development of the analytic faculty in those who later become great scientists—an observation that borders on tautology.

The inexactitude of McClelland's key propositions concerning the avoidance of intimate personal relations and complex emotions (including interpersonal aggressivity) ought in itself eliminate the need to examine the author's central hypothesis—namely, that the personality of the creative physical scientist is shaped by a repression of feelings of love toward the mother and an excessive identification with the father. We cannot resist, however, citing one example: Newton's father died when the child was three months old, and Newton's quasi-morbid attachment to his mother right up to the end of her life has been noted by all of his biographers.[128] When, after his mother remarried, a new father appeared, the young Newton conceived so much affection toward him that he wished nothing more than to set fire to his house, hoping no doubt to burn the stepfather along with it![129]

This brief critical discussion of McClelland's typology raises a methodological problem concerning psychohistorical typologies. McClelland established his typology on the basis of a series of experimental studies involving a large number of contemporary physical scientists; these studies, therefore, have a certain statistical validity. In criticizing the conclusions drawn from these studies, we ourselves considered three historical cases of especially eminent physical scientists; and, since in the three cases shown—which, by their eminence, represent the very quintessence of the type under investigation—the hypotheses proved to be invalid, the characteristics of the proposed typology appear to be incorrect. But can one invalidate a typology founded on a large number of contemporary cases by citing three particularly brilliant historical cases, or must one, in order to test the typology, refer to a very large number of historical examples, given the fact that in this instance one is not dealing with laws similar to those of the natural sciences, in which a single anomaly is enough to invalidate a hypothesis? Indeed, how can we know if the number of historical cases chosen in order to confirm or to invalidate an existing typology, or else to found a new typology, is large enough? And how can we prove that the examples chosen, whose number is inevitably limited, do not represent cases arbitrarily selected in order to verify a thesis, or, conversely, are not plausible exceptions to a typology that is generally valid?

We shall base our answer on the evidence rather than on logically impregnable arguments. Let us consider once again our critique of McClelland's typology: if, in order to show that it is invalid, we had chosen three cases of creative physical scientists whose rank was nevertheless only of the second order in the history of physics, our method would have been open to challenge. But as it happens, it is three of the most eminent physicists of all times who, in one way or another, do not fit into the typology in question; in such a case, it seems to us, the numerical comparability of the "samples" becomes totally irrelevant. Let us imagine that someone established the psychodynamic characteristics of creative musicians based on a list of contemporaries, but it turned out that neither Bach nor Mozart nor Beethoven could fit into the typology; would we have to add a whole series of other names to make our refutation convincing?

One can use the same reasoning for the positive demonstration (i.e., the confirmation) of a typology. Let us take the example of composers once again, and suppose that the study included not only Bach, Mozart, and Beethoven but also Schubert, Brahms, Schumann, Wagner, Berlioz, Ravel, and Debussy. Let us further suppose that the data converged so that we could define a type of composer's personality. We could then present this incomplete series as a typological hypothesis, on the grounds that the choice of composers *universally recognized* to be among the greatest made the addition of further names unnecessary; but in such a case the proof always hinges on some major contradiction, and in the last analysis it is only intuitively that one can decide to what extent a series is sufficiently representative—or, conversely, to what extent a refutation is conclusive.

As an example of a positive demonstration, let us take the type of the political "hawk," who in the technical terminology of game theory is known as the "defector." In the case of most conflicts, game theory divides the possible strategies into two major categories: strategies of cooperation and strategies of "defection." The political personality who opts for a strategy of "defection" is not ready to make any concessions in the pursuit of his goals, and if necessary he will resort to force or to any other kind of pressure required by the situation. The political personality who opts for cooperation will emphasize the common interest of the parties in conflict and the possibilities of a compromise.

Research in social psychology shows that, in experimental conflict situations, there is a marked correlation between certain personality traits and the choice of a preferred strategy. Thus, the "defectors" manifest authoritarian characteristics, a pronounced liking for risk, and a very low threshold of tolerance for ambiguous situations.[130] In other words, experimental social psychology offers us a typology of the "defector" that it is up to the historian to test and possibly to complete, through the use of biographical material concerning major political figures.

We shall not enter into the details concerning the technical problems posed by a study of this type.[131] It will be enough to sketch in the outline of the typology itself.

The first question we must ask is obvious: can we find, among the major political figures of the contemporary period (19th and 20th centuries) any who systematically opted for a policy of "defection" throughout their career? Are we, in other words, justified in speaking of a typology on the basis of the historical material available? The answer is yes, and we have chosen fourteen political figures who seem to us to have systematically opted for this kind of policy (with the exception of a few marginal situations) throughout the course of their career: Napoleon Bonaparte, Napoleon III, Clemenceau, and Poincaré for France; Theodore Roosevelt, Forrestal, and Dulles for the United States; Crispi for Italy; William II and Hitler for Germany; Beck for Poland; Palmerston, Duff Cooper, and Churchill for England. In most of these cases, the choice of a policy of "defection" operated not only on the level of international affairs, but also in the domestic affairs in which these men were involved. In certain cases, one finds the same attitude even when the men in question were in the opposition.

Once we have identified this type of politician, the second question we must ask is whether certain personality traits are found in the majority of the "defectors," based on the historical data available. Here again the answer is positive, and we can discern the repetition of the following characteristics: a rebellious attitude toward authority when the person in question finds himself in a position of inferiority, and the intransigent, quasi-dictatorial exercise of authority when the person is himself in a position of authority; a preference for violent solutions and the use of violent language in a conflict situation; timidity, at least during the years preceding the rise to positions of power, and in general a difficulty in establishing harmonious interpersonal relations; in certain cases, paranoid tendencies. These characteristics diverge at several points from those determined on the basis of experimental research. Thus, the experimental data suggest a marked correlation between the tendency toward "defection" and a love of risk. Historical investigation, on the other hand, indicates that more than half of the figures studied showed a great deal of prudence in their politics, even while generally opting for "defection." In this instance, historical investigation brings a corrective to the hypotheses of experimental psychology. But, as we noted earlier, our aim here is to go beyond the merely critical function: based on the biographical material at our disposal, we have tried to set up a complete typology, in other words one whose evolutionary aspect can be documented and made explicit. In the political figures we have studied, one finds two distinct developmental contexts, most of the time separate but occasionally combined in strange configurations: in one context, the mother's role and authority predominate, due either to the father's absence or to his weakness; the other context is essentially authoritarian in the classic sense of the term. In at least one case, that of Adolf Hitler, the second (authoritarian) context dominates until the age of thirteen, and is then replaced by the dominance of the mother after the father's sudden death.

The first context, in which the mother is dominant due to the absence or the weak character of the father, can generally lead to a fixation on the mother and therefore to a submissive and self-effacing personality, but it can also lead—and it is the latter case that interests us here—to a process of compensatory masculinity: since the child has no clearly defined male model to follow but is at the same time pushed by the demands of the society toward masculine behavior, he will naturally tend to exaggerate the masculine traits of his personality, emphasizing the elements of domination, force, competition, etc.[132] This in turn leads to a "defector's" behavior as we have defined it.

As regards the consequences, for the personality, of a typically authoritarian context, they are too well known for us to dwell on them: repression of any expression of emotional ambivalence, displacement of the aggressivity thus repressed onto people outside the family and, later, outside the group, often resulting in a generalized hostility toward anything that does not belong to the "in-group" as such.

The study of types cannot replace biography or the complex methods of investigation required by collective phenomena, but it can occasionally confirm (or invalidate) the results obtained in both of these domains; above all, it can develop into an autonomous branch of psychohistory (more exactly, of the intermediate field between psychohistory and psychosociology) and, based on the requirements of a strict comparative method, become the model and the constant reminder of the methodological imperative in psychohistory.

3. Collective Phenomena

In his admirable preface to Jacques Lafaye's book on the formation of national consciousness in Mexico,[1] Octavio Paz summed up the various meanings attributed to the ancient Goddess Tonantzin, later known as the Virgin of Guadalupe, by the diverse groups that came to constitute modern Mexico:

> Mother of the gods and of men, of the stars and of ants, of corn and of agave, Tonantzin-Guadalupe was the Indians' imaginary compensation for the orphaned state into which the conquest had cast them. Having seen their priests massacred and their idols destroyed, their links with the past and with their supernatural world broken, they took refuge in the bosom of Tonantzin-Guadalupe: the bosom of the mother-mountain, the bosom of the mother-ocean. The ambiguous situation of the New Spain led to a similar reaction: the Creoles sought in Tonantzin-Guadalupe their veritable mother. A natural and supernatural mother, made of American earth and European theology. For the Creoles, the brown Virgin represented the possibility of rootedness in the earth of the Anahuac. She was both the womb and the tomb: to become rooted is to penetrate into the earth. . . . For the half-castes, the feeling of abandonment was and remains more total and more dramatic. For the half-caste, the question of origin is primordial, a question of life or death. In the imagination of the half-castes, Tonantzin-Guadalupe has her infernal counterpart: Chingada. She is the raped mother, exposed to the outside world, torn apart by the conquest: the Virgin Mother, on the other hand, is intact, invulnerable, and carries a son in her womb. The secret life of the half-caste oscillates between Chingada and Tonantzin-Guadalupe.

If one could, by means of a single example, summarize the objectives of a wide-ranging and complex method, one would define the primary aim of the psychohistory of collective phenomena as the investigation, in a society that can be studied historically, of the unconscious meaning of fundamental myths such as that of Tonantzin-Guadalupe, their hidden relationships, their manifestation on the level of ritualized behavior and everyday beliefs, and finally their place in the symbolic network which includes the culture as a whole.

But this would be only the end of the road; in the meantime, in order to allow us to treat more simple problems, our field of investigation will be broader and our objectives more attainable. One can, in fact, conceive the psychohistorical study of collective phenomena[2] on several distinct levels: meta-history, macro-history, and micro-history.

Meta-history is the interpretation of the underlying tendencies in the evolution of a civilization, the outline of the development of universal institutions or—after all, why not?—of humanity as such; in a word, it is the series of speculations of which Freud gave us some examples and which, still today, proliferate under the most diverse titles.[3] It is not psychohistory as we understand the term.

Macro-history, to which the above-quoted example belongs, attempts to define the unconscious characteristics of a culture or a collective mentality. It represents the most fascinating area of investigation in this domain, but we shall be able to offer only very general suggestions as far as it is concerned. In any case, in this context, quasi-intuitive extrapolations, even if they are borne out by a few texts, cannot lead us very far. The occasional remarks by William Langer, E. R. Dodds or Zevedei Barbu[4] on the anguish felt by a whole society would most likely require a more detailed formulation. A different, more systematic kind of inquiry is perhaps possible.

Whether one is dealing with perceptions, symbolic expressions or collective behavior, micro-history remains, by comparison with macro-history, the domain of what is definable and comparable, and therefore, to a far greater degree, analyzable as well. This is essentially the category of isolated phenomena in heterogeneous groups and in homogeneous groups, whether stable or temporary.

Finally, there is a whole other side to the psychohistory of collective phenomena, which is perhaps the most interesting one; we will treat it in detail in a subsequent work, not only because of the complexity of the subject but also because it requires a separate discussion. The problem is that of the unconscious ties that link societies to their own past—in other words, the mode of elaboration of a collective past. What is involved here is the question of the hidden foundations of the historical process, on the individual level but above all on the collective one.

In the discussion that follows, we shall take up our previous distinction between homogeneous and heterogeneous groups as well as the theoeretical models we proposed in chapter 1, treating them in a more explicit and detailed way. Our manner of proceeding will be, in a sense, circular: beginning with the analysis of stable homogeneous groups, where culture and society coincide in a limited and isolated sphere, we shall go on to the necessarily more fragmented analyses of temporary homogeneous groups and heterogeneous groups, ending up with the global analysis of the cultures (and mentalities) of heterogeneous groups. Along the way, we shall stop to consider the particular problems posed by the study of generational age groups and of the various stages of personality development in different historical periods. These are all cases that put psychohistorical investigation to the test, allowing one to see its possibilities as well as its limits.

Homogeneous Groups

Let us recall the characteristics of homogeneous groups: absence of sharp social differentiation, considerable isolation in relation to the outside world, or else the total domination of an ideology, an institution or an individual who, for a more or less limited time, provides the group with a manifest identity in behavior and with psychological self-isolation in relation to the outside environment.

One notes that when the first two criteria co-occur with common primary institutions, the result is a relatively stable homogeneous group, while the third criterion allows us to identify the temporary homogeneous groups, whose specific characteristics can be of the most diverse kinds: temporary homogeneous groups include the "groupe en fusion" that Sartre talks about, the blind but short-lived solidarity of "believers" in a sect or a totalitarian party under the influence of a charismatic personality, as well as the uniform attitudes, on the whole, of the members of a "total institution," in the sense in which Irving Goffman uses that term.[5] As for stable homogeneous groups, they include primitive societies as well as certain advanced communities whose physical or ideological isolation has made them into closed societies over a period sufficiently long to allow for the development of common primary institutions. It is only in the case of stable groups that the "culture and personality" paradigm is really applicable.[6] In temporary homogeneous groups, on the other hand, the uniformity of behavior is due, as we suggested in the first chapter, to the internalization, by most members of the group, of certain fundamental norms which may have been edicted by a charismatic personality or else be the result of the particular interpretation of an ideology (in the broadest sense of the term).

Stable homogeneous groups are rare in societies that can be studied historically. Historical evolution as such implies the action of powerful social forces which, by definition, eliminate the bases of the "stability" of the group, namely the common primary institutions. A French psychoanalyst has identified the characteristics of a genuine "basic personality" rooted in a specific, well-defined family environment in contemporary Malagasy society.[7] As for us, we have chosen two studies that are more clearly historical in character. In the first case, the homogeneity of the group is reinforced by the domination of a "total" ideology that influences every aspect of existence: the group here is that of the New England Puritans of the 17th century, more specifically the inhabitants of Plymouth Colony, studied by John Demos.[8] In the second case, that of the black slaves in the American South, the study we shall discuss[9] emphasizes not the relationship between primary institutions and the personality, but rather the phenomena of identification with, and internalization of, the norms of the masters; this, despite the fact that the family organization of the slaves could have been related to the black personality in this type of society.

According to Demos, the Puritans of Plymouth Colony believed in great severity toward children, starting at the time of the child's first interest in the world around him and his first manifestations of independence, between the ages of one and two years. The first expressions of the child's will were interpreted as a trace of original sin and of man's rebellion against God. Thus, in his second year of life the Puritan child experienced an essentially repressive environment. This second year was also, in most cases, the one in which the child experienced a more or less pronounced loss of affection, for it was around then that the next child was born in those very large families.

Using Erikson's model, Demos points out that excessive severity toward a child or a withdrawal of affection in the second phase of his evolution are likely to fixate the child in an attitude of doubt and shame instead of allowing for the harmonious development of individual autonomy. Aggressivity, directed toward oneself or others, becomes a dominant characteristic of the personality.

In light of this, what do we observe among the adult Puritans of Plymouth Colony? Contrary to what was long believed, it is not sexual problems that constituted their major preoccupation, but rather problems linked to aggressivity—more precisely still, situations that concerned matters of honor ("face-saving"), and that were obviously closely linked to shame and doubt: "Such considerations," writes Demos, "are manifest, for example, throughout the legion of Court cases that had to do with personal disputes and rivalries. Many of these cases involved suits for slander or defamation—where the issue of public exposure, the risk of shame, was absolutely central. Moreover, when a conviction was obtained, the defendant was normally required to withdraw his slanderous statements, and to apologize for them, *in public.*"

We know that, according to Erikson, the fixation at a particular stage of development implies, later on, a strong preoccupation with certain specific aspects of social organization. Corresponding to the second stage of development is the concern for "law and order." And of course, "few people have shown as much concern for 'law and order' as the Puritans."[10]

Here then is a stable homogeneous group, due to its cultural unity, its relative isolation in relation to the outside world (at least during the first decades of its settlement in New England), the absence of major social subdivisions, and above all the domination of a "totalitarian" ideology in the genuine sense of the term: the Puritan religion. The result was a set of specific mothering and child-rearing practices which had a decisive effect on the development of the personality, and consequently on certain important aspects of adult behavior—consequences that, according to John Demos, were also manifest in a certain conception of the social order and of the role of institutions.

It must be said, however, that the univocal causal relationship Demos establishes between certain mothering practices of the group and characteristics such as the preoccupation with "law and order" is not altogether justified. The Puritan religion itself implied a concern for "law and order," and any attempt to find a psychoanalytic explanation for it is superfluous. On the other hand, the aggressive behavior of the inhabitants of Plymouth Colony is less easily explained by Puritanism alone; similarly, the strong emphasis on questions of honor can be identified as a characteristic of a significant "basic personality." Still, one must note that when Kardiner and Linton studied the Alorese or the Comanches, the relations they found between primary institutions, the basic personality and the secondary institutions formed a detailed and complex configuration, one that was sufficiently idiosyncratic so that it could not be attributed to general and commonly observable sociocultural conditions. This is not true in the case of Plymouth Colony. Only a comparative study of several groups of this type would allow one, perhaps, to resolve the problem.

On the other hand, Stanley Elkins' study of black slaves in the United States could have resulted in a more convincing explanation than the one he proposes, if he had invoked the influence of a specific family structure on the formation of the slave personality.[11]

Stanley Elkins establishes a fundamental distinction between the "open system" of slavery as it was practiced in Latin America, where various institutions eased the existence of the slave and made him partially independent of his master, and the "closed system" of slavery practiced on the plantations of the South, in which nothing could weaken the total dependence of the slave on his white master. According to Elkins, the slave entered this closed system after having experienced the basic psychological shock of being torn from Africa and from his ancestral culture; as a result, he knew no other values or other meaningful norms than those imposed on him by his masters. Like certain prisoners of the Nazi concentration camps, the black slave internalized the norms of the master and accepted, paradoxically, the latter as his "father," identifying with him and regressing, in relation to this cruel father, to the emotional stage of the child. This accounted for the appearance of the specific personality of the black American slave, "Sambo." Elkins writes: "Sambo, the typical plantation slave, was docile but irresponsible, loyal but lazy, humble but chronically given to lying and stealing; his behavior was full of infantile silliness and his talk inflated with childish exaggeration. His relationship with his master was one of utter dependence and childlike attachment: it was indeed this childlike quality that was the very key to his being."[12]

Elkins' "closed system" endows the slavery of the American South with one of the essential characteristics of homogeneous groups, but the absence of any systematic reference to the primary institutions raises the question of the stability of this group. In his book, Elkins himself made a detailed comparison between slavery and the system of the Nazi concentration camps and found many similarities in the psychological processes at work in both contexts, which would suggest a temporary homogeneous group. On the other hand, in his reply to his critics Elkins practically abandoned the comparison with the Nazi camps in favor of the more flexible notion of "total institution" proposed by Goffman; this comes even closer to the temporary group. But Elkins' initial study contained an allusion to the specific family situation of the slave:

For the Negro child, in particular, the plantation offered no real satisfactory father-image other than the master. The "real" father was virtually without authority over his child, since discipline, parental responsibility, and control of rewards and punishments all rested in other hands; the slave father could not even protect the mother of his children except by appealing directly to the master. Indeed, the mother's own role loomed far larger for the slave child than did that of the father. She controlled those few activities . . . that were left to the slave family. For that matter, the very etiquette of plantation life removed even the honorific attributes of fatherhood from the Negro male, who was addressed as "boy"—until, when the vigorous years of his prime were past, he was allowed to assume the title of "uncle."[13]

We can see here the outlines of a unique family structure, in which the problem of the identity formation of the black male child was to become, of necessity, the focal point of intense neurotic conflicts.[14] It seems to us plausible to consider this family structure as an essential factor in the formation of the personality of the black slave, whether of the Sambo type or not. It would have been important to analyze the relationship between this kind of "basic personality" and various aspects of the black subculture on the plantations; the results would doubtless have suggested that we were dealing with a stable homogeneous group, characterized by the interaction between culture and personality. This kind of analysis would still have allowed Elkins to utilize the conceptions of Sullivan and those of role theory, but the specifically psychoanalytic part of his study would have been strengthened, even while allowing him to answer a question that one cannot fail to raise after reading his book: How is it that temporary institutions, such as those that Elkins used as models, could give rise to a personality as stable in its essential characteristics (over several generations, moreover) as that of Sambo? Why not look, in trying to answer this question, at the most stable of institutions, that of the specific family structure?

The stable homogeneous groups that interest the historian are few in number, and the method of analysis that we propose to apply to them here is clear. It is evident that the essential characteristics of the basic personality of such a group must be found, with all of its idiosyncratic elements, in a significant number of individuals belonging to the group. We can therefore formulate the verification criteria for the psychohistorical study of stable homogeneous groups in one sentence: *Any psychohistorical explanation concerning these groups must be formulable in terms of typology and verifiable in terms of biography.*

If the analysis of family structure and of specific primary institutions forms the center of graviy of the psychohistorical study of stable homogeneous groups, the center of gravity of unstable or temporary homogeneous groups varies according to the nature of the factor that dominates in the formation of the group: a dominant personality or an isolated collective obsession on the one hand, or the psychological effect of a total institution on the other.

The influence of a personality on a group of "believers" and the influence of an obsession in the absence of a dominant personality (more exactly, without the continuous presence of a dominant personality[15]) seem to be governed by an identical mechanism: the members of the group seem to renounce their individuality, and the injunctions of the dominant personality or of the obsessive ideology, like the norms of the total institution, often lead them to the most aberrant and sometimes even the most criminal behavior without their manifesting the least resistance, as if they were under the effect of hypnosis.

In the category of groups dominated by a personality, we recognize the prophet and his disciples or the head of a sect and its members, ready to follow their leader even into death; such groups include the millenarians of the late Middle Ages,[16] as well as Hitler and the "true believers" of the Nazi party.[17] If the leader is replaced by a dominant fantasy, we have the bands of flagellants or the groups of the possessed (or of witches) in Loudon, in Salem—a multitude of similar examples dot the history of the Western world.[18] Although they are more homogeneous than all the others, these groups are nevertheless astonishingly short-lived. If the dominant personality disappears, the group disintegrates; if the circumstances change, the collective obsession suddenly dies down: "normalcy" returns, as if nothing had happened.[19]

We must admit from the start that it is extremely difficult to explain the behavior of temporary homogeneous groups of this type. The classical explanation is the one proposed by Freud in *Group Psychology and the Analysis of the Ego.*[20] It is not an acceptable explanation, as we shall see.

Freud too seems to admit that an "idea" can replace a dominant personality and have the same psychic effect on a group, even though he considers this a minor point. What interests him is the relation of the group to its leader, and the relation of the members of the group to each other. Two explanations, which are interdependent, allow him to resolve the problem to his satisfaction. First, "A primary group of this kind is a number of individuals who have put one and the same object in the place of their ego ideal and have consequently identified themselves with one another in their ego."[21] In other words, in this kind of group the members have abandoned their individual superegos (their ego ideal) in favor of a collective superego, founded on the process of identification among the various members of the group. Why does this substitution of the leader's superego for the superego of each member occur? Freud replies with a phylogenetic explanation: "Thus the group appears to us as a revival of the primal horde. Just as a primitive man survives potentially in every individual, so the primal horde may arise once more out of any random collection. . . ."[22] And above all: "The uncanny and coercive characteristics of group formations, which are shown in the phenomena of suggestion that accompany them, may therefore with justice be traced back to the fact of their origin from the primal horde. The leader of the group is still the dreaded primal father; the group still wishes to be governed by unrestricted force. . . ."[23]

Thus, in order to explain the influence of the leader on the group, Freud must have recourse to a phylogenetic theory with no basis whatsoever. Furthermore, if one recalls that ideas can impose themselves on a group with the same power as individuals, it becomes hard to see how the analogy with the father of the primal horde can apply. And how would it apply to groups dominated by a woman? Of Freud's explanation, we can retain therefore two elements: the libidinal nature of the bonds formed between the members of a group of this kind, and the introjection of the leader's values by each member of the group. These notions, which are more descriptive than explicative, are close to what we wrote earlier about the relationship between the charismatic personality and the group; several possible avenues for psychohistorical investigation are suggested by it.

Even without knowing the exact nature of the process involved, but simply after observing that among the members of a group of this type there is a total introjection of the leader's values or an absolute sharing of the same obsession, the historian can interpret the basic elements of these shared fantasies in terms of their unconscious mechanisms, and establish a link between them and the manifest behavior of the group. This is what I myself tried to do in *L'Antisémitisme nazi,* in which I showed that the fantasy of the Jew as a germ was shared by Hitler and his followers, and that this fantasy led to a behavior of identification and purification (a combination well known to students of individual obsessions), whose final form was to be the physical elimination of the Jews, the "final solution."[24]

The functioning of total institutions is similar, as one can see from certain first-person accounts of the evolution of the behavior of inmates in the concentration camps. We may take as an example the one analyzed by Bruno Bettelheim in *The Informed Heart.* According to Bettelheim, the aim of the Nazi concentration camp system was to break the individuality of the prisoners, "and to change them into a docile mass from which no individual or group act of resistance could arise."[25] The various methods employed to this end by the SS succeeded in a certain number of cases, and the group of prisoners came to manifest similar psychic characteristics of which the most important was an infantile regression combined with a more or less strong identification with the aggressor: "Since old prisoners had accepted, or been forced to accept, a childlike dependency on the SS, many of them seemed to want to feel that at least some of the people they were accepting as all-powerful father images were just and kind."[26] Bettelheim does not, of course, suggest that all of the prisoners arrived at that point; but a certain fraction, or subgroup, did.

Temporary homogeneous groups, whatever the differences between them, all present, therefore, an identical configuration: at a given moment, an individual, an idea, or an institution brings together a number of individuals in a group which, under this influence, adopts a form of behavior due to a sudden transformation of the personality of the members of the group. But once the dominant personality, the idea or the institution disappears, the group as a whole disintegrates and the behavior of its members reverts, most often, to what it was before the formation of the group.

These empirical data do not lend themselves to a single theoretical explanation. One can opt for the theory of continuous identification and internalization, but how then can we explain the restructuring of the personality? This restructuring is altogether paradoxical, for it is both unconscious and profound, yet is at the same time ephemeral. In cases of this kind, the historian can do no more than attempt a description and a few partial explanations, such as the influence of the charismatic personality. Taken as a whole, temporary homogeneous groups are not yet amenable to systematic psychohistorical analysis.[27]

Heterogeneous Groups: The Study of Isolated Phenomena

The study of heterogeneous groups presupposes the primacy of sociological explanation.[28] The contribution of psychology can be only secondary, but, as we emphasized earlier, it is essential to an understanding of the phenomenon in all its aspects.

In this context, the study of isolated phenomena—whether a collective attitude, a ritual, or some enduring form of symbolization on the level of the group—represents the first and logically the simplest stage. Thus, David McClelland attempted to isolate and analyze the extent and the origins of the "need for achievement" in various societies.[29] The psychohistorical objective (although the term "psychohistory" is not used) of McClelland's study is explicitly stated: "The present effort . . . should be viewed as a first attempt by a psychologist interested primarily in human motivation to shed some light on a problem of historic importance [i.e., that of economic growth—S.F.]."[28] According to McClelland, there exists an essential causal relationship between a high degree of the "need for achievement" in the majority of the individuals in a group and a high rate of economic growth, the inverse also being true. McClelland attempted to measure, by means of various projective tests, the "need for achievement" in several contemporary societies; he attempted to do the same for several societies of the past as well, chiefly through a content analysis of literary and artistic themes. Children's literature plays an important role in the identification of the degree of the "need for achievement" in various modern societies, whereas classical literature and vase drawings play a similar role in the study of Greek society in the Golden Age.

It is with the explanation of the origins of the "need for achievement" that we enter fully into the domain of psychohistory as we understand it. McClelland establishes a link between this type of motivation and a specific family context: the mother of a child who in later life will manifest a high degree of the "need for achievement" encourages the child, from a very young age, to show a great deal of independence. At the same time, the attitude of the father in this family context must not be restrictive or authoritarian.[31] Generally speaking, the interference of the mother is tolerated and will allow for higher achievement, whereas the interference of the father (in the case of a male child) will have the opposite effect.[32]

One notes that the Protestant ethic tends to favor the kind of family behavior that stimulates the "need for achievement;" this allows us to add a psychological dimension to Max Weber's famous theory concerning the role of Protestantism in the development of modern capitalism.

McClelland's theses provoked some controversy, and his quantitative demonstrations are not always convincing. In this instance, however, what matters is not the rigorousness of the demonstration but the formulation of the question, which opens up a whole field of inquiry. To suggest that there is a relationship between profound psychological attitudes and economic develop-ment is to open up new horizons for economic history, and to demonstrate that even a phenomenon seemingly as independent of psychology as economic growth can, through the psychohistorical analysis of a specific attitude (the "need for achievement") take on a new significance. It goes without saying, however, that it is in the domain of collective disorders—what Georges Devereux calls "ethnic disorders" and "typical disorders," linked to a specific cultural model or a particular social structure[33]—that the psychohistorical study of isolated phenomena will find an immense field of application.

"Every culture," writes Devereux, "allows certain fantasies, drives and other psychic manifestations to reach and remain on the conscious level, while repressing others. That is why all the members of a given culture have in common a certain number of unconscious conflicts."[34] We shall return to this essential notion in discussing the global analysis of cultures, but it is funda-mental for the study of isolated phenomena as well, for the psychohistorian will want to investigate the relationship between the global culture and the predominance of a given fantasy or basic attitude; he will also attempt to analyze a given characteristic trait in its various stages of manifestation, or else compare it to a similar trait in a different sociocultural context. Could one not study, for example, the evolution of paternal authoritarianism in the German family from the eighteenth century to the present, or else compare the characteristic traits of this widespread phenomenon in German culture with the doubtless different traits that it manifests in Russian society? Or again, to cite another of Georges Devereux's suggestions, could we not examine, *through time,* the way in which various cultures "masculinize" their men, "feminize" their women and make their children "childlike"?[35]

If we turn to psychic disorders in the clinical sense of the term, it is again Georges Devereux who points out that the most common neurosis in our societies at the turn of the century involved symptomatic disorders; during the 1930's, it was replaced by characterial disorders, whereas today patients suffer rather from "an alteration in their sense of their own identity."[36] It is the manifestly irrational or morbid kinds of behavior that provide a rich material for study. Is not the first task of psychohistory to narrate the history of, and furnish an explanation for, the evolution of neurotic and psychotic disorders in various cultures, as a function of the evolution of the global sociocultural context?[37]

The great movements of collective irrationality require the same kind of analysis as the clinical disorders. Among the most evident of such pheno-mena, we may mention the witch-crazes and the witch-hunts,[38] or anti-Semitism and the persecution of the Jews. We shall consider in some detail two of these examples, to show how, in each case, psychohistory can add a new dimension to the traditional and essential sociocultural analysis.

A few years ago, the British historian Hugh Trevor-Roper published his study on *The European Witchcraze of the Sixteenth and Seventeenth Centuries*. His work meets all the traditional canons of historiography, for it describes perfectly the social and intellectual context of the phenomenon in question: ancient Manichean notions as well as various pagan traditions survived in the midst of marginal groups which feudal Christianity had assimilated only very partially, especially in the mountainous regions of Europe. In the context of a general struggle against heresies, the Dominicans, seeking to delimit and wipe out these heterodox beliefs, erected an elaborate system out of their diffuse notions and thus created an increasingly complex mythology concerning the practices of witchcraft and the nature of witches. But as the mythology of the defenders of the faith became more elaborate, it in turn attracted psychopaths of all kinds (according to Trevor-Roper), thus contributing to its own propagation.

It matters little to us what other social, intellectual, and political factors contributed to the growth of the witch-craze and later to its decline, as long as the psychological dimension of this immense harvest of collective fantasies is absent. Although Trevor-Roper, in discussing the fantasies of the witches themselves, mentions in passing that they belong to the domain of psychopathology, when it comes to the monks who created the whole system he does no more than describe a kind of theological-intellectual process without even raising the question of psychopathology.[39] And yet, a work such as the *Malleus Maleficarum* (*The Hammer of the Witches*), an encyclopedia of witchcraft written by two Dominicans and listing all the practices of witches and the measures used to counteract them, certainly calls for psychohistorical interpretation. The aim of such an interpretation would be to lay bare at least part of the irrational foundations of the movement.

Amand Danet, in his Introduction to a new critical edition of the *Malleus*,[40] has in fact attempted a psychohistorical interpretation. Danet seeks to define the anguish that lies at the very source of the inquisitors' obsession, an anguish that has often been described as characteristic of the late Middle Ages, when the end of the world seemed just around the corner. This obsession gave rise to a compensatory fantasy about the Church and the motherly Virgin, as well as to its necessary counterpart, the fantasy of the maleficent woman, the witch who must be thrown into the fire and who is "herself fire, a hot and evil flame." Here we enter into the obscure dialectic between the sexual fantasies of the inquisitor and those of the witch herself—a dialectic that doubtless reflects conflicts of an altogether different order. For what is the aim of the inquisitor, asks Danet, if not to dishonor this woman (the witch) and her sexuality? But in that case, he asks, what is the "underlying motive for this operation?" The explanation Danet offers is most suggestive: "Could it be a question of responding to an obscure cultural movement of masculine revenge, directed against an Indo-European (Celtic and Germanic) matriarchal *culture* in which the mother had some of the attributes of the priest and the prophet? A whole tradition of folklore has persisted over the centuries, heavy with the symbolism of an obscure battle between maleficent women who castrate men or change them into beasts, and men who attribute to women only the phallic flight of impotence, riding on a demon, an animal, or a ridiculous stick. . . ."[41] Finally, the *Malleus* completes this picture with an image of God the Father. The figure that emerges is that of a divinity full of duplicity and sadism:

> Beneath the watchful eyes of such a cunning father, what can the sons be if not desperate, impotent men with sado-masochistic tendencies? The image of transgression is linked, in their minds, with that of dissimulation and perversion. The desire of such sons is directed toward the forbidden fruit, which appears all the more "infinitely desirable" since it bathes in the fantasy of the unattainable and is guarded by the interdiction of a wrathful Father. Under the pressure of an always ill-resolved crisis, man is then tempted to scorn the forbidden pleasure, to dishonor sexuality. In trying to win the good graces of the Father, he even goes so far as to practice a certain sadism toward others and ultimately a castrating masochism toward himself.[42]

As a matter of fact, Amand Danet merely touches the tip of the iceberg, and one can imagine a much more detailed and in-depth analysis of the same fantasies. That would have been beyond the scope of an introduction, however; and in any case, we are far from Trevor-Roper and his explanation of the demonological system of the inquisitors as part of the "rationalism of the period."[43] One would like to complete this discussion by an analysis of the fantasies evoked in Michelet's *La Sorcière,* but as we suggested earlier, Alain Besançon's brilliant reading of that text presents a methodological problem which, as far as we are concerned, is not resolved.

Turning now to another species of collective "craze," that of anti-Semitism, we note that witches and Jews were amalgamated in the fantastic imagery of evil. But even at a time when witches and demons had disappeared, the Jew remained; indeed, he is the most enduring symbol of Evil known to Christianity. One could go so far as to say that in the sociocultural context of the Christian world as a whole, the myth of the Jew fulfills a single function from the sociological and the psychological points of view: he allows the society in question to distinguish Good from Evil, the Pure from the Impure, what is itself from what is "other." From the sociological point of view, the Jews represent above all the deviant group that allows a society to define its own limits.[45] From a psychological point of view, the identifying function of the Jew is even clearer: he is the "group's counter-ideal," whose essential function is to "serve as a negative counterpart to the group ideal, an embodiment—as an example to be avoided—of everything that the group ideal is not, and must at all cost avoid being."[46]

But even on the most general level, an explanation of the hostility directed against the Jew in terms of the latter's double identifying function is insufficient. We are dealing here with an overdetermined phenomenon, and it is the effect of overdetermination that explains the stability of this collective attitude and the endurance of the symbol. The religious and cultural origins of this negative symbol are well known; they were constantly reactivated on the social level by a particular structure of relationships between Jews and non-Jews, as well as by certain additional functions of the Jew in situations of change and crisis. On the general psychological level, the negative symbol owes its permanence not only to its identifying function, but also to its particular overtones in the unconscious and to its offering an outlet for the projective tendencies of specific categories of neurotic or psychotic personalities.

Thus, in sociological terms, as concerns the relations between Jews and non-Jews, the religious auto-segregation of the former helped to arouse hostility, as did their conviction of being a "chosen people"; their group solidarity allowed others to identify them with all that was "foreign," and to imagine them capable of the worst betrayals; above all, their professional concentration in the most visible sectors of the society (finance, in medieval and in modern times; cultural affairs in modern times), their unusually rapid upward social mobility in comparison with neighboring groups, and finally their participation in certain extremist ideological movements—all these factors reinforced the negative attitudes of the society around them.

During the endogenous social transformations of a non-Jewish society in a situation of *anomie* and crisis, the hatred of the Jew fulfills an important integrative function: "This sentence: 'I hate the Jews' is a sentence which is said in chorus; by saying it one connects oneself with a tradition and a community," wrote Sartre.[47] And in my own previous study, I added: "For a society or a class in the midst of rapid transformation, when the old bonds of community have disappeared and new bonds have not yet been created, to attach oneself to a tradition and a community becomes a vital need."[48] Furthermore, in a situation of crisis, the tension between the Jew and his environment becomes exacerbated: certain classes in the society lose their status and their prestige, and in their eyes any success on the part of the Jew becomes infuriating as professional rivalries increase. Finally, in the eyes of the society as a whole the role of the Jew becomes more threatening as the social order disintegrates, and people begin to wonder whether the Jew himself is not the cause of that disintegration.

The astonishing stability of the negative symbol of the Jew is due perhaps above all to the particular psychological coloring of the imagery that surrounds the Jew in the collective unconscious. The remarks that follow are hypothetical, but in a society that is both fundamentally Christian (at least until very recently) and fundamentally patriarchal, they have a certain logic that cannot be easily dismissed. Thus, to the extent that one accepts the notion of Oedipal conflict, and to the extent that in many individuals the problem of Oedipal ambivalence is never wholly resolved, the Jew becomes—for cultural reasons that are readily understandable—the symbol, in a Christian world, of the "bad father." Indeed, as has often been noted, the Jews are considered as the representatives of God the Father, in opposition to God the Son, with whom the Christian child identifies. But God the Father is the Law of Retaliation as opposed to the Law of Love; he represents strict justice and the commandments of an authoritarian ethic, as opposed to charity. The Jews are the ancestors, those whom the Christian child readily assimilates to the father. Thus, the Christian imagination sees (more or less consciously) in the conflict between the Jews and Christ a reflection of old personal conflicts with the father, and this conflict comes to symbolize, on an unconscious level, the Oedipal situation. Certain Jewish practices can only reinforce, moreover, this identification of the Jew with the father in the Oedipal conflict. Circumcision, for example, can evoke the threat of castration and even of death, a threat that is intimately linked to the Oedipal conflict. One finds the trace of these identifications and these fears under the most various forms in Western culture, from the myth of ritual murder to the image of the Jew as a frightening old man, as Ahasverus the Wandering Jew or some other similar figure.[49]

Finally, in general psychological terms the hostility directed against the Jew serves as an outlet for the projections caused by certain specific deformations of the personality. We obviously have no sufficient data to determine whether virulent anti-Semites are for the most part neurotic or psychotic personalities, but the clinical studies by Ackermann and Marie Lazarsfeld-Jahoda,[50] by Adorno and his associates, by Gough[51] and by Loewenstein[52] tend to confirm that hypothesis, just as my own brief survey in *L'Antisémitisme nazi* does: the biographies of some twenty notorious anti-Semites, most of whom lived in the nineteenth and the beginning of the twentieth centuries, seem in fact to indicate a correlation between a fanatical hatred of the Jews and various personality disorders.[53] The correlation, moreover, is not between extreme anti-Semitism and certain specific disorders, but—and this confirms the clinical hypotheses of Ackermann and Jahoda—between anti-Semitism and a whole potential range of neurotic or psychotic characteristics.

The identification of the general sociological and psychological functions of anti-Semitism and the study of their interrelationship does not amount to a psychohistorical study in the true sense of the term, for the diachronic element is still missing. That is precisely where specific questions come into play: *one must study the transformation of the general functions in specific, and changing, historical contexts.*

We have already mentioned, for example, the role of anti-Semitism as a factor of social cohesion in situations of *anomie* or crisis. The psychological dimension of this role is particularly easy to illustrate when the society in question is undergoing a prolonged crisis or when the identity of the group is still uncertain: in such cases, the negative symbol serves to emphasize the positive traits of the collective identity, by means of contrast. This process, discernible in various groups of European society during the period of radical transformation in the second half of the 19th century, was particularly evident in Germany, where the changes were more rapid and more intense than elsewhere and where the formation of a stable collective identity was prevented by very serious obstacles. Thus, many Germans became conscious of their own "German-ness" thanks to the imaginary Jew. "The German people," wrote the racist anti-Semite Böckel, "must, thanks to anti-Semitism, learn to be aware of itself once again as the Germanic race opposed to the Jewish race." Irving Fetscher, who quoted this statement by Böckel, adds: "The imaginary counter-image [*Gegenbild*] of the Jewish people appears, for a people such as the Germans, whose national consciousness is very weak, as a welcome means whereby to achieve, indirectly, a growth of this national consciousness."[54] One could cite a whole list of quotations on this theme by German anti-Semites: Jörges, Paul de Lagarde, and many others. Commenting on the examples she cites on this subject, Eva Reichmann notes: "An inner disharmony, a lack of unity, was at the bottom of the intellectual pre-War anti-Semitism in Germany. An artificial homogeneity based on the selection of a common foe was to be substituted for the natural homogeneity based on national feeling which had had no chance of developing before the disintegrating influence of a highly developed industrialism began to shatter it."[55]

Another psychological factor that reinforced anti-Semitism in Germany during the nineteenth and twentieth centuries—especially in the middle classes—was the high frequency of the authoritarian family context, and hence of the "authoritarian personality." We know that a tendency to be prejudiced, and especially a tendency toward anti-Semitism, is one of the essential characteristics of the authoritarian personality. Consequently, wherever this type of personality is especially frequent, anti-Semitism is especially widespread. The authoritarian personality, we may note, represents a specific variant of the general psychological foundations of anti-Semitism based on personality factors.

In *L'Antisémitisme nazi,* I studied both the sociological and the psychological factors, in order to show their cumulative effect in a crisis-ridden Germany. The basic functions fulfilled by a hatred of the Jew remained unchanged, but the variants introduced by the rapid transformation of the social and psychological context became more numerous, and the interaction of various factors became more pronounced; nevertheless, the method of investigation remained logically the same, allowing us to understand the reality involved in all its complexity and in its historical evolution. There is no need for us to repeat here the details of an argument sufficiently documented elsewhere.[56]

Heterogeneous Groups: The Study of Change

The transformation of heterogeneous groups, which makes up practically all of the situations of social change that interest us, is far from being explained by a single, unanimously accepted sociological theory. The various theories that have been proposed can be classified according to the "content" of the change (theories of progress or of decline),[57] but a formal classification is more useful if one wants to see to what degree they take account of psychological factors.

We can thus distinguish three fundamental types: 1) theories of "nonchange"; 2) theories of progressive and continuous change; 3) theories of sudden and discontinuous change.

In the first category, we may place the structuralism of Lévi-Strauss and its potential application to advanced societies. It is possible that the structuralists will eventually arrive at a theory of the transformation of structures that will account for the laws of these transformations; at present, however, these laws are neither precise nor even perceivable. Structural analysis provides an important tool, however, from our point of view; to the extent that, as Robert Nisbet has noted, one can study change only in relation to a certain stability in the identity of the institution or the group that is changing, structuralism allows us to analyze the fundamental components of this stable identity. In this context, the contribution of psychology is clear: the basic structure reflects certain fundamental aspects of the human mind, whether we are dealing with formal binary oppositions or with yet another restatement of the incest taboo. On the level of the analysis of fundamental structures, psychology is predominant, even if its contribution can be expressed only in general terms. Any analysis of social change should in fact begin with an attempt to define the permanent structures of certain symbolic manifestations of the group (for example), but that is a step that the non-structuralists usually omit; they prefer to emphasize the permanence of certain institutional or cultural elements before turning to a study of the processes of transformation themselves.

The modalities of change have given rise to rival theories: in one camp are those who espouse the theory of gradual and continuous change; in the other, those who maintain that no genuine change is possible without a sharp break with the past, a sudden transformation in structure, paradigm, or norms. The theory of continuous change, in which one can include some of Marx's models as well as those of Talcott Parsons if one remains on the formal level of analysis, is based on the simple idea that the sources of change are found in the structure of the society itself: the tensions and "dysfunctions" that arise between elements in the social structure provoke an unstable situation in which certain elements became maladapted; the system will then tend to resolve the situation by readapting and transforming its constituent elements.[58] Societies advance, thus, in a continuous movement from one system of equilibrium to another, passing through necessary temporary stages of tension and disequilibrium in the process; these stages of disequilibrium can even be revolutionary crises in the Marxist sense of the term.

According to the theorists of discontinuous change, the processes we have just described exist, to be sure, but they can lead only to a "reordering" of the system without any genuine transformation. Genuine change, whether it is provoked by a social crisis, a technological advance, or the discovery of an anomaly in the existing scientific concepts, can be none other than a total break with the past and a sudden mutation of the structure or the paradigm.[59]

Some historians are not aware of this theoretical debate,[60] but their implicit or explicitly stated conceptions nevertheless place them either in the camp of change-through-modification-of-structures, or in that of sudden-passage-from-one-structure-to-another. In opposition to the traditional Marxist school of historians, one can quote, among many others, Emmanuel Le Roy Ladurie. After having emphasized the coherence which, despite all the variations, one can find in any given historical structure, Le Roy Ladurie remarks that the passage from one structure to another is, in the final analysis, a "random" phenomenon: "*Mutation*, in history as in ideology, remains, in most cases, that scandalous zone where chance reigns supreme: from this zone, factors that are often mysterious carve out, in the field of possibilities, large areas of necessity which impose themselves as inevitable, but which a moment before their appearance were as unpredictable as they were unimaginable."[61]

Is there not, in fact, a possible synthesis between the "dialectical" position and the "mutationist" one? Is there not, among the "mutationists," a certain confusion between the *unpredictable* nature of the event which produces the change in structure, and the *ex post facto explicability* of the event in terms of the structure whose disappearance it provokes? Robert Nisbet cites as examples the French Revolution and the Russian Revolution. But in fact the French Revolution can be seen as the result of a slow process of disintegration of the *ancien régime* and of the growing tensions and disequilibrium within the system, *and* as the result of an immediate crisis, the event (or the series of events) which provoked the change in the system; this event was unpredictable, to be sure, but it could be explained afterward in the context of the evolution that preceded it and without which it could not have taken place, or would not have had the consequences it had.

In the framework of this kind of synthesis, one can raise the problem of the influence of psychological factors on the processes of change. We may summarize here the model of change that we proposed in chapter 1.[62] We argued that the "reordering" of a system implies, in general, the abolition and the replacement of certain common symbols of power and the like, without any change in the fundamental norms, whereas the passage from one system to another can be accomplished only with the disintegration and the restructuring of these norms. Our conclusion was as follows: "The essential causes of the reordering or the transformation of a social system are social, not psychological, in nature. However, the integration of a new symbolic system (in the case of reordering) or of new norms (in the case of transformation) into the society in question depends not only on social factors, but also on the affective reactions of a majority of the members of that society—facts that are interpretable only in psychological terms."

Let us take as an example German society in the twentieth century. We can distinguish three essential norms that were expressed by different symbolic systems: unconditional obedience to hierarchical authority, the acceptance of self-sacrifice for the glory of the group, and an active commitment to the supremacy of the group. Under the Empire as under the Weimar Republic and the Third Reich, these norms were represented by a symbolic system whose bases were constituted by elements relating to the head of State, the army and the national territory.

Under the Empire, the three fundamental norms were accepted and invested with powerful positive affects; the symbolic system that represented them was accepted as a whole, despite a growing disaffection with the person of Wilhelm II as Emperor. When defeat brought about the replacement of the Empire by the Weimar Republic, the weakening of the Imperial army (reduced to a hundred thousand men), and the amputation of some national territories both on the eastern and the western frontiers, the result was a veritable exacerbation of the positive feelings invested in the three norms in question, together with a total rejection, by the majority of Germans, of the new symbols that expressed these norms. Thus, the reordering of the system did not succeed, and it was only with the coming of the Third Reich, when the symbolic system satisfied the aspirations of the masses, that one can speak of a genuine reordering. Nevertheless, the fundamental norms remained the same, and still carried a powerful emotional charge. After Germany's second defeat, the situation became altogether different: not only was the old symbolic system discarded, but the fundamental norms of the preceding systems lost their affective charge; the society of the Federal Republic seems to be in the process of assimilating new norms, closer to those of American society or of Western society in general than were the norms of the past.

In this particular case the processes of emotional investment and dis-investment are evident, and one can easily perceive the difference between a reordering of the system which does not succeed (Weimar) and a reordering that does, and is therefore accepted on the emotional level (Third Reich); one can also see the difference between these reorderings which preserve the fundamental norms, and a transformation of the system which involves a rejection of the old norms (the Federal Republic). But the underlying causes of these affective changes are not evident at first glance, and that is precisely the most significant question from a psychohistorical point of view.

In effect, the process of internalization is a general process which allows us to relate social structure to individual structure, but in itself it does not tell us anything about the reasons why a new norm is accepted or rejected. It is by analyzing the changes in attitude that accompany the evolution of some insti-tutions (the transformation of family structures, for example) that we can understand their relation to changes in norms when they occur. Let us again take Germany as an example. We can ask why, after the collapse of the Empire, the need for a despotic leader was felt as a profound necessity by most Germans even though the Weimar Republic offered them the novelty of a liberal system; why this leader was accepted with such enthusiasm under the Third Reich; and finally, why that same need for an authoritarian regime was easily replaced by the liberal system of the Federal Republic. In other words, we can ask why the traditional authoritarian norms were so easily abandoned at the end of the 1940's. To answer that question, we must examine the relationship to authority on two distinct levels: that of political structures and ideological injunctions on the one hand, and that of family structure on the other. In the absence of detailed studies on the evolution of the German family from the beginning of the century to the present day, we must content ourselves with a general discussion, citing facts that are known to and accepted by specialists in the field. Thus we may note that at the beginning of the century there was still a strong correlation between the level of political structures and that of family structure (especially in the middle classes), with the norm of authority generally preached and accepted in both; the following decades, however, saw an evolution in the Germany family toward greater liberalization, as well as the rapid disappearance of hierarchical feudal structures in a great many areas. The Third Reich, contrary to what is generally believed, did not prevent this transformation but encouraged it.[63] The German child born in 1930 grew up in an environment that was much more "fraternal" and much less "paternal" than the environment of a child born in 1920, let alone one born in 1900 or 1910. As a result, although one can understand the problems of group identity which led to the preservation of the norm of authority on the political level until the end of the Second World War, one can also see that the general emotional foundations of this norm were weakened by the evolution of the family structure; the ground was therefore ready, in an ever-growing segment of the German population, for the internalization of the new liberal norms implied by the change in the system that occurred in 1945. Without this evolution, the Federal Republic might have suffered the same fate as the republic of Weimar. These hypotheses will have to be confirmed by a series of systematic analyses; but for psychohistory there can be no definitive explanation of the social change that has taken place in Germany over the past few decades without an in-depth study of the changes in attitude toward authority in the German family, and of the repercussions of these transformations on individual development.

We shall not discuss here the role of psychological factors in a process of limited social change, such as the birth and the evolution of a political movement. What is involved is a relatively simple kind of analysis, the model for which has already been presented by Neil Smelser.[64] We shall consider the essential points of his model, which seems to us applicable to a large number of phenomena of partial change that the historian might study.

Logically, the analysis of change should proceed in four stages, the phenomenon under study being considered each time from a sociological and from a psychological point of view: a definition of the structural context, both on the sociological and the psychological level, should be followed by an analysis of the immediate cause of the phenomenon (usually, a lack felt by a fairly large number of people); this in turn should be followed by a study of the ideology or belief which serves as a rallying point for the members of the new movement; finally, the analyst must examine mechanisms of social and personal control that are activated by the formation and the development of the movement in question.

Remaining within the field of German history, we may analyze the birth and evolution of the Nazi Party according to the four stages outlined above. The social context that facilitated the spread of Nazism is well known; we can add to it an equally evident psychological context: there was the need for revenge, of course, but also the search for identity on the part of a society in full disarray, and a desire both for submission and domination, this last tendency being strongest in the authoritarian personality that seems to characterize the German middle classes of the period.

In social terms, the lack which functioned as the immediate cause was the destruction of a sense of national honor, as well as the economic, political, and social chaos of Weimar. In psychological terms, the lack can be defined as the reinforcement of the above-mentioned factors (problem of identity, aspirations of the authoritarian personality) by the social and political upheavals of the time.

As concerns the process of mobilization whereby the group most affected by the above changes rallied around an idea or a personality, we find that the explanation must be stated in psychological rather than in social terms, for what is involved here is the formation of a temporary homogeneous group (which we discussed earlier).

The same is true of the final stage of analysis, concerning the activation of mechanisms of social and individual control. Within the Nazi group, there occurs a weakening of the mechanisms of control of the ego; this is the collective regression typical of temporary homogeneous groups, with its usual psychological consequences: the acceptance of the fantasies of the leader and the development of a collective obsession of identification and purification in the face of the group's mythical enemy.

Obviously, not every phenomenon of limited change can be analyzed according to this model, but it does provide an example of a method that the historian can adapt to various contexts. Similarly, the phenomena of change that the historian seeks to interpret do not all fall into one of the two categories we have discussed here; some will be more general than the study of the birth of a political movement, without amounting to a transformation of the social system as a whole. What we have tried to propose are two different models whose elements can be combined according to the specific characteristics of the phenomena under study.

Before going on to discuss macro-history or the global analysis of cultures, let us stop for a moment to consider the possible contribution of psychohistory to the explanation of a unique phenomenon: that of generational age groups, or, to use the technical sociological term, cohorts.

Age Groups

The significance of a particular age group, and sometimes even its existence as a distinct stage, varies from culture to culture and period to period. According to Philippe Ariès, "the distinguishing marks of childhood" did not exist in medieval society. Children passed from the care of the mother or the wet nurse, in other words from the stage of infancy, to full—albeit passive—participation in the life of adults.[65]

It was in the sixteenth century that people began to distinguish childhood as a specific category. "The child, or at least the child of quality, whether noble or middle class, henceforth had an outfit reserved for his age group, which set him apart from the adults. The adoption of a special childhood costume, which became generalized throughout the upper classes from the end of the 16th century, marked a very important date in the formation of the idea of childhood."[66]

If childhood appeared as a distinct category during the sixteenth century, "adolescence," which plays such an important role in current psychoanalytic thought, did not make its definitive appearance, according to Philippe Ariès, until the end of the nineteenth century! Already in the eighteenth century, to be sure, Cherubino and the new recruit were present as two prototypes of the modern adolescent, but it was with Wagner's *Siegfried* that the adolescent really came into his own: "The music of *Siegfried*," writes Ariès, "expressed for the first time that combination of (provisional) purity, physical strength, naturism, spontaneity and joie de vivre which was to make the adolescent the hero of our twentieth century, the century of adolescence."[67]

One can of course dispute the exact date of the appearance of the "adolescent" in Western culture. The German *Bildungsroman* ("novel of education") of the early nineteenth century, of which Goethe's *Wilhelm Meister* is the most famous example, seems already to have been concerned with the basic problems of adolescence. We may fix the latter's appearance, therefore, rather at the end of the eighteenth century, in the works of Rousseau.[68] But the quarrel over dates is a minor matter. What matters is that we understand the historical and cultural variations imposed on some of the most important developmental phases of our existence. Depending on the society, certain developmental phases can be blocked or eliminated; conversely, some societies will create, as Kenneth Keniston has noted, developmental phases that do not exist in others.[69] This fact naturally leads to various hypotheses; thus, according to Keniston, "in societies where adolescence does not occur many of the psychological characteristics which we consider the results of an adolescent experience should be extremely rare: for example, a high degree of emancipation from the family, a well-developed self-identity, a belief system based upon a reexamination of the cultural assumptions learned in childhood, and, perhaps, the cognitive capacity for formal operation."[70] This type of correlation is not self-evident, but it is the kind of question that the historian can ask about age groups in various societies. In fact, the historian ought to establish the give-and-take between the age group and the society at large, explaining the characteristics of the former by the evolution of the latter, and, conversely, examining the possible influence of the age group on some of the attitudes of the society. Thus, in his study of childhood in France in the seventeenth century,[71] David Hunt shows both the particularities of the behavior toward children in the society, and the influence of this behavior on certain aspects of the society itself.

Hunt maintains that, contrary to Ariès's thesis (according to which parents were indifferent to the behavior of their children as long as the latter remained outside the adult world), French parents in the seventeenth century showed a strong interest in their children's reactions, beginning as early as infancy.[72] He even perceives an interaction between adult behavior, the reaction of the child, and certain crucial aspects of the social structure as a whole: "In particular, I have the impression," he writes, "that the second Eriksonian stage has been the most pertinent to the study of childhood in the old regime."[73] Hunt then provides an abundance of first-person accounts about the harshness of the methods employed to break the child's "autonomy" as soon as it manifested itself. As for the social consequences of this treatment, Hunt sums it up by showing the vicious circle it created: the father's harshness led to the same harshness in the son; in the society at large it led to the passive acceptance of a hierarchical order indifferent to the dignity of the individual and founded for the most part on coercive methods. By repressing the child's tendencies toward autonomy in the second stage of development, monarchic society could ensure, *to some extent,* the submission of adults: "In this way, a repressive status quo [was] anchored in the conflicts of the anal stage."[74]

In context, the sentence we have just quoted is not as "simplistic" as it might appear. Even so, one notes a certain absence of subtle discriminations (which is perhaps the inevitable weakness of psychohistory). Having said that, we must immediately go on: is Hunt's hypothesis verifiable? Can one demonstrate the existence of the correlation he suggests?

The developmental stage that Hunt found to be significant is the second stage of the Eriksonian model—the anal stage in orthodox psychoanalytic terminology. This was also the stage that John Demos found most pertinent in his study of Plymouth Colony. As Hunt notes: "There are several possible explanations for the particular salience of this aspect of Erikson's theory. For example, one might argue that because of its distinctive characteristics, seventeenth-century society chose to define with a special clarity issues associated with the second stage of childhood. It is also possible that *all* societies tend to stress these issues and that the emphasis found in the present study is related to a universal fact of childrearing."[75] This is an important observation, not because the emphasis placed on the problem of the second stage in Erikson's model doubtless reflects the fact that this stage, when the child's autonomy first manifests itself, elicits special attention from the parents, but rather because it seems that the attitudes acquired at this stage are—together with the formation of the identity—*those whose effects on the social behavior of the adult are the most readily identifiable.* In primitive societies or in certain homogeneous groups as we have defined them, it is possible to discover in adult behavior the consequences of a specific manner of resolving the problems of the first developmental stage (the oral stage, with its antithetical attitudes of trust and suspicion), or the consequences of the mode of resolution of the Oedipal conflict. The complex social organization of heterogeneous groups, on the other hand, places greater emphasis on attitudes toward authority on every level of behavior, and on the question of individual and collective self-image—hence on the solution of the problem of identity. If this is in fact the case, then Hunt's extrapolations, which are difficult to support in the context of an isolated study, would become altogether more significant in the framework of a comparative study.

We can obviously not present, in these pages, a comparative study of this kind. We will, however, after some general remarks on the characteristics of the stage of "youth" in contemporary societies, examine a particular aspect of this stage in German society at the beginning of the twentieth century; we will also suggest some possible comparisons between the German case and certain kinds of youthful behavior in more recent times, notably in American society during the 1960's.

Regardless of the exact period when adolescence and early youth emerged as a culturally distinct stage in the developmental cycle, it is only at the end of the nineteenth century that one finds the first expressions of the psychological and cultural exigencies of youth *as youth,* that is as a group with its own values, a distinct generation in the sense in which Karl Mannheim defined the term.[76] As several scholars have noted, most of the "rebellions of youth" up to that time ("Young Italy," "Young Turks," etc.) had been fought in the name of universal revolutionary ideals, rather than with the deliberate aim of expressing the aspirations of youth as such.[77]

Among the sociological criteria that characterize this age group, we must distinguish between the general criteria that define the function of youth in the global structure of modern societies on the one hand (these criteria, being "universalistic" in nature, do not allocate status and roles in terms of family or clan membership), and the social conditions of conflict between youth and the society at large on the other hand; this latter criterion is the more important one from our point of view.

Generally speaking, one can consider adolescence and youth in modern societies as the age during which the individual separates himself from the familial norms that defined his existence until then, without at the same time integrating himself into so-called "adult" society and accepting all of its norms. The adolescent tends to seek the company of his peers in organizations of various kinds, and to use these groups as environments in which to prepare for adult life. Naturally, not all such groups provide adequate preparation for adult life, and some provide very inadequate preparation indeed; nevertheless, it is in these groups that the adolescent can experience a whole series of roles that will be necessary for his integration into adult society. By definition, then, "Youth as an age span becomes a special period of discontinuity and resocialization in which past and future identifications and roles are sharply contrasted, often mutually incompatible."[78] Thus, the period of adolescence and youth implies, in modern industrial societies, an element of tension and of conflict with the adult society. This tension becomes especially pronounced when the society is undergoing rapid changes that give rise to major conflicts of values.[79] It is in such situations that the psychological tensions characteristic of this developmental stage become especially significant.

Before discussing the psychology of adolescence, we must emphasize once again that certain characteristics of the psychic transformation that occurs during this period of human development have taken on importance only very recently, and for the most part in industrial societies. It remains true, however, that the physiological transformations of adolescence, and the fact that these transformations are in all cultures accompanied by a change in status (the more or less harmonious and more or less rapid entry of the child into the adult world) make this a difficult period, characterized by certain psychological disturbances whose intensity can vary greatly from individual to individual.[80]

Even in industrial societies, differences in social status and sudden changes in the sociocultural context have a considerable influence on the behavior of adolescents; this influence is easy to account for theoretically, if one admits that this is the developmental stage during which the individual must define his identity, both by integrating the diverse elements of his own past history and by referring to the norms of the group to which he belongs—in other words, his sociocultural context.

It has been argued recently that a perpetual change in identity is becoming a normal psychological characteristic of modern man, who is obliged to adapt to a constantly changing environment.[81] Whether or not this is in fact the case, it is certain that during the first half of this century—and, for a great majority of young people, right to up to this day—the search for a stable identity has been an overriding concern. But we should note that the solution to this problem can take on three different forms (excluding a fourth, pathological possibility— that of permanent irresolution):

1) the acceptance of the social and ideological realities of the environment, together with its fundamental norms;

2) the rejection of these realities and the perpetuation of an attitude of revolt within the framework of "revolutionary" ideological and political institutions;

3) the rejection both of social reality and of all revolutionary solutions in the name of a more or less extreme degree of disinvolvement or "privatism"; the latter can be expressed in various forms, ranging from religious mysticism to absolute estheticism.

The first of these solutions is the one that the liberal bourgeois society of the West considers normal: it is the one adopted, as a rule, by the great majority of young people. As for the other two possibilities, it has seemed to us that the "ideological" deviant solution was more characteristic of the 1920's and 1930's, whereas the "privatist" solution has been more frequent in the recent past. If this change could be demonstrated, some fundamental questions would arise concerning the evolution of large-scale social structures, but above all the evolution of family structures in Western society.

If we examine the German youth of the first three decades of this century, we note that the movements of protest and revolt which developed in Germany were more structured than in neighboring countries; at the same time, these movements were simply a more emphatic expression of a malaise that was also evident among middle class youth in other Western countries. The social origins of this notable increase in the opposition of young people to the existing system have been well summed up by Kingsley Davis: the acceleration of the rhythm of social change, the growing complexity of the system, the appearance of conflicting norms within the society, and the acceleration of social mobility.[82] These conditions were particularly evident in Germany, where industrialization had been more rapid and on a larger scale than in other European countries, and where, by the beginning of the twentieth century, the messianic dreams attached to the foundation of the Reich were no more than a vague memory; furthermore, the conflicting norms thus produced—on the one hand, the demands of the new industrial society; on the other, the traditions of rural life, which still exercised a powerful attraction—gave rise to insurmountable divisions within the society.

But in Germany as elsewhere, the behavior of young people is far from being uniform, and the three solutions to the identity crisis that we mentioned above can be distinctly discerned. We shall not analyze here the significance of the first solution—that of acceptance and compromise—with all its possible variations: this was the traditional liberal solution finally chosen by the hero of Thomas Mann's *The Magic Mountain,* Hans Castorp, as well as by Mann himself. Nor shall we analyze the "privatist" solution, for the history of the period shows that it was adopted only by a minority. The second solution, implying the rejection of bourgeois reality and the perpetuation of utopian aspirations and of an attitude of revolt, seems to us far more significant: politically, it led to fascism or to communism, the two great revolutionary options of the period. It is by studying the youth movements that we shall discover the psychological bases of this option.

The history of the German youth movements has often been told.[83] It was in 1901 that the movement of the *Wandervögel* ("migratory birds") was officially founded, in a basement in Berlin-Steglitz. Under the leadership of the movement's founder, Karl Fischer, a few dozen youths aged from twelve or thirteen to nineteen went on organized hikes far from the cities, first in Germany and later in other parts of Europe. Hikes formed the basis of the movement's activities: there were the camp fires, the singing, the nights spent under the stars, the return to nature and to the sources of life. Soon after its founding, the movement, which grew from a few dozen to a few hundred and then to several thousand members[84] (most of them male), broke up into rival factions. Karl Fischer resigned and others took his place. At the great meeting of the youth movements that took place on the Hohe Meissner in 1913, there were not one, but several distinct groups present. Yet, the aspirations and the fundamental problems remained the same in all the groups and continued to be so after the war, when the movements became politicized and their influence was felt by a good part of the country's bourgeois youth. In the magazines of all kinds published by the various factions, as well as in their songbooks and in the novels, the poetry and the painting that they adopted, one finds the same fears and aspirations despite their apparent diversity.

"The time of the *Wandervögel's* foundation," writes the first historian of the movement, Hans Blüher, "was characterized by a struggle of young people against the world of adults."[85] Recently, some writers on the subject have tried to minimize the importance of this aspect of the movement, claiming that the youth of the *Wandervögel* were not in principle opposed to the world of their fathers and that their apparent rejection of it was only true of a few theoreticians within the movement.[86] In fact, all the evidence suggests the contrary: the movement was first of all an attempt to liberate young people from the world of adults, a world whose values and customs they rejected. Their opposition to that world was intense, so much so that during the war many young people demanded the exclusion of the first members of the movement—

who had in the meantime become adults—in the name of the natural opposition between generations.[87] But against what, exactly, were these young men revolting? What were the values and the behavior that they rejected?

In a very general way, we could reply, as Peter Gay does, that the *"Wandervögel"* sought an escape from the lies spawned by petty bourgeois culture, a clean way of life unmarked by the use of alcohol or tobacco, and, above all, a common existence that could rise above self-interest and shabby party politics."[88] Thus it was the lies, the routine, the often sordid character of petty bourgeois life—in the home, at school and in the larger social context—that were rejected. But this radical refusal, to which one should add a systematic anti-materialism and the horror of large modern cities, was accompanied by specific themes that were quite strange but quite important from our point of view. Here was a group of young people who, in the great majority, revolted against the "impurity" of the adult world in a very precise sense: they rejected alcohol and tobacco, but they also rejected the "impurity" of adult sexual life. The evidence for this is massive.

Among the favorite novels of the members of the youth movements, *Wiltfeber* was ambiguous on the question of the rejection of "impurity," but *Helmut Harringa* was a veritable call to arms against alcohol and eroticism.[89] But let us look, rather, at the writings of the *Wandervögel* or the *Bünde* themselves, and above all at the behavior of their members. "One of the principal targets of the attacks of the youth movements," writes someone who knew the movements first-hand, "was bourgeois social life, especially the coarseness of sexual mores both public and private, which assailed their deep longing for chastity at practically every streetcorner. Disgusted by the abject omnipresence of these corrupt morals, the young people, in their need for purity, at first saw no other solution than a total rejection of all sexuality. . . ."[90] In his introduction to a volume of writings of the youth movements, Theodor Wilhelm, while voicing skepticism about the role of the "generation conflict" in the constitution of the movements, maintains that "sexual asceticism" was one of their essential characteristics. But in reading the texts themselves, one is astonished by the arguments employed by these youth-movement members of forty years ago. Their rejection of sexuality was, they claim, a reaction against the "corrupt" morals of adults, but also an ordinary consequence of the fact that the young girls who founded their own groups, distinct from the male groups, were not very attractive![91] Curious rationalizations, these. Whatever one thinks of them, the rejection of a sexual freedom that today would be considered normal and desirable characterizes a considerable segment of the German youth movements of the beginning of the century, and (although to a lesser extent) of the 1920's as well. "Young people," writes Wyneken, "found no other solution to their sexual problem than to profess sexual abstinence and set up comaraderie as the relation between the sexes. . . ."[92] This statement, which seems to be a criticism, is in fact a kind of proclamation of faith by the author himself. As Walter Laqueur has noted, "Wyneken was on the whole in favor of 'heroic asceticism' and frequently stressed his belief that in the existing social order the sexual question was insoluble. . . . Heimann and the few others who went on record before the outbreak of the First World War favored abstinence before marriage, out of an 'erotic-mystical orientation' which, they insisted, was not at all identical with the spirit of abstinence preached by the professional philistine abstentionists.'"[93]

In conflict with the world of adults and wary of the opposite sex, the young Germans who joined the ranks of the youth movements naturally sought refuge, consolation, and a goal in life in their own group, the group of young men united under an idealized leader. In fact, more than the desire to return to nature, more than the flight toward a mythical past or a utopic future, it was the involvement with the group, the exaltation of comaraderie and the community of young men that marked the *Wandervögel* and the movements that followed it. Much has been said about the homosexual character (either latent or active) of the German youth movements. It is probable that the sexual reticence toward women, the immersion in a group of men at an age when young men often experience homosexual inclinations, and the influence of certain leaders contributed to the creation of a more or less overtly homosexual atmosphere in the movements, and perhaps even to certain homosexual practices.[94] We shall look in a while at the larger implications of these tendencies; first, however, let us consider the core of the movements: the community of peers and their leader.

The community, the group, was itself a program: as one of their manifestos declared, "Where lively people are together no one needs a programme. . . . There is nothing more wonderful and fruitful than communion in a small circle of confidants where no plan and no 'order of the day' hems in spontaneous vitality and the spirit . . . 'blowing where it listeth.' "[95] Or again, as one of the participants, Wilhelm Stählin, put it: "The new instinct that awoke, the instinct of community, found its perfect realization in the bonds of friendship within these small groups. . . ."[96] But without a leader, group action was impossible: the idealized, inspired leader was the center, the uniting bond and the activating element of each section of the movement.

It was a relationship of this kind that existed between the first *Wandervögel* and their leader, Karl Fischer, and it was the same relationship that united the members of the successive groups that made up the movements and those who led them: "At a time when democracy is conquering the whole world," wrote one of the leaders, Robert Oelbermann, in 1922, "at a time when the masses think they can rule and when the value of a person is judged by his pocket-book, . . . the awareness of leadership [*Führertum*] and the sense of loyalty in those who follow the leader [*Gefolgschafstreue*] have been reawakened in the youth movement. . . ."[97] The mystical and erotic character of the bonds between the group's leader and his young followers, which has been noted by Blüher and others, incontestably reflects a deep emotional involvement: "Oh, my leader," writes a young man beset by sexual problems which seemed to him irresolvable, "do not turn away from me, help me to be pure!"[98] These young "rebels" were waiting for a savior, on the personal level and on the collective one as well.

Before going further, we should emphasize that the themes of alienation, revolt, idealism, and utopia, expressed in extreme terms by the German youth movements of the first three decades of this century, were in fact the amplified echo of the fears and aspirations of a large segment of German society—or at least of German youth—at the time. Antimaterialism, the loss of confidence in the values of the bourgeois world, the determination to break out of the authoritarian straitjacket of the family and the larger social institutions (even if that involved accepting the authority of a charismatic leader)—these are among the great subjects treated in the art and literature of the period, by the Expressionists above all but by others as well. The most popular novel of the pre-war period, Burte's *Wiltfeber,* depicts the fundamental antagonism between the young Germanic hero and the rigid, suspicion-ridden, petty world of adults. Hessenclever's *Der Sohn* and Arnolt Bronnen's *Vatermord* express not only the son's revolt against the father, but, in the latter novel, the son's murder of the father. In his study of German culture during the Weimar Republic, Peter Gay devotes a whole chapter to the "revolt of the sons,"[99] which he sees as one of the fundamental psychological characteristics of the time. The same theme appears as an essential leitmotiv in the post-war German cinema: the hateful, demented nature of authority is one of the central themes of the most famous German film of the twenties, *The Cabinet of Dr. Caligari.*[100] As for the desire for a new community, for a charismatic leader and a liberating form of action, we know how deeply entrenched it was in the aspirations of German society during this period; those aspirations had their roots, to be sure, in a remote past, but were already manifest at the beginning of the century. The youth movements thus appeared as a kind of seismograph that registered a very deep upheaval.

We have already mentioned the sociological foundations of this revolt of the young. The sociological explanation is not sufficient, however, for it leaves aside the factors we have just described; a psychological analysis is necessary to complete the picture.

Let us return to our point of departure: the revolt of the young that became widespread in Germany after the beginning of the century was due to general social factors, but also to a new attitude toward the authoritarianism of German society and of the German family. This questioning of authoritarian norms can be attributed, it would seem, to a falling-off of the emotional charge associated with the hierarchical framework both on the general and the familial level, this falling-off being itself due to the intrusion of egalitarian norms imposed by industrial society as well as to the incipient transformation of the German middle-class family. In the framework of rural life or in the world of small craftsmen, the authority of the father was that of someone who was present at every hour of the day; in the framework of the new industrial society, that authority belonged to a man who was absent more and more of the time: it became more arbitrary, more blind, but more feeble as well. Furthermore, the ease of access to education gave the sons a sudden advantage over the fathers. Thus, the psychological foundations of revolt appear evident.

Before attempting to interpret them, let us recall the essential aspects of this revolt: 1) isolation of the young in an autonomous culture that emphasized the particular values of youth (*Jugendkultur*); 2) an insistence on ascetic ideals with a more or less strong homosexual coloration—in general, an idealized homosexuality; 3) the cult of the peer group and a quasi-mystical submission to the authority of the leader.

The isolation of the young in an autonomous culture appears as an obvious form of rejection of the surrounding reality, and at the same time as an extreme manifestation of the narcissistic regression that marks the normal development of the adolescent. But in this case we can speak of a narcissistic fixation, evidenced by exaggerated attitudes of self-admiration: the idealization of the values of youth within an autonomous culture; the idealization of the beauty of young bodies and of the physical environment of youth in the illustrations of books and magazines (especially in the stylized engravings of the movement's most famous illustrator, Fidus); the proliferation of rites and ceremonies that perpetuated the mythical, "all-powerful" world of youth by denying the very existence of another reality; finally, the narcissistic cult of the peer group and its leaders—idealized and aggrandized images of the self.

The narcissism of the members of the youth movement leads us to one of the essential components of their ascetic self-discipline as concerned alcohol and cigarettes, and above all, sex. Asceticism, in effect, is the rejection of uncleanness or pollution, be it by alcohol or sex (for alcohol and the sex life of adults were seen as forms of pollution); in other words, it is the perpetuation of one's original purity, which is the most intense form of narcissism. Asceticism is also the rejection of "debauchery" (interpreted as a loss of strength), the will to preserve one's erotic energy in all its magical fullness in order to devote it to a higher end (this theme recurs constantly in discussions concerning Eros and sex); in a word, it is the narcissistic preservation of a mythical plenitude of the self.

But the asceticism of the youth movements has, I believe, yet another psychological source: the fear of instinctual chaos. In his analysis of German films of the inter-war period, Siegfried Kracauer has convincingly shown that Germans at this time, and especially the young, felt confronted by a fundamental dilemma: traditional tyrannical authority was hateful, but if he abandoned it, man would find himself in chaos—social chaos and instinctual chaos—and chaos meant death.[101] The symbol of chaos in *The Cabinet of Dr. Caligari* is the carnival where Caligari hides out and from where Cesare sets out to strangle his victims. Thus, the disaffection with the authoritarian structure of the family and of society triggered revolt, but it also threatened the individual with fatal disintegration due to the chaotic irruption of instinctual forces that a weakened superego could no longer contain. Against this threat, the young rebel had only one recourse: he replaced external authority by an internal authority that was even stricter, but that appeared freely chosen.

Narcissism, ascetic discipline, and the imperious instinctual needs of youth account for the sublimated homosexuality that characterized the movement: the idealization of the peer group, the idealization of the male body, the myth of Eros as the antithesis of sexual debauchery, the cult of discipline—all of these factors converge toward the same end. Finally, these same factors account for the remarkable psychological compromise represented by submission to the leader.

The leader, in fact, was barely older than the members of the movement, but he was surrounded by a genuinely mystical aura. This cult of the leader amounted, it seems to me, to a psychic compromise between three pairs of contradictory impulses:

1) A compromise between the need to submit and the need to revolt. The initial authoritarian structure and the authoritarian family had inculcated the young with a profound need for submission, which tended to negate the will to revolt caused by other, independent factors. Now the leader was not a father figure, but a member of the same generation whom his followers idealized and whose leadership they "freely" accepted.

2) A compromise between total narcissistic regression and the facing of reality. The leader satisfied the narcissistic need, for he was the idealized image of the members themselves; that in turn allowed them to face certain real problems that the leader chose to bring up for discussion or to confront directly.

3) A compromise between asceticism and libidinal needs. The leader helped the young men to turn their backs on debauchery and became himself the object of the erotic desire of the members; these desires were then sublimated, their energy placed at the service of the group.

We may note, finally, that two of the principal psychological traits we have attributed to the members of the youth movements—latent homosexuality and the fear of instinctual chaos, whence the need for discipline and order—are characteristic traits of the "authoritarian personality," whose development is encouraged by the type of family structure that was prevalent in Germany during this period.[102]

It is impossible for us to undertake here the detailed comparative study that is needed between the German youth movements of the beginning of the century and the student movements of the 1960's. We can nevertheless suggest some directions for exploration. The similarities between these movements have sometimes been emphasized; in fact, the differences between them strike us as more important. But as to the reasons for these differences, we can only venture some very general hypotheses on the subject.

The student revolts of the 1960's involved a definite minority, but, as in the case of the German youth movements, this minority seems to have expressed, in an extreme way, a state of mind shared by a great majority of its peers. Very schematically, the opposition of these young people to contemporary society can be seen as having taken three different forms: 1) the bohemianism of the "hippies;" 2) radical activism; 3) a vague disengagement. The first two of these attracted attention because of their eccentricity or their political repercussions; the third, however, was probably much more representative of the general state of mind.[104] Indeed, the hippies and the radicals seem to have disappeared from the scene, whereas the feeling of vague alienation and disengagement has persisted.

It is obvious that once they reach adulthood, the great majority of today's "alienated" youth will adapt to the society around them; but the particular way in which they live their youth remains significant: *whereas at the beginning of the century the opposition of the young led to ideology (even if the ideology remained ill-defined) and to the desire to become involved in some kind of struggle, today their opposition seems to be leading to indifference, to personal disinvolvement.* One could, of course, simply say that we live in an era that has seen the "end of ideology,"[105] so that disengagement is, for many people, the only logical stance possible. That may be so, but in that case we have to ask whether this development is not also due to unconscious causes, over and above the simple rejection of the idols of the past and the obvious effects of a consumer society.

Kenneth Keniston has studied the psychological structure of "uncommitted" students in several American universities during the 1960's. These young people emerge as "rebels without a cause," incapable of defining the positive values to which they are attached, searching for an uncertain identity.[106] Their case histories are marked by a very clear repetitive pattern: strong attachment to the mother, whom they see as a victim, a woman who was not able to realize all her potential; a scornful attitude toward the father, who for the most part appears weak, incompetent, and always distant. The mother is not considered responsible for her own failures in life; the father, on the other hand, is.[107] In the psychoanalytic interviews and the projective tests given to these young people the predominant themes are oral, which corresponds to an attachment to the mother; but these oral themes are themes of dependence and passivity in relation to women. This dependence can be dangerous, for the fantasies that come up imply a struggle with the male rival; although the outcome of the struggle is always victory for the young hero, it is accompanied by guilt feelings and a profound fear of the conquered mother, whose demands the young man will be unable to meet.[108]

One can ask whether these attitudes, however extreme they may be, are not linked to a fundamental transformation of family structures in Western society—specifically, to a change in the sex roles of the two parents. In the German family at the beginning of the century, but also, to a somewhat lesser extent perhaps, in the American family, the central role of the father was an undisputed fact—this despite the reaction against various forms of authority on the part of the young people of the period. Admittedly, the social evolution that eventually led to the "disappearance" of the father had already begun, but until the Second World War the father's central position was only shaken, not eliminated altogether. The conflict between generations developed, therefore, according to the relatively simple pattern we described earlier: the rebellion of the sons was accompanied by a fear of the chaotic consequences of their rebellion, whence their asceticism and their need to channel their repressed energies into a different but still authoritarian direction; the leader of the peer group allowed young men to submit to authority, but the particular nature of the ego ideal he represented allowed for a remarkable compromise between rebellion and submission.

The definitive displacement of the father from his central role can be explained as the result of a clear sociological trend. As Alexander Mitscherlich has convincingly demonstrated, the father, who in traditional society was constantly present and visible, a source of authority but also a living example, has become more and more cut off from the family because of the demands of professional life in advanced industrial societies.[109] In fact, one can distinguish three successive and distinct phases in this transformation: the phase of close physical and cultural proximity between father and son, which is the phase where paternal authority was accepted and assimilated in the context of a continuous tradition and a feeling of reciprocity; the phase of physical and professional distantiation between father and son, which manifested itself more clearly during the second half of the nineteenth century than during the first half, and in which the absence of reciprocity, of continuous exchange between father and son gave rise to a seemingly arbitrary and distant authoritarianism as well as to the first signs of rebellion on the part of the sons, a rebellion which became widespread at the beginning of the twentieth century; finally, the third phase, which is the phase of the disappearance of the father: he becomes, in his son's eyes, a ridiculous personage and the object of scorn (since, as Keniston showed, he is so easily vanquished and displaced from his position near the mother), a phenomenon that exists not only in America but in the West in general.

Macro-history: Collective Mentality and Culture

The discussion of macro-history is all the more difficult because of the confusion that abounds concerning the exact nature and meaning of the phenomena covered by such terms as "collective mentality" or "national character"—yet it is precisely these phenomena which, insofar as they are analyzable, are the province of macro-historical analysis.

The term "collective mentality" was coined by the French school of historians, but its definition is hazy. Thus, in a recent essay, Jacques Le Goff speaks of religious mentalities and of the medieval mentality, but when he tries to explain exactly what he means by these terms, he does so in a very roundabout way:

> The level of the history of mentalities is the level of the ordinary and the automatic; it lies outside the control of the individual subjects of history because it reveals the impersonal content of their thinking: it is what Caesar and the last of his soldiers, Saint Louis and his serf, Christopher Columbus and the sailor of his fleet have in common. The history of mentalities is to the history of ideas what the history of material culture is to economic history. The reaction of the men of the fourteenth century to the plague, that divine punishment, grows out of the age-old, unconscious message of Christian thinkers from Saint Augustine to

Saint Thomas Aquinas; it can be explained in terms of the equation between illness and sin, formulated by the monks of the late Middle Ages, but it does away with every kind of logical articulation, every subtle form of reasoning, and keeps only the rough cast of the idea. Thus, the utensils of everyday life and the clothing of the poor derive from prestigious models created by the surface developments of the economy, of fashion and of taste. The style of a period lies below that, on the deep level of ordinary life.[110]

It is not surprising after this to learn that the word "mentality" is not listed in the indexes of contemporary works of psychology, anthropology, or sociology.[111] Yet, in speaking of mentalities the historian is not dreaming: there is certainly something there. Is that all we can say?

It will be readily admitted that the collective mentality includes certain commonly shared perceptions, as well as certain commonly accepted attitudes. Now is it not this community of perceptions and attitudes that gives a society—whether large or small—its sense of identity? And the notion of identity carries with it an essential element: that of *internal coherence.* Le Goff himself recognizes this when he speaks of the "style of a period." Lucien Febvre alludes implicitly to this same coherence when he asks whether certain periods or cultures do not exhibit identifiable emotional tendencies—toward cruelty or pity, toward hatred or love.[112] According to Alphonse Dupront, this coherence is the key concept (the "baptismal notion," in his words) in the study of collective mentalities.[113] But can a coherence in mentalities exist in a vacuum? Does the coherence of a collective mentality not express the structural unity of the underlying culture? We thus arrive at a quasi self-evident definition: the collective mentality is the common denominator of perceptions and attitudes produced by a specific culture, or by one aspect of that culture,[114] at a given period.

The culture in question can be national or transnational, and we note immediately that in the case of a collective mentality related to a national culture we can speak of a "national mentality," which is none other than the much-maligned "national character." But in that case, what do we do with the objections raised against the notion of national character? Do these objections not apply to collective mentalities as well?[115]

The objections are obvious: the heterogeneity of a national group, the multiplicity of social distinctions, of sub-groups of all kinds, make it impossible to define a "national character," hence a collective mentality on the national level, hence any collective mentality related to a vast and diversified cultural whole. It was David Riesman who noted that in the United States if one took as a constant the median annual income of four thousand dollars (this was in 1953), one would find many more differences than similarities between a Methodist accountant in Wichita, a Jewish bartender in Brooklyn, a Greek restaurateur in Chicago, and an Irish Catholic policeman in Boston.[116] But the United States, one could reply, is a special case, and the ethnic differences that persist despite the pressure of the American "melting pot" suggest precisely that it makes sense to study national character. Such is not the opinion of Riesman, however: "There are Jews who are very 'Irish'. . . .

'The' Swedes were 'warlike' not so many generations ago; now they produce peacemakers. 'The' English have gone through fantastic transformations from Elizabethan times to the present. From Merrie England to the Cromwellian sobersides, from eighteenth-century license to mid-Victorian rigidity, and from this to mid-twentieth century 'spontaneous collectivism'—these are immense shifts of the emotional center of life for millions of people."[117]

Important as it was at the time it was written—because it tempered the excesses[118] of the studies on national character—Riesman's statement is nevertheless incorrect. The notion of national character or collective mentality does not imply stability over time: mentalities change, just as the sociocultural contexts that underlie them change. As for the objection concerning social divisions, Louis Dumont once remarked that "proletarians and capitalists speak French in France, otherwise they couldn't confront their ideas; in general, they have much more in common than they think, in comparison to a Hindu, for example."[119]

As a matter of fact, this common denominator is implicit in the very notion of culture; there is a necessary link between the coherence of a social structure (which can be the structure of a whole nation), the coherence of the culture that expresses it, and the coherence of certain characteristics of the collective mentality that is a manifestation of it. And since every society must confront certain specific problems linked to the manner in which it adapts to general human and natural limitations, as well as to specific human and natural limitations, a culture will necessarily be "a closed system of questions and answers concerning the universe and human behavior."[120] A collective mentality corresponding to a given culture can be recognized as much by the kinds of questions it asks as by the manner it formulates them and the answers it gives to them. When Serge Moscovici tells us, with brilliant concision, that "through every century there runs an essential questioning which mobilizes its vital forces," and goes on to remark that "the eighteenth century can be said to have been set in motion by the *political question.* . . , the nineteenth century emphasizes the *social question* [and] the two currents converge in our century to raise the *natural question,*"[121] then one sees what is perhaps the common denominator of modern Western culture. The "sub-questions" that result from these great interrogative currents will be reflected in a collective mentality on the level of this transnational culture, which is more vast even than the culture of the Christian Middle Ages, but is no less real. Just as there exists a hierarchy of social and culture contexts, so one must take into account a hierarchy of essential questions and a hierarchy of traits in collective mentalities.

Now questions and answers are formulated not only on the conscious level. Every fundamental answer is expressed in symbolic terms, and the latter resound in a particular way in the unconscious, in function of a specific culture which "allows certain fantasies, drives and other psychic manifestations to reach and remain on the conscious level, and demands that others be repressed"[122]—in other words, in function of the unconscious mode of interpretation that a culture gives of its most general symbols. But how then is one to study both the conscious level and the level of the unconscious foundations of a culture or a collective mentality? And first of all, what documents can the historian use?

We have already mentioned the variety and the polysemous character of psychohistorical documentation, but it goes without saying that every subject has its own privileged sources. As concerns the study of mentalities, Lucien Febvre, who envisaged it on the level of surface phenomena, cited as sources the ethical documents (especially judicial archives) and the artistic and literary documents of a culture.[123] That is too limited a view, even if one remains on the conscious level. Jacques Lafaye has shown how important it is to analyze the great myths of a collectivity, in order to discern the permanent themes around which the disparate elements of the collective mentality are crystallized; he himself studied the role of the myth of the god Quetzalcoatl, who became Saint Thomas, and of the goddess Tonantzin, transformed into the Virgin of Guadalupe, in the creation of national consciousness in Mexico—in other words, as the foundation of Mexican collective mentality.[124] Jacques Le Goff went one step further in emphasizing the role of "documents which bear witness to those feelings or those paroxystic or marginal forms of behavior which, through their deviation from the norm, bring out more clearly the underlying common mentality."[125] In the case of the medieval mentality, these include hagiographies and the various manifestations of demonic behavior such as possession or heresy, as well as the opposite kind of behavior which is just as marginal and no less significant: witch-hunts, or the behavior of the judges toward their victims. As we saw earlier in discussing the work of Georges Devereux, the psychic disorder that runs through a culture represents an essential index of the fundamental structures of that culture—hence of its most common forms of expression—even though it does so on the pathological level.[126] One can also cite here documents that represent certain rites which characterize, over a very long timespan, a whole cultural area, such as the "tarantism" that Ernesto De Martino has so masterfully described and analyzed. This rite not only illustrates the specific ritual context elaborated by a culture in order to allow for the expression and, eventually, for the reintegration of certain idiosyncratic psychic disorders, but also tells us a great deal about the underlying mental characteristics of a Mediterranean culture which experienced, and still experiences, the clash between Christianity and pagan orgiastic cults.[127]

Literary[128] and artistic documents are an inexhaustible source for thematic analysis, but it may be even more useful to study the characteristic forms (or styles) of the art of a period, relating them to other essential currents in the collective sensibility in order to discover their common underlying significance.[129] Finally, one must attempt to discover, through a study of its historiography, the vision that a society has of itself and of the world. As Alphonse Dupront has noted, "An inventory of the types of historical nostalgia for an original past . . . would provide us with an extraordinary document on the ways the human imagination has conceived of the notion of return; it would also provide a rich psychic documentation on the modes of refusal to live in one's own time. The temporal horizon of a period and of a society is like a code indicating its need for balance, its particular emotional resources, and its awareness of its own existence. Societies with a long history and societies with a short history constitute two general types of collective behavior toward the past; the same is true of societies that live in the eternal—and naturally, in the surging diversity of the human, of all the intermediary types in between."[130]

This enumeration of documentary sources, which is by no means exhaustive, brings us back to the essential question: the method of investigation.

One method, obviously, is simply to describe surface phenomena. Some of the best historians have stopped at that level, Huizinga's *The Waning of the Middle Ages* being a classic example.[131] Perhaps a purely descriptive stage is necessary even if one aims for a more in-depth analysis, for it is description alone that preserves the impalpable "je ne sais quoi" which characterizes the phenomena of collective mentality. Even on this level, however, one must ask the "unifying" questions and discover the "style" of the period, of the culture or of the mentality one is studying: Huizinga, for example, speaks of the "bittersweetness of life," and sees in that particular emotional contrast the chief characteristic of the waning medieval world. But, as we have already suggested, the unconscious level also calls for study. Some contemporary historians recognize this necessity. Michel Vovelle, in his volume of essays on collective attitudes toward death in the seventeenth and eighteenth centuries, mentions right at the outset that ". . . the history of mentalities . . . is turning more and more toward the collective unconscious."[132] Vovelle's own work, however, remains exclusively on the level of conscious thought. The most recent study of English collective mentality in the sixteenth and seventeenth centuries, Keith Thomas' *Religion and the Decline of Magic,* shows the same partial awareness of the need to study unconscious structures, without actually attempting to do so: Thomas mentions Freud's theses in passing, but that is all. Although the awareness of a new dimension exists, then, in most cases it has not brought about a reorientation in the methods of research themselves.

The first of the two methods we ourselves are about to propose is somewhat hazardous: it risks falling into the simplistic approach of studies on the basic personality, even though the heterogeneous context makes such an approach invalid.[133] The method involves an analysis on three distinct levels: first, the definition of the characteristics of the group's "modal personality;" second, the analysis of certain common elements in the primary institutions; third, an interpretation of the dominant elements in the symbolic expressions of the community. An attempt at synthesis would consist in interpreting the traits of the modal personality as the consequence of typical emotional reactions aroused by certain dominant elements in the group's network of symbolic expressions, and possibly as the consequence of certain common characteristics in the group's primary institutions.

The term "modal personality" is meant here in the sense proposed by Inkeles and Levinson: "It appears unlikely that any specific personality characteristic, or any character type, will be found in as much as 60 to 70 percent of any modern national population. However, it is still a reasonable hypothesis that a nation may be characterized in terms of a limited number of modes, say five or six, some of which apply to perhaps 10 to 15 percent, others to perhaps 30 percent of the total population. Such a conception of national character can accommodate the subcultural variations of socioeconomic class, geosocial region, ethnic group, and the like, which appear to exist in all modern nations."[134]

A study on the modal personality of a group can be meaningful only if it is comparative, that is, if it succeeds in pinpointing notable differences concerning certain crucial aspects in the life of every individual and every community: for example, the typical attitude toward authority, toward oneself, and toward the dilemmas posed by the various stages of personality development (in the Eriksonian sense).[135] We could perhaps add to this list the typical attitudes toward existential situations such as love, illness, or death. Emmanuel Le Roy Ladurie recently noted the fundamental differences between the contemporary attitude of Western cultures toward death, and their attitude two centuries ago. He also noted the widespread interest of European historians in the phenomenon of death, even though nothing of the sort was apparent in American historiography.[136] Could that be the symptom of more profound differences on the level of mentalities?

Whereas the comparison between contemporary mentalities is essentially the work of anthropologists and sociologists, the historian will concern himself above all with comparisons between periods in the past, either in the context of a single culture or in different cultural contexts.

Parallel to the comparative study of manifest attitudes, the historian will undertake a comparative study of social structures, as well as family structures and modes of childrearing, aiming once again to pinpoint significant differences among groups.[137] If it turns out that, over and above the differences due to the social subdivisions within each heterogeneous group, certain childrearing practices existing on the level of a complex sociocultural entity can be distinguished from the practices of other entities of the same kind, then one can venture a hypothesis relating a given characteristic of the modal personality to a given socio-familial context. At the same time, one must always be aware of the influence of socialization processes outside the family, which may be of decisive importance.[138]

The correlations between the group's primary institutions and the characteristics of the modal personality would be only a first step; it would have to be followed by an examination of how the dominant elements of the group's symbolic system can in turn determine certain characteristics of the modal personality, even if the origins of the symbolic system itself remain unclear. *A synthesis relating these three levels of investigation to each other would, as we mentioned earlier, constitute the most complete global analysis one could undertake of the unconscious foundations of a "collective mentality," whether on the national or on some other level.*[139]

If the attempt to relate the characteristics of the modal personality to the primary institutions in a heterogeneous context appears toc hazardous, there remains the second method, which is the analysis of symbolic networks alone. The documentary sources we enumerated earlier provide, each in its own domain, some essential symbolic indices, and the analysis would concentrate on the concordance of the different networks: hagiography, literature, political thought and historiography, art, and so on. We shall take as our example a study that illustrates precisely this kind of method: Alain Besançon's *Le Tsarévitch immolé* (*The Immolated Tsarevitch*). Through this concrete example we shall rediscover all the appeal of psychoanalytic structuralism, but we shall also see its most evident pitfalls.

Le Tsarévitch immolé is, as its subtitle indicates, a study on the "symbolism of the law in Russian culture." Alain Besançon examines the symbolic theme which, according to him, is apparent in the relation of the Russians to God as well as in their relation to the sovereign. The same theme and the same structure of unconscious psychic elements can be discerned, it would seem, in the great works of Russian literature. What is involved here is a specifically Russian way of approaching the Oedipal problem, namely, an inability to resolve the problem due to a kind of paralysis and self-punitive submission on the part of the son, in the face of an all-powerful and inaccessible father. Whereas, on the religious level, Christ's life and self-sacrifice represent, for Western man, symbols of liberation, for the Russian the encounter with God is annihilating and seems to lead to death.[140] On the political level the same symbolism is evident, and it is the immolation of the Tsarevitch by the Tsar which occupies the center of the stage: Ivan is the victim of his father, Ivan the Terrible, Dimitri is killed by Boris Godunov, Alexis is killed by Peter the Great, Ivan is killed by Catherine II.[141]

The relationship between the underlying theme on the religious level and on the political level is clear. One finds in Russian literature an expression of the same inability to attain autonomy, to resolve the problem of Oedipus and to leave the father behind: "Just as Russian culture, in its original treatment of Christianity and royalty, seems to have drawn its inspiration from the critical phase of the Oedipal conflict, so Gogol, Dostoevsky, Rozanov, and Blok came ever closer to the Oedipal crisis in their works . . . without ever attempting to overcome it. That was not their aim. They developed an ideology of acceptance and a philosophy of self-sacrifice which is not the most vital part of their work, but which covers up and rationalizes their veritable motive: to relive, in tears and terror, that incandescent moment of human life. They come fearlessly close to Oedipus, but only in order to savor the experience. . . . They use the Pantocrator and the Tsar, the cruel facts of serfdom and of the patriarchal world, everything that is specific to their culture and their nation, in order to play out a drama perpetually re-enacted by all of humanity. Their works, so specifically rooted in a time and place, acquire thereby a universal resonance. They did not change Russian history, but transmuted it into song. . . ."[142]

It was from this context, argues Besançon, that the Russian Revolution derived its particular form: despite a certain development, the Revolution seems to have encountered an obstacle, and its first phase, that of parricide, was never surmounted; but in this instance, it is the Russian people who are paying the debt, not the tyrant.[143]

Alain Besançon obviously does not deny the possibility of interpreting Russian culture in sociological terms, but he proposes another interpretation, another meaning, independent of the sociological one: "I have taken special care," he writes, "to separate the two levels: on the one hand, the level of economic, political and social history, which obeys its own laws; on the other, running parallel to the first and accompanying it in counterpoint, this other history, marching to a different drummer. . . ."[144]

That such a reading of a symbolic system is fascinating, and that it opens up new perspectives, will readily be admitted. But, as we have already emphasized, a structuralist analysis can be convincing only if it is sufficiently rigorous in its demonstrations. Now in terms of Alain Besançon's own analysis of Russian culture, one notices that Dostoevsky, the most Russian of Russian writers, lends himself to a reading that suggests a very different Russian approach to the Oedipal conflict from the one that Besançon proposes: if, in *Crime and Punishment,* the relationship between the judge Porfiry and Raskolnikov seems to fit the structural model proposed by Besançon, can't one argue, on the contrary, that in *A Raw Youth* the son confronts the father, that in *The Possessed* he gets the better of him, and that in *The Brothers Karamazov* he kills him? In all of Dostoevsky's novels, there is not a single paternal figure who is not ridiculous, debauched, or absent. There is certainly no one who resembles the divine Pantocrator or the inaccessible Tsar, the terrible torturer, the muzhik brandishing his ax. There is nothing that would allow for a univocal interpretation of this sort.[145]

The same difficulties could be found in the political field. What are we to conclude from them?

A collective mentality (or, as in this instance, a culture considered as a single phenomenon) lends itself to the kind of global analysis characteristic of structuralism in general, and of psychoanalytic structuralism in particular. In order to be convincing, such an analysis must give evidence of an extremely high degree of rigorousness. Only the accumulation of a whole series of studies of this type will show whether such rigorousness is in fact possible. Otherwise, the method will yield some fascinating connections between symbols, some new insights that could not have been arrived at by description alone, but it will not necessarily produce conviction. . . .

Can we not say that we have just defined the problem of psychohistory itself?

Conclusion

What, then, is the value of psychohistory? The preceding pages are full of hesitations, warnings, expressions of approval immediately qualified by reservations. It is time to pronounce a more definite conclusion.

We may give a general reply to the question by considering the term "psychohistory" in its broadest theoretical sense, not as the current application of psychoanalysis to history. If one defines psychohistory as the utilization of psychological theories in history, without considering the present state of these theories but rather their possible future development, whatever that might be, then one can reply that the value of psychohistory is the same as the value of a systematic explanation of human behavior applied to an understanding of the past. For those who do not reject a history of this kind, tending toward generalizing explanations, psychohistory thus defined offers an unlimited field of possibilities. In such a case, the reply about its value must be positive, without qualification. But in fact, it is not with the abstract principle of psychohistory that we are dealing here. Our question concerns the utilization of psychoanalytic theories in history—envisaging, to be sure, the possibility of new developments in psychoanalysis, but not the radical transformation of the general framework of current psychoanalytic thought.

The weak spot of psychohistory remains the verification of its explanations. We have suggested the use of various verification criteria, but we must recall that, whatever their degree of convergence, psychohistorical explanation will necessarily, by its very nature, remain indirect. This not withstanding, our aim has been to show that even in psychohistory one could not prove just anything by using just any method: a coherent framework does exist, and its internal logic is discernible. The best examples of a concrete application of psychoanalysis (examples that are admittedly still too rare) differ from traditional historiography only by the slightly greater degree of indeterminacy that characterizes their explanations.

That, I would suggest, is a small enough price to pay; the reasons for it have been implicitly adduced throughout this book, but they must now be made explicit. First of all, psychohistory throws a new light on traditional problems; second, it makes possible the study of new problems; finally, it makes an important contribution to the integration of various historical methods into a global approach tending toward a total history.

For the reader of this book, the first reason I have mentioned should require no demonstration. One can argue, to be sure, about the validity of psychohistorical explanations, but it seems incontestable that, in the field of biography as in that of collective behavior, psychohistory can approach traditional subjects from a new perspective. We need but recall the hypotheses concerning the structure of Wilson's personality and its influence on his political behavior, or the relationship between childrearing practices and adult behavior in Plymouth Colony, or again the relationship between family structure and the "need to achieve" in certain societies. We may also recall the demonstration of possible links between personality disorders and virulent anti-Semitism and the significance of this phenomenon for the explanation of anti-Semitism in general, or the possible psychohistorical explanation of witch-hunts, or the explanation that psychohistory can provide for certain peer group phenomena, or, finally, its explanation of the underlying significance of a "collective mentality."

The second reason must not be confused with the first: here we are no longer dealing with a new conception of traditional historical problems, but rather, thanks to psychohistory itself, with the formulation of altogether new questions. Thus, two recent new fields of inquiry probably owe their development to the preoccupations of psychoanalysis: the history of childhood and of the family, and the history of sexual mores. But have we not also suggested a history of the authority relations between fathers and sons in a given society, or a history of mental disorders or of collective neuroses? Could we not have a more in-depth history of attitudes toward death? Can we not envisage, thanks to psychohistory, the rehabilitation of biography and the systematic study of types (either historical typology or the historical verification of empirically derived types)? More generally, doesn't psychohistory suggest and make possible *the comparative study of the psychological phenomena of the past?*

The third reason, concerning the contribution of psychohistory to the elaboration of a total history, introduces a wholly different dimension. Throughout this book we have above all insisted on the interdisciplinary nature of history, on the possible modes of convergence between history, sociology, and psychoanalysis. But this is only a step in the direction of an even more encompassing historical inquiry: the complete investigation of an individual or social phenomenon is, in effect, possible only if the explicative approach, the view from the outside—in other words, the approach of systematic history—supplements and complements the intuitive approach, the view from the inside. Systematic explanation must not replace intuition, it must complete it. Only a dual approach of this kind can be called total history: the understanding of a phenomenon both as a network of data accessible to systematic inquiry *and* as the existential, irreducible reality of a person or of a group. Now from this perspective, the methodological weakness of psychoanalysis and consequently of psychohistory appears, paradoxically, as their strongest point: they are really situated between *Erklären* and *Verstehen,* linked both to the pole of systematization and to that of intuitive understanding. Psychoanalysis partakes of both, and at the same time these two approaches are not simply juxtaposed in it: they are integrated into a unified interpretation of the phenomenon. Despite the weaknesses of psychoanalytic theory itself, and despite the methodological difficulties posed by its application outside the therapeutic context, the unified approach that it imposes on us can be considered, from this point of view, exemplary.

But the contribution of psychohistory to the creation of a total history is not only methodological, it is substantive as well. Historians have no trouble establishing plausible correlations between the social life, the economic activity, and even the scientific and technological evolution of a society; the history of ideas and cultural or artistic history constitute a distinct area that can also be presented in a unified way; finally, political and military history constitute a third distinct area. Historians have succeeded in relating these diverse domains to each other, either in a unified Marxist context or in various more recent sociological contexts. But in every one of these cases, a crucial element remains unexplained: the sociological "input" can be identified, and so can the "output" in terms of collective behavior; but the mechanism that allows one to link the "input" to the "output" is not explained, or at best is explained more or less tautologically. Now the models we proposed in chapter 1 and developed in chapter 3 are perhaps no more than embryonic outlines of possible solutions. Nevertheless, they indicate a direction to be followed if one wishes to explain the interaction between society and collective behavior, on the level of static analysis as well as on that of dynamic analysis or historical change.

Finally, we may recall that in chapter 2 we tried to show that psychohistory made a fundamental contribution to the study of certain "total social facts" (in Marcel Mauss's terminology), in particular of works of art, political decision-making, and the elaboration of a collective identity norm. It is here that the historian ought to grasp, in the most concrete way possible, the convergence of the social and the psychological (on the various levels of both these factors), in the context of a genuinely integrated history.

Were we to stop here, we would have to conclude that psychohistory is valuable indeed, opening vast perspectives for future development and the breaking of new ground. But there remains one last problem which bodes less well for the future.

We have seen that those psychoanalysts who launched upon historical studies produced, for the most part, works of dubious value, and sometimes even works that were totally unacceptable from the point of view of the historian. Quite understandably, it is difficult if not impossible to devote the major portion of one's time to clinical work and be able to acquire, at the same time, a solid historical background. It is thus up to historians who are well informed about psychology in general and psychoanalysis in particular to develop the discipline of psychohistory. But what does it mean to be "well-informed" in this instance? It seems to be generally agreed that a purely bookish knowledge of psychoanalysis is insufficient, and that analysis is a process one must have lived through in order to understand its nuances and its veritable significance. In short, in order to understand psychoanalysis, one must have been psychoanalyzed.

In theory, the pesonal experience of psychoanalysis ought to allow one to avoid the misuse or the purely mechanical application of concepts which, as we now know, are extremely complex and have multiple meanings. But that is precisely where the difficulty arises: psychoanalysis is a process which involves the whole person, and involves him emotionally on the deepest level. It is true that a successful analysis ought to end with the resolution of the patient's transference toward the analyst *and toward psychoanalysis as well,* but the notion of a "complete" or "perfect" analysis remains an abstraction. In fact, historians who have been psychoanalyzed maintain, and will for the most part continue to maintain, an attitude of intense emotional involvement with psychoanalysis; this makes it extremely difficult for them to exercise that critical faculty without which, as we have seen, psychohistory cannot hope to develop into a scientific discipline worthy of the name. Thus, if he is not analyzed, the historian risks having only a superficial understanding of analytic theories; and if he is analyzed, he risks not being able to exercise, in this new domain, a critical faculty that is absolutely essential. I would not have raised this problem if I had not noticed, in certain political scientists or historians who undertook and finished an analysis both for personal and for professional reasons, the development of an intense "ideological" extremism.

This dilemma appears unresolvable, and only future works in psychohistory will show whether certain historians are able to find the necessary equilibrium between analytic experience and critical detachment. It is not merely for the sake of paradox that I would suggest, in conclusion, that the real difficulties of psychohistory do not reside only in the nature of the subject, in the state of psychoanalysis, or in the problem of proofs and criteria for verification; they are inherent in the ambiguous situation of the psycho-historian.

Notes—Introduction

1. Lucien Febvre, *Combats pour l'histoire,* p. 235 (Febrve's italics). (Unless otherwise indicated, all translations from French works cited in this book are by Susan Suleiman.)

2. Frank E. Manuel, "The Use and Abuse of Psychology in History," *Daedalus,* no. 100 (winter 1971): 192. Along the same lines, Gaston Bachelard quotes Remy de Gourmont who found that "as one reads the *Chants de Maldoror,* consciousness slips away, slips away. . . ." (Gaston Bachelard, *Lautréamont,* p. 104).

3. Lucien Febvre, *Combats pour l'histoire,* p. 230.

4. W. B. Gallie, *Philosophy and the Historical Understanding,* p. 116.

5. This is the distinction established by Leopold von Ranke: "The writing of history cannot be expected to possess the same free development of its subject which, in theory at least, is expected in a work of literature." (Quoted in Fritz Stern, *The Varieties of History from Voltaire to the Present,* p. 57.) The same distinction was particularly well made by Fred Weinstein and Gerald M. Platt in their article, "History and Theory: The Question of Psychoanalysis," *The Journal of Interdisciplinary History* 2, no. 4 (spring 1972). We cannot, however, invoke here the psychoanalytic arguments used by Weinstein and Platt, for that would be circular.

6. The notion of the unconscious, for example, is already to be found in antiquity, notably in the Upanishad and in Greece. See on this subject L. L. Whyte, *The Unconscious before Freud.*

7. Jean Piaget, *Epistémologie des sciences de l'homme,* pp. 93ff.

8. Carl Hempel, "The Function of General Laws in History," reprinted in Patrick Gardiner, *Theories of History,* pp. 344ff.

9. For a good definition of "laws" in the contemporary social sciences, see Hans Reichenbach, "Probability Methods in Social Science," in Daniel Lerner and Harold D. Lasswell, *The Policy Sciences: Recent Developments in Scope and Method.*

10. Paul Veyne, *Comment on écrit l'histoire,* pp. 111ff., 203–205; for the phrase about laws *in* history, see p. 279.

11. *L'historien entre l'ethnologue et le futurologue* (collective work), p. 277.

12. Jean Piaget, *Epistémologie des sciences de l'homme,* p. 21.

13. Abraham Kaplan, *The Conduct of Inquiry: Methodology for Behavioral Sciences,* pp. 86, 117.

14. See in particular on this subject Raymond Aron, *Introduction to the Philosophy of History,* p. 49; and Maurice Mandelbaum, *The Problem of Historical Knowledge,* pp. 64–66.

15. Among French specialists in psychohistory, one can mention the example of Alphonse Dupront, who in the course of a few years evolved from a very "classical" position on the question

to a position favoring the use of psychoanalysis in history. See Alphonse Dupront, "Problèmes et méthodes d'une histoire de la psychologie collective," *Annales ESC,* Jan. 1967; and "L'histoire après Freud," *Revue de l'enseignement supérieur,* nos. 44–45 (1969).

16.   William L. Langer, "The Next Assignment," in Bruce Mazlish, *Psychoanalysis and History,* pp. 89–90.

17.   See especially Lewis Namier, *Personalities and Powers,* as well as Lewis Namier and John Brook, *Charles Townshend.* As for E. R. Dodds, his two chief works in this context are *The Greeks and the Irrational* and *Pagan and Christian in an Age of Anxiety.*

18.   Cushing Strout, "Ego Psychology and the Historian," *History and Theory,* 7, no. 3 (1968), p. 281.

19.   Alan Bullock, for example, recently declared that he found Erikson's book on Luther less instructive than most of the other works he had read on the subject. Generally speaking, he found the results obtained by the use of psychoanalysis in history disappointing, and only some fruitful applications of the method in question would, according to him, confirm its validity (*L'historien entre l'ethnologue et le futurologue,* p. 192).

20.   Jacques Barzun, "The Muse and Her Doctors," *The American Historical Review* 77, no. 1 (1972).

21.   Ibid., pp. 37–39.

22.   Ibid.

23.   Sidney Rattner, "The Historian's Approach to Psychology," *Journal of the History of Ideas* 2, no. 1 (1941).

24.   Jacques Barzun, "The Muse and Her Doctors," p. 50.

25.   Carl E. Rogers, "Toward a Science of the Person," in T. W. Wann, *Behaviorism and Phenomenology: Contrasting Bases of Modern Psychology,* p. 109.

26.   For an excellent illustration of the possible overlapping between various psychological theories, see Gardner Murphy, "Psychological Views of Personality and Contributions to Its Study," in Edward Norbeck, Douglas Price-Williams, and William M. McCord, *The Study of Personality: An Interdisciplinary Appraisal,* especially pp. 24ff. In fact, the problem of the diversity of explicative theories is not unique to psychology. It also exists in economics, and economic history is none the worse for it. Quoting Henri Guitton, Jean Bouvier writes that the multitude of theories of economic crisis can "make one dizzy. . . ." At the same time, "all of the theories (including Marxist ones) have allowed us to bring out some of the principal traits of industrial-capitalist economic development. . . ." (Jean Bouvier, "Problématique des crises économiques du XIXe siècle et analyses historiques: le cas de la France," in Jacques Le Goff and Pierre Nora, *Faire de l'histoire. II. Nouvelles approches,* p. 27.

27.   There exist currently several volumes of essays devoted to psychohistory, but with the exception of Alain Besançon's, they are all, in our judgment, too heterogeneous. The reader will nevertheless find some useful insights in the following: Bruce Mazlish, *Psychoanalysis and History;* Benjamin B. Wolfman, *The Psychoanalytic Interpretation of History;* Hans-Ulrich Wehler, *Geschichte und Psychoanalyse;* Alain Besançon, *Histoire et expérience du moi.* The volume by Alain Besançon, although it too is a collection of the author's previously published articles, offers a coherent and brilliant demonstration of the possibilities of a psychoanalytic reading of historical texts, as well as of the possibilities of a method of interpretation that can be qualified as "psychoanalytic structuralism."

Notes—Chapter One

1. It is true that certain experiments in individual psychology, and especially in social psychology, allow us to explain some historical phenomena whose characteristics would otherwise be difficult to grasp. Thus the notorious refusal of certain political figures to perceive an unequivocal reality (as was the case with Chamberlain in early 1939), or the growing accumulation of decisions based on a unilateral and false perception (Chamberlain in 1938 or Stalin in 1940–1941) can be explained, at least in part, by Leon Festinger's theories abut "cognitive dissonance." The extraordinary success of a pamphlet like the *Protocol of the Elders of Zion* in Germany in the 1920's can also, *in part,* be explained by these theories (see Leon Festinger, *A Theory of Cognitive Dissonance*). Similarly, the cohesion or the disintegration of certain groups, especially governing groups experiencing a crisis situation, can find a partial interpretation in Hamblin's experiments on groups in crisis (see Robert L. Hamblin, "Group Integration during a Crisis," in J. David Singer, *Human Behavior and International Politics*). One could cite other examples as well. Their limited importance, however, is due to the fact that they are unrelated to each other, that they explain only very limited phenomena, and that often they simply define more clearly ambiguous aspects of a phenomenon that is already understood. We may note that H. Stuart Hughes, who is among those contemporary historians most interested in the possible application of the social sciences to history, reached the same negative conclusions concerning experimental psychology, although for slightly different reasons (see H. Stuart Hughes, "The Historian and the Social Scientist," *American Historical Review* 66, no. 3 [1960]: 34).

2. Robert Coles, "How Good is Psychohistory?" *The New York Review of Books,* March 8, 1973.

3. On the relation between Piaget's theories and psychoanalysis, see the very detailed study by P. Wolff, "The Developmental Psychology of Jean Piaget and Psychoanalysis," *Psychological Issues,* 1960.

4. The validity of these criteria was "confirmed" when I discovered that they corresponded almost exactly word for word to the criteria formulated by the historian Robert F. Berkhofer, who was attempting to define the conditions for the application of the behavioral sciences to history. (See Robert F. Berkhofer, *Behavioral Approach to Historical Analysis.*)

5. Sheldon's theories, like those of Le Senne, can nevertheless provide secondary confirmations, and sometimes they throw light on certain characteristics that psychoanalysis, for example, hardly treats at all. Thus Anthony Storr's psychoanalytic interpretation of Churchill's personality is also based on some of Sheldon's concepts. (See Anthony Storr, "The Man," in A. J. P. Taylor et al., *Churchill Revised: A Critical Assessment,* p. 236.) Generally speaking, the attempts to establish a correlation between bodily characteristics and personality traits are as old

as psychology itself. Having mentioned the American Sheldon and the Frenchman Le Senne, we must in the interest of fairness mention the German Ernst Kretschmer, whose best known work is *Körperbau und Charakter (Body Structure and Character).*

6.   The necessary convergence of the most diverse disciplines and methods in the systematic study of the personality is cogently argued in Edward Norbeck, Douglas Price-Williams, and William M. McCord, *The Study of Personality.*

7.   One would like to have Sartre in one's camp in this enterprise, and yet. . . . When he tells us, for example, that Baudelaire, *at the age of six* (my italics), finding himself alone and rejected upon the remarriage of his beloved mother, instead of "passively supporting" his isolation, "embraced it with fury . . . and, since he was condemned to it hoped that at any rate his condemnation was final," we cannot but wonder at the precociousness of the boy; the same is true when we are told that "this brings us to the point at which Baudelaire chose the sort of person he would be—that irrevocable choice by which each of us decides in a particular situation what he will be and what he is. . . ." (Jean-Paul Sartre, *Baudelaire,* trans. Martin Turnell, p. 18). And what would have happened if Caroline Baudelaire had gotten remarried when young Charles was only two years old? He could not, in that case, have consciously assumed his destiny, but is it certain that he would not have reacted? We know that very young children who experience powerful emotional frustrations fall ill and sometimes die. We also know that an "abandonment" of the kind experienced by Baudelaire—if it takes place at the age of two or three years—often provokes immediate somatic reactions and can subsequently leave neurotic traces that last a lifetime. The rejection of unconscious processes leads Sartre to elaborate developmental schemata that are empirically indefensible, at least from our point of view.

8.   H. Stuart Hughes, *History as Art and as Science,* p. 42.

9.   Hans Meyerhoff, "On Psychoanalysis and History," *Psychoanalysis and the Psychoanalytic Review* 49, no. 2 (1962), p. 5. For a more systematic study of the "historical" character of psychoanalytic therapy, see Samuel Novey, *The Second Look: The Reconstruction of Personal History in Psychiatry and Psychoanalysis.*.

10.   Philip Rieff, "The Meaning of History and Religion in Freud's Thought," in Bruce Mazlish, *Psychoanalysis and History,* p. 25. The "historical" conception of psychoanalysis is not accepted by everyone, however; Page Smith, for example, has noted the *repetitive* character of the Freudian interpretation of certain collective phenomena (*The Historian and History,* p. 128). But this criticism confuses Freud's metahistorical theories, which can easily be rejected without any repercussions for psychoanalytic theory, with the use of psychoanalytic theory itself in historical explanation on the individual or collective level. Smith has also argued that the notion of Oedipal conflict is ahistorical, for it implies a break between father and son, whereas history is founded on the transmission of values from father to son (*The Historian and History,* p. 130). This strange argument shows that the ignorance of historians in matters of psychoanalysis is at least as great as the ignorance of psychoanalysts in matters of history. The fact is that the resolution of the Oedipal conflict leads to the formation of the superego, which is precisely the internalization of paternal values by the son.

Admittedly, other historians, much more knowledgeable about psychoanalysis, have pointed out the ahistorical character of the interpretation of a specific situation by reference to an unvarying Oedipal conflict that would somehow exist outside of time (Carl E. Schorske, "Politique et parricide dans *l'Interprétation des rêves* de Freud," *Annales ESC* 28 [March-April, 1977], p. 328). The Oedipus complex can, in itself, be considered as an invariable psychic conflict, but there are as many ways of experiencing it as there are individuals. A different analysis of the dreams in *The Interpretation of Dreams* would have allowed Schorske to perceive the specific, historical character of this vision of the conflict between father and son in Freud himself.

11.   I am assuming here that the reader is familiar with the essential principles of the psychoanalytic theory of the personality, or if not that he can familiarize himself with them by consulting one of the many works available on the subject. For a very complete description of the principal schools of thought that dominate contemporary psychoanalysis, see Ruth L. Munroe, *Schools of Psychoanalytic Thought.* Orthodox Freudian theory is well presented in a large number of textbooks, to wit: Charles Brenner, *An Elementary Textbook of Psychoanalysis;*

Robert Waelder, *Basic Theory of Psychoanalysis*; Gerald S. Blum, *Psychodynamics: The Science of Unconscious Mental Forces;* Daniel Lagache, *La Psychanalyse.* A good summary of the neo-Freudian point of view can be found in Clara Thompson's history of psychoanalysis, *Psychoanalysis: Evolution and Development.*

12.   Karl R. Popper, *Conjectures and Refutations: The Growth of Scientific Knowledge,* p. 38.

13.   Anatol Rapoport, "Various Meanings of Theory," *The American Political Science Review* 52, no. 4 (1958), p. 982.

14.   The number of publications devoted to this subject is immense; I shall of necessity mention only the most important arguments, giving a minimum of references.

15.   Cf. Philip E. Vernon, *Personality Assessment,* p. 121.

16.   Ernest L. Hilgard, "Psychoanalysis: Experimental Studies," in D. L. Sills, *International Encyclopaedia of the Social Sciences,* p. 40.

17.   This is in fact the opinion of a great many psychoanalysts, including Ernst Kris, Lawrence Kublie, Gittelson and others. See Björn Christiansen, "The Scientific Status of Psychoanalytic Clinical Evidence," *Inquiry,* no. 7 (1964): 64.

18.   Michael Martin, "The Scientific Status of Psychoanalytic Evidence," *Inquiry,* no. 7 (1964): 32.

19.   Ibid., p. 24.

20.   Christiansen, "The Scientific Status of Psychoanalytic Clinical Evidence," p. 65.

21.   Ibid., p. 75.

22.   Paul E. Meehl, *Clinical versus Statistical Prediction: A Theoretical Analysis and a Review of Evidence.*

23.   See in particular McKeachie and C. L. Doyle, *Psychology,* p. 448, and Harrison H. Gough, "Clinical versus Statistical Prediction in Psychology," in Leo Postman, *Psychology in the Making,* p. 576.

24.   The number of publications on this subject is considerable. For a relatively old but very systematic evaluation of experimental studies of psychoanalytic concepts, see Robert R. Sears, *Survey of Objective Studies of Psychoanalytic Concepts*; for a study that tends more toward the justification of psychoanalysis on these grounds, see E. Pumpian-Mindlin, *Psychoanalysis as Science.* For a very recent synthesis, see Ernest L. Hilgard, "Psychoanalysis: experimental studies"; see also Germald S. Blum, *Psychodynamics: The Science of Unconscious Mental Forces,* pp. 25ff.; Philip E. Vernon, *Personality Assessment,* p. 92; and especially I. Sarnoff, *Testing Freudian Concepts: An Experimental Social Approach.*

25.   It is worth mentioning, however, that over the past few years some quasi-experimental studies on young children, and especially in ethology, "have gradually confirmed some analytic theories that seemed to be purely speculative" (Anthony Storr, *Human Destructiveness,* p. 78; see also I. Sarnoff, *Testing Freudian Concepts*).

26.   Robert Waelder, *Basic Theory of Psychoanalysis,* p. 19.

27.   Karl R. Popper, "Philosophy of Science: A Personal Report," in C. A. Mace, *British Philosophy in the Midcentury,* pp. 158–159.

28.   Abraham Kaplan, *The New World of Philosophy,* pp. 150–151, and, by the same author, *The Conduct of Inquiry,* p. 100.

29.   Saul E. Harrison, "Is Psychoanalysis 'Our Science'? Reflections on the Scientific Status of Psychoanalysis," *Journal of the American Psychoanalytic Association* 18 (1970), p. 132.

30.   See, on this subject, Ernest Nagel, "Methodological Issues in Psychoanalytic Theory," in Sidney Hook, *Psychoanalysis, Scientific Method and Philosophy,* p. 41. A particularly massive and ferocious attack on the imprecision of many psychoanalytic terms, especially those of ego psychology, was recently published by an author who has himself systematically applied psychoanalysis to the study of politics, Nathan Leites. See his *The New Ego: Pitfalls in Current Thinking about Patients in Psychoanalysis.*

31.   Certain psychoanalysts have attempted to bypass the whole problem of the scientific status of psychoanalysis, by proposing a "semantic theory" of psychoanalysis: the patient's symptoms and various aspects of his behavior are not "caused" by such and such an event or by a past situation, but rather they constitute a language that the patient creates but does not understand; it is the analyst's task to interpret this language, to say clearly what the patient says, as it were, in code. (See especially, on this subject, Charles Rycroft, *Psychoanalysis Observed.*) The problem of causality, of explanatory theory, seems thus to be surmounted; but it is surmounted in appearance only, for the psychoanalyst cannot decipher the patient's language without referring, explicitly or implicitly, to a theoretical system that will provide him with the key to the code. This theoretical system brings us right back to the problem of the scientific verification of psychoanalytic propositions.

32.   The basic concepts of ego psychology are discussed in most general works on psychoanalysis (see note 11 above). For more complete theoretical discussions, see the following classic works: Anna Freud, *The Ego and the Mechanisms of Defense;* Erik H. Erikson, *Childhood and Society;* Heinz Hartmann, *Ego Psychology and Problems of Adaptation;* and, by the same author, *Essays on Ego Psychology: Selected Problems in Psychoanalytic Theory.*.

33.   Bruno Bettelheim, *The Informed Heart.*.

34.   This existential conception of the integrity of the self is well described in Rollo May's work, *Psychology and the Human Dilemma;* concerning the application of this concept to a better understanding of extreme situations, see Victor E. Frankl, *Man's Search for Meaning: An Introduction to Logo-therapy,* a new and revised edition of *From Death-Camp to Existentialism.*

35.   Ludwig Binswanger's study on "the case of Ellen West" is justly famous. It is perhaps the best example of the possible contribution of existential analysis to psychohistory. (See Ludwig Binswanger, "The Case of Ellen West: An Anthropological-Clinical Study," in Rollo May et al., *Existence: A New Dimension in Psychiatry and Psychology.*) The major difficulty of existential analysis remains, however, unchanged: such analysis falls easily into vagueness, imprecision, and purely intuitive procedures. If one had to point to an equivalent of this kind of analysis in France—one that exhibited both its strongest and its weakest points—the name that would most readily come to mind is that of Minkowski.

36.   For an excellent summary, see Anthony Storr, *Jung.*

37.   Georges Devereux would doubtless disagree with this point: in his *From Anxiety to Method in the Behavioral Sciences,* he discovers the distorting effects of unconscious countertransference even in the relation between the experimental scientist and his subject. Devereux is right in theory, but in practice this kind of countertransferential distortion is often so minimal that we can speak of objective analysis.

38.   Jacques Hassoun, "Avant-propos" in Theodor Reik, *Le Rituel: Psychanalyse des rites religieux,* p. 13.

39.   Alain Besançon, *Histoire et expérience du moi,* p. 77.

40.   Ibid., pp. 77–78.

41.   My position here is identical to the one explicitly formulated by Erik H. Erikson in his article, "On the Nature of Psychohistorical Evidence: In Search of Gandhi," *Daedalus,* no. 97 (summer 1968), p. 713.

42.   Milton Singer, "A Survey of Culture and Personality Theory and Research," in Bert Kaplan, *Studying Personality Cross-Culturally,* p. 19. Concerning mental disturbances, Georges Devereux has convincingly shown that, even if every culture has its own way of expressing deviant behavior, the distinctions between normal and abnormal derive from universal criteria. (See Georges Devereux, *Essais d'ethnopsychiatrie générale.*)

43.   Anne Parsons, "Is the Oedipus Complex Universal?" in Werner Muensterberger and Sidney Axelrad, *The Psychoanalytic Study of Society.*.

44.   Bronislaw Malinowski, *Sex and Repression in Savage Society.*

45.   *The Standard Edition of the Complete Psychological Works of Sigmund Freud,* published by James Strachey (with the collaboration of Anna Freud), vol. XI, pp. 63ff. (All subsequent references to this edition will be indicated as *SE*).

46.   This was a common practice without any particular individual significance, unless one can show the existence of thematic repetition in the unfinished works, in opposition to the finished ones. Freud made no comparative analysis of this kind. Dominique Fernandez, on the other hand, arrives at some interesting results along these lines in his study of Michelangelo. See his *l'Arbre jusqu'aux racines: Psychanalyse et Création,* pp. 140–141.

47.   Abraham Kaplan, *The Conduct of Inquiry,* p. 314.

48.   Jean Laplanche and J.-B. Pontalis, *The Language of Psychoanalysis,* trans. Donald Nicholson-Smith, p. 292.

49.   Ibid.

50.   Robert Waelder, *Basic Theory of Psychoanalysis,* p. 5.

51.   Fritz Schmidl, "Psychoanalysis and History," *Psychoanalytic Quarterly* 31, no. 4 (1962), p. 539.

52.   Alexander L. George and Juliette L. George, *Woodrow Wilson and Colonel House: A Personality Study.*.

53.   Arthur S. Link, *Woodrow Wilson,* vol. 1, *The Road to the White House,* pp. 90–91.

54.   For an interesting example of a repetitive structure of behavior, as well as a brief discussion of the methodological questions implied by the use of this type of psychohistorical proof, see Richard L. Bushman's article on Benjamin Franklin: "On the Uses of Psychology: Conflict and Conciliation in Benjamin Franklin," *History and Theory* 6, no. 1 (1966).

55.   See especially Alfred L. Baldwin, "Personal Structure Analysis: A Statistical Method for Investigating the Single Personality," *Journal of Abnormal and Social Psychology* 37 (1942).

56.   The methodology in question is too technical and too varied to be discussed here. The interested reader will find examples of the various approaches in George Gerbner et al., *The Analysis of Communication Content.* The difficulty, from our point of view, is that the analysis of content or the analysis of the logical structures of individual communication cannot be univocally correlated with a particular type of personality.

57.   H.-I. Marrou, *The Meaning of History,* p. 81. Obviously, it is the traditional type of personal documents—letters, diaries, etc.—that form the bulk of the documents to be used by the psychohistorian, especially in the domain of biography and typology. The use of such documents has always been considered difficult, and one would do well to consult the study by Louis Gottschalk, Clyde Kluckhohn, Robert Angell, *The Use of Personal Documents in History, Anthropology and Sociology.* Even more important from our point of view is the study by Gordon W. Allport, *The Use of Personal Documents in Psychological Science.*

58.   Alphonse Dupront, "L'histoire après Freud," p. 29.

59.   Dominique Fernandez, "Introduction à la psychobiographie," *Incidences de la psychanalyse* 1 (1970): 42.

60.   Jean-Paul Sartre, *L'Idiot de la famille.*

61.   Erik H. Erikson, *Youth Man Luther: A Study in Psychoanalysis and History,* pp. 72–73. Erikson attempts at least to reconstruct by means of inference the unknown events of childhood; certain psychohistorians have decided to facilitate their task by simply inventing the unknown elements, with no attempt at inference whatsoever. This is how Rudolph Binion proceeds from the very first pages of his biography of Lou Andreas-Salomé (*Frau Lou: Nietzsche's Wayward Disciple,* p. 6). We will return to this problem in the next chapter.

62.   Fyodor Dostoevsky, *Crime and Punishment,* part I, chapter 5.

63.   Fyodor Dostoevsky, *The Diary of a Writer,* p. 186.

64.   Ibid., p. 19.

65.   Alain Besançon, *Histoire et expérience du moi,* p. 115.

66.   Dominique Arban, *Dostoievski par lui-même,* p. 22. The interpretation of literary documents becomes even more uncertain when one is dealing with texts that are on the surface "revelatory," but that were written by writers familiar with psychoanalytic theories. The interpretation of Kafka's work, for example, in terms of a father-son conflict is in a sense

obligatory; *Das Urteil* (*The Judgment*) occupies a central place in this kind of interpretation, and is often cited. Kafka himself, however wrote in his *Diaries*, precisely about *Das Urteil*: "Many emotions carried along in the writing, joy, for example, that I shall have something beautiful for Max's *Arkadia*, thoughts about Freud, of course . . ." vol. 1, p. 276.

67.   This uncertainty is increased further by the fact that the symbolic significance of the mare cannot be proven, except by the similarity in structure between the signifying sequence and the signified sequence. Contrary to the position advanced by Freud in *The Interpretation of Dreams,* I believe that there is no fixed relation between a given symbol and a specific unconscious configuration. The choice of symbols is always subjective, and therefore itself subject to interpretation. This variable and purely subjective relation between signifier and signified eliminates certain recent arguments against psychoanalytic interpretation, notably those developed by Dan Sperber in his book, *Rethinking Symbolism.* .

68.   On this subject, see Bruce Mazlish, "Clio on the Couch," *Encounter* 31, no. 3 (1968).

69.   Thus Durkheim relates a high suicide rate to the absence of religion, bachelorhood, or living in an urban environment; he establishes, in other words, a correlation between the tendency to suicide and cohesion, or the degree of the individual's social integration. But, as Jean Maisonneuve notes, "does this give us an explanation of suicide? No, for we must still understand . . . the psychological mechanisms whereby cohesion or the absence of cohesion restrain one from, or push one to, suicide." (Jean Maisonneuve, *Introduction à la psychosociologie,* p. 10.) See also, on this subject, the article by Alex Inkeles, "Personality and Social Structure," in Robert K. Merton et al., *Sociology Today,* pp. 252ff.

70.   Marcel Mauss, *Sociologie et Anthropologie,* pp. 291–292.

71.   Ibid.

72.   Claude Lévi-Strauss, "Introduction à l'oeuvre de Marcel Mauss," in Marcel Mauss, *Sociologie et Anthropologie,* pp. 16ff., and especially p. 23.

73.   Talcott Parsons, *Social Structure and Personality.*

74.   Neil J. Smelser, *Theory of Collective Behavior.*

75.   Neil J. Smelser, *Essays in Sociological Explanation*; and Robert S. Wallerstein and Neil J. Smelser, "Psychoanalysis and Sociology: Articulations and Applications," *International Journal of Psycho-analysis* 50 (1969).

76.   Wallerstein and Smelser, "Psychoanalysis and Sociology," p. 694.

77.   Much has been written about the way Freud interpreted the past and envisaged history. We shall mention only those points that are immediately relevant to our discussion; for a more general treatment, see Paul Ricoeur, *Freud and Philosophy,* and Philip Rieff, *Freud, the Mind of the Moralist.* It is Alain Besançon, however, who offers the best introduction to the subject in the first chapter of his book, *Histoire et expérience du moi.*

78.   *SE,* vol. 13, p. 157.

79.   *SE,* vol. 23, p. 80.

80.   *SE,* vol. 21, pp. 42–43.

81.   *SE,* vol. 23, p. 99.

82.   See especially, on this subject, Gerard Mendel, *La Révolte contre le père,* pp. 15ff., pp. 144ff.

83.   Gerard Mendel, *La Crise des générations,* p. 57. The same hypothesis is convincingly presented by Georges Devereux in his *Essais d'ethnopsychiatrie générale,* especially pp. 143ff., and p. 160.

84.   See Roger Dadoun, *Géza Roheim et l'essor de l'anthropologie psychanalytique,* p. 48.

85.   Géza Roheim, *The Origin and Function of Culture,* p. 99.

86.   Wilhelm Reich, *The Mass Psychology of Fascism,* p. 154.

87.   Norman O. Brown, *Life against Death,* pp. 292ff. The reader will find dozens of similar examples, applied to every conceivable field, in Robert Bastide, *Sociologie et Psychanalyse.*

88.   Hanns Sachs, "The Delay of the Machine Age," *Psychoanalytic Quarterly* 4, no. 2 (1933): 404ff.

89.   Kurt R. Eissler, *Medical Orthodoxy and the Future of Psychoanalysis,* pp. 230ff. It is amusing to see Eissler's simplemindedness on this point criticized, in the name of historical rigor, by another psychoanalyst, Robert Waelder, who then turns around and explains (in the name of the same historical rigor, no doubt) the collapse of Austrian allegiance to the imperial institution in terms of a "castration complex." See Robert Waelder, "Psychoanalysis and History: Application of Psychoanalysis to Historiography," in Benjamin B. Wolman, *The Psychoanalytic Interpretation of History,* pp. 4, 24.

90.   Raymond de Saussure, "Psychoanalysis and History," in Géza Roheim, *Psychoanalysis and the Social Sciences,* vol. II, p. 25.

91.   Talcott Parsons, "Psychoanalysis and the Social Structure," *Psychoanalytic Quarterly* 19, no. 3 (1950), pp. 372–375.

92.   The structuralist paradigm of psychohistorical explanation has few adherents at present, and as far as I know the only studies attempting to develop this mode of inquiry are those published in France. The works of Alain Besançon represent, in this respect, the most complete statement of a conception that one also finds, on a more restricted level, in the work of other French psychoanalysts. Despite its limited field of application, this model of psychohistorical explanation seems sufficiently original and coherent to be considered as a separate category.

93.   Alain Besançon, *Histoire et expérience du moi,* pp. 9, 91.

94.   Ibid., p. 94.

95.   See, for example, the definition of structure according to Piaget: "Le problème de l'explication," in Leo Apostel et al., *L'Explication dans les sciences,* p. 9.

96.   See in particular the criticisms formulated by Edmund Leach, in his book, *Lévi-Strauss.* Leach himself is a convinced structuralist, but his analysis of various Biblical texts, although brilliant, does not altogether dispel one's doubts about the structuralist method. (See Edmund Leach, *Genesis as Myth and Other Essays.*)

97.   The difference between formal structures and thematic configurations, or even configurations of object relations, represents all the difference between structuralism *strictu sensu* and psychoanalytic structuralism. It is obvious, contrary to the thesis advanced by Janine Chasseguet-Smirgel, that a given configuration of any individual's object relations is understandable only in terms of content. As concerns the similarities and differences between Freud and Lévi-Strauss in their conception of the unconscious, see especially Ino Rossi, "The Unconscious in the Anthropology of Claude Lévi-Strauss," *American Anthropologist* 25 (1973).

98.   It is high time we proposed some definitions: 1) A society is a group of individuals (a group of variable size), whose members have established mutual relations that differentiate them in some way from those not belonging to that society; generally, what is distinctive about a society is the elaboration or the assimilation of a specific culture. 2) A culture corresponds, here, to the set of representations and symbolic expressions (language, institutions, norms, art, religious and philosophical system, etc.) of a society. (The definitions of culture are, of course, legion.) 3) The term "collective behavior" designates two different types of behavior: on the one hand, the behavior of the members of a group, conscious of belonging to that group and acting according to certain common perceptions and goals; on the other hand, the behavior of individuals who have the same perceptions and act in similar ways, without necessarily identifying themselves as members of the same group. It goes without saying that, in both cases, the conscious perceptions and goals can also have an unconscious meaning. Thus, in the broadest sense, it is a certain unity in perceptions, behavior and goals among a small or large number of individuals that allows us to speak of "collective behavior."

99.   This term, current in American sociology, will be explained in chapter 3.

100.   The relation between culture and personality has become a vast field of research, a good part of which has nothing to do with psychoanalytic theory. Milton Singer's article, "A Survey of Culture and Personality Theory and Research," contains an excellent summary of the various kinds of research in this field.

101.   The aim of this formulation, as of the pages that follow, is to allow for a synthesis (a rather unusual one) between the conceptions of Erik H. Erikson and those of Abram Kardiner and Ralph Linton. For Erikson's theses on this point, see especially *Childhood and Society*; for the theories of Kardiner and Linton, see their two works: *The Individual and His Society* and *The Psychological Frontiers of Society.* .

I am perfectly aware of the considerable differences between Erikson's notions and those of Kardiner, as well as of the fact that Erikson can be considered as part of the mainstream of psychoanalytic thought, while Kardiner is always characterized as a neo-Freudian. Yet, in the perspective of our paradigm, the inherent logic of their analyses is almost identical.

102.   Mikel Dufrenne, *La personnalité de base*, p. 128. We may recall that in France the importance of studies on the basic personality as a unifying ground between psychoanalysis and sociology was already noted in the 1950s by Roger Bastide (cf. his *Sociologie et psychanalyse*).

103.   The distinction between homogeneous and heterogeneous groups is absolutely essential if one is to understand the relation between primary and secondary institutions. In attempting, on the basis of a study conducted in a small American town ("Plainville, USA"), to describe the characteristics of a basic Western personality—as if Western society constituted a homogeneous group—Kardiner comes close to being ridiculous (see *The Psychological Frontiers of Society*). Furthermore, a certain uniformity in family structures is not in itself a sufficient index to explain or determine the homogeneity of a group; at most one can attempt to look within the secondary institutions for some reflections, more or less distorted by other social factors, of these common family traits. There is therefore nothing surprising about the fact demonstrated by Robert Bellah, namely, that certain common traits in the family structure and family ethos of Christian society and Chinese society are not directly reflected on the level of religious expression in these two societies (see Robert N. Bellah, *Beyond Belief: Essays on Religion in a Post-Traditional World*, pp. 76ff.).

104.   Abram Kardiner and Ralph Linton, *The Psychological Frontiers of Society.* .

105.   Mikel Dufrenne, *La Personnalité de base*, p. 179. It would be easy to reformulate this example in "orthodox" Freudian terms.

106.   The empirical studies concerning the validity of the notion of basic personality have been interpreted in contradictory ways. Milton Singer, for example, maintains that there is no conclusive proof that the majority of the members of a given sociocultural entity possess a sufficient number of similar characteristics to allow one to speak unequivocally of the existence of a "basic personality," despite certain noticeable similarities; Bert Kaplan, on the other hand, writing in the same year, arrived at the conclusion that the notion of basic personality was strongly reinforced by the empirical studies, which nevertheless were not absolutely conclusive. For these two opposing views, see Milton Singer, "A Survey of Culture and Personality Theory and Research," p. 41, and Bert Kaplan, "Cross-Cultural Use of Projective Techniques," in Francis L. K. Hsu, *Psychological Anthropology*.

107.   John Bowlby, "The Nature of the Child's Tie to Its Mother," *International Journal of Psycho-analysis* 39 (1958).

108.   See Talcott Parsons, *Social Structure and Personality*. As concerns the relation between social structure and the specific activity of the id, one can cite some studies on dreams in various societies: it is not only the manifest content of these dreams that varies from society to society, but—insofar as the kind of classical analysis that can be used is correct—their latent content as well. It has been noted, for example, that Americans and Japanese suffer from different anxieties, manifesting themselves differently on the level of dreams—hence on the level of primary processes of the id. See R. Burke, "Histoire sociale des rêves," *Annales ESC* 28 (March-April 1973): 332.

As for the formation of the ego by means of successive internalizations of idealized objects, notably of the idealized characteristics of the parents, Heinz Kohut's recent studies on narcissim confirm the essential character of this process. See especially Kohut's *The Analysis of the Self: A Systematic Approach to the Psychoanalytic Treatment of Narcissistic Personality Disorders*.

109.   Fred Weinstein and Gerald M. Platt, *Psychoanalytic Sociology: An Essay on the Interpretation of Historical Data and the Phenomena of Collective Behavior*.

110.   Roy Schafer, *Aspects of Internalization,* p. 9.

111.   The paradigm I shall propose here is inspired only in part by the one that Fred Weinstein and Gerald M. Platt presented in *The Wish to be Free: Society, Psyche and Value Change,* and in *Psychoanalytic Sociology.* Their conception taken as a whole seems in effect very much open to doubt. In our perspective, the id remains, on the whole, an area inaccessible to the process of internalization, whereas in Weinstein's and Platt's second book (*Psychoanalytic Sociology*) the generalized character of processes of internalization at *all* levels of the personality practically eliminates the need for a psychoanalytic study of social change.

112.   I use the general term "affective needs" for the sake of convenience; it is evident that we are dealing here with the result of complex interactions implying, in particular, various compromises between the instinctual tendencies and the demands of the superego and the ego of the members of the group.

113.   Ludwig Immergluck, "Determinism versus Freedom in Contemporary Psychology: An Ancient Problem Revisited," *American Psychologist* 19 (1964): 270.

114.   Ernest Jones, *Essays in Applied Psychoanalysis,* vol. II, p. 186.

115.   Jean Laplanche and J.-B. Pontalis, *Vocabulary of Psychoanalysis,* p. 130.

116.   One finds this notion expressed, in one form or another, in a great many articles. Among the latter, we may cite: Ernest Hartmann, "The Psychophysiology of Free Will: An Example of Vertical Research," in Rudolph M. Loewenstein et al., *Psychoanalysis as a General Psychology,* pp. 521ff.; John Hospers, "Free Will and Psychoanalysis," in W. Sellers and J. Hospers, *Readings in Ethical Theory,* pp. 560ff.; Samuel D. Lipton, "A Note on the Compatibility of Psychic Determinism and Freedom of Will," *International Journal of Psychoanalysis* 36, no. 2 (1955).

117.   Erik H. Erikson, *Identity, Youth and Crisis,* p. 109.

118.   Heinz Hartmann, *Ego Psychology and the Problem of Adaptation,* pp. 8–9.

119.   Merton Gill and G. S. Klein, *The Collected Papers of David Rapaport,* pp. 22–23.

120.   Ibid., pp. 352, 294, 830. An almost identical notion is convincingly expressed by Abraham Kaplan in *The Conduct of Inquiry,* p. 121.

121.   Abraham H. Maslow, *Toward a Psychology of Being,* pp. 103ff.

122.   Erik H. Erikson, *Childhood and Society,* p. 228.

Notes—Chapter Two

1. See Herman Nunberg and Ernst Federn, *Minutes of the Vienna Psychoanalytic Society. I. 1906–1908; II. 1908–1910.*

2. Sigmund Freud, "Leonardo da Vinci and a Memory of His Childhood," *SE*, vol. 11. A few years later Freud devoted a very brief psychobiographical study to Dostoevsky: "Dostoevsky and Parricide," *SE*, vol. 21. The very first psychobiographical interpretation made by Freud came well before these two essays, however; it was in a letter to Fliess, June 20, 1898, in which Freud spoke about the novelist Konrad Fredinand Meyer. (See Sigmund Freud, *The Origins of Psychoanalysis: Letters to Wilhelm Fliess, Drafts and Notes,* pp. 256–257.)

3. Sigmund Freud and William C. Bullitt, *Thomas Woodrow Wilson, Twenty-Eighth President of the United States: A Psychological Study.*

4. Psychobiographies of all sizes come literally by the hundreds; the fact that most of these studies are now forgotten is no reflection on psychohistory. Readers with a collector's or archivist's bent will find some of the titles of psychobiographies published during the First World War and the 1920's interesting. (See John A. Garraty, *The Nature of Biography,* pp. 115ff., 230ff.) Many psychobiographical studies have also used classicial psychiatry, existential psychoanalysis, or various idiosyncratic derivatives of psychoanalysis. To the titles we have already mentioned, we may add Karl Jaspers' *Strindberg und Van Gogh,* as well as the huge catalogue of "pathographies" published by W. Lange-Eichbaum: *The Problem of Genius.*

5. The extent of Freud's error as well as the other weaknesses of his study have been particularly well demonstrated by Meyer Schapiro, "Leonardo and Freud: An Art Historical Study," *Journal of the History of Ideas* 17 (1956). But the polemic is by no means over, and the die-hard Freudians have in turn refuted Schapiro's theses (see in particular Kurt R. Eissler, *Leonardo da Vinci. Psychoanalytic Notes on the Enigma*). An interesting Jungian analysis of Leonardo's work and personality is to be found in Erich Neumann, *Art and the Creative Unconscious.*

6. M. S. Guttmacher, *America's Last King: An Interpretation of the Madness of George III.*

7. Ida McAlpine and Richard Hunter, *George III and the Mad Business,* pp. 354–363. See also E. J. Hundert, "History, Psychology and the Study of Deviant Behavior," *The Journal of Interdisciplinary History* 2, no. 4 (1972), pp. 453 ff. But one ought to mention that the thesis of the king's organic illness (actually, porphyria) propounded by the opponents of the psychoanalytic interpretation is itself considered unfounded by various medical experts as well as by many historians (see J. H. Plumb, "The Wolf's Clothing," *The New York Review of Books,* Dec. 14, 1972).

8.   Sibylle K. Escalona and Grace Heider, *Prediction and Outcome: A Study in Child Development*, p. 9. This fundamental continuity found in every individual manifests itself particularly strikingly in personalities that have experienced "conversion." It was Lucien Goldmann—who, as we shall see, cannot be accused of a bias in favor of biographical studies—who gave an excellent demonstration of the unity of Pascal's quest, for example, despite Pascal's famous conversion (see Lucien Goldmann, *The Hidden God*). From our point of view, the continuity is not only that of form and style, but is expressed through essential characteristics and tendencies of the personality.

9.   The most recent study on this subject is David Shapiro's *Neurotic Styles*.

10.   Quoted (and illustrated) in H. J. Eysenck, *Crime and Personality*, p. 51.

11.   Erik H. Erikson, *Childhood and Society*, p. 348.

12.   Gertrud M. Kurth, "The Jew and Adolf Hitler," in Sandor Lorand, *The Yearbook of Psychoanalysis* 4 (1949), pp. 266ff.

13.   Georges Devereux, "La psychanalyse appliquée à l'histoire de Sparte," *Annales ESC* (Jan.-Feb. 1965), p. 29.

14.   Gustav Byshowski, *Dictators and Disciplines*, p. 147.

15.   Rudolph Binion, "Research Note," *Newsletter: Group for the Use of Psychology in History* 1, no. 3 (July 1972).

16.   Walter C. Langer, *The Mind of Adolf Hitler: The Secret Wartime Report*, pp. 194–196. Since my aim here is not to analyze these studies individually but rather to compare them, I will not mention the numerous factual errors, and above all the unfounded suppositions contained in Langer's work; these are for the most part attributable to the early date of its writing. For a critique of Langer see Hans W. Gatzke, "Hitler and Psychohistory," *American Historical Review* 78, no. 4 (1973).

17.   According to many historians, however, this decision was made in March or April 1941.

18.   Robert C. L. Waite, "Adolf Hitler's Antisemitism," in Benjamin B. Wolman, *The Psychoanalytic Interpretation of History*, pp. 203ff.

19.   Saul Friedländer, *L'Antisémitisme nazi: Histoire d'une psychose collective*, pp. 133ff.

20.   This is also the age at which some future political leaders compose plays and poems, whose importance for psychobiography is evident—as is amply shown by Saint-Just's *Organt* or De Gaulle's *Une Mauvaise rencontre*.

21.   "A problem, once suggested, carries its own impetus," writes a biographer of Nietzsche, "and the thinker is driven on by it to new problems and solutions. To understand these, we must follow the development of his thought—and that is best done separately from the survey of his life, as any joint treatment will almost inevitably suggest a false notion of causal relationship between life and philosophy." (Walter Kaufmann, *Nietzsche, Philosopher, Psychologist, Antichrist*, p. 21.) The dichotomy between life and work is too sharply drawn, but Kaufmann makes clear the nature of the indeterminacy that the biographer must confront.

23.   See on this subject the excellent biography by Quentin Bell: *Virginia Woolf* (2 vols.).

24.   Werner Maser, *Adolf Hitler, Legende, Mythos, Wirklichkeit*, p. 333.

25.   Werner Maser, *Adolf Hitler*, pp. 334ff.

26.   Lord Moran, *Winston Churchill: The Struggle for Survival, 1940–1965*.

27.   Edwin A. Weinstein, "Woodrow Wilson's Neurological Illness," *Journal of American History* 57 (1970–1971).

28.   Edwin A. Weinstein, "Woodrow Wilson's Neurological Illness."

29.   T. S. Eliot, *Selected Essays*, pp. 21–22.

30.   Raymond Picard, *Pourquoi la nouvelle critique?*, p. 117.

31.   Serge Doubrovsky, *The New Criticism in France*, trans. Derek Coltman, p. 94.

32.   For a more complete picture of the various currents of "la nouvelle critique," see the

excellent volume containing the proceedings of the Cerisy colloquium, *Les Chemins actuels de la critique.*

33.   Lucien Goldmann, *Pour une sociologie du roman,* p. 431.

34.   "The greatest of all pictures based on the facts of vision wasn't painted in the scientific atmosphere of Holland, but in the superstitious, convention-ridden court of Philip IV of Spain: *Las Meninas,* 'The Ladies in Waiting,' which was painted by Velasquez about five years before Vermeer's finest interiors. . . . Although one may use works of art to illustrate the history of civilization, one must not pretend that social conditions produce works of art or inevitably influence their form." (Kenneth Clark, *Civilization: A Personal View,* p. 213.)

35.   Lucien Goldmann, *Structures mentales et Création culturelle,* p. 16.

36.   Ernst Kris, *Psychoanalytic Explorations in Art,* p. 61.

37.   Sarah Kofman, *L'Enfance de l'art: Une interprétation de l'esthétique freudienne,* pp. 125–126.

38.   Janine Chasseguet-Smirgel, *Pour une psychanalyse de l'art et de la créativite,* pp. 44–46, 60–62. The same thesis is stated, among others, by Yvon Beleval in his preface to the study by Anne Clancier, *Psychanalyse et Critique littéraire,* p. 19.

39.   Kofman, *L'Enfance de l'art,* p. 127.

40.   Chasseguet-Smirgel, *Pour une psychanalyse de l'art,* p. 62. One finds this necessary synthesis between the structuralist and genetic methods in biography in the most unexpected places. Thus, in his inaugural speech at the Académie Française, Claude Lévi-Strauss, paying homage to his predecessor, Henry de Montherlant, began with a structural analysis of Montherlant's works—an analysis that led, according to him, to an evident conclusion whose "internal logic" manifested itself in "the need to short-circuit the mediation of the mother: the carnal act, performed either actually or figuratively, results in a metaphoric or actual death. And life, understood in this metaphoric or actual sense, can result only from a renunciation of the carnal act, either actually or figuratively."

Lévi-Strauss then turned to a direct thematic analysis, taking into account the biographical origins of the work: "The plot of *La Reine morte (The Dead Queen)* lays bare, I believe, this well-spring of my predecessor's thought. To the question 'Who is the dead Queen?' few spectators would hesitate to reply: Ines de Castro. Is she not seen, after all, at the end of the last act, dead and wearing a crown? Yet, during the play itself the words of the title appear only once, and they refer to another woman: the dead wife of Ferrante, who says to his son: 'From the time you were five years old to when you were thirteen, I loved you tenderly. The Queen, your mother, died very young.' The ambiguity here is more than a matter of chance. Pedro, therefore, is a son without a mother, like Philippe in *Les Jeunes Filles* and Alcacer in *Don Juan,* like the son that Alban invents for himself at the end of *Le Songe* or the one to whom is addressed the *Lettre d'un père (Letter from a Father),* or the one who engages in a dialogue with the stranger of *L'Equinoxe de septembre*; just as Celestino's daughter is a daughter without a mother, her mother having 'died in giving her birth.' But, unlike the author, who, as is well known, always rejected marriage, Pedro succeeds in replacing his mother, who died while he was a baby, by a wife: Ines, who, as if to confirm this continuity, becomes in turn the dead Queen. She must die, in fact, not only in order to reproduce the Queen mother, whom she replaces (we must not forget her belly, which alone bears the crown), but also and above all because the author, even more than Ferrante, wants to eliminate the solution chosen by Pedro—a solution he rejects, to a problem that is also his own. . . ." (Claude Lévi-Strauss, "Discours de réception à l'Académie française," *Le Monde,* June 28, 1974.)

41.   Anthony Storr, *The Dynamics of Creation*; David McClelland, *The Roots of Consciousness.*

42.   *SE,* vol. 13, p. 187.

43.   Jean Delay, "Névrose et création," in *Aspects de la psychiatrie moderne.*

44.   For Melanie Klein's thought on this subject, as well as for the theses advanced by Janine Chasseguet-Smirgel, see the latter's work, previously cited: *Psychanalyse de l'art et de la créativité.*

45. Storr, *The Dynamics of Creation.*

46. Chasseguet-Smirgel, *Psychanalyse de l'art et de la créativite,* p. 102.

47. Storr, *The Dynamics of Creation,* p. 203ff.

48. Jean Starobinski, *La Relation critique,* p. 283 (my italics).

49. Ibid., p. 63.

50. Roland Barthes, *Michelet,* p. 5.

51. Marie Bonaparte, *Edgar Poe, sa vie, son oeuvre, Etude analytique,* pp. 763–764. Other scholars have arrived at similar conclusions. Thus, Leopold Bellak establishes a distinction between writers who constantly treat the same story in various forms (extreme subjectivity) and those who are able to express several themes (see Leopold Bellak, "Somerset Maugham: A Thematic Analysis of Ten Short Stories," in Robert W. White, *The Study of Lives,* p. 157.) When, in the case of a writer with a single theme, the theme is very often reworked, the historian can attempt to capture its essence by using the method of the superposition of texts advocated by Charles Mauron. For a very clear summary of Mauron's method, see his essay, "Les origines d'un mythe personnel chez l'écrivain," in *Critique sociologique et Critique psychanalytique,* pp. 91ff. For a systematic and detailed demonstration of the method, see Mauron's book, *Des métaphores obsédantes au mythe personnel: Introduction à la psychocritique.*

52. George D. Painter, *Proust: The Early Years,* p. 16.

53. In certain cases, which are by definition rare, the fundamental problem is so particular that it is possible to determine rather exactly its influence on the level of the work. Thus, Marc Soriano has admirably demonstrated, in the life and works of Charles Perrault, the importance of Perrault's having been a twin. See Marc Soriano, *Les Contes de Perrault, Culture savante et Traditions populaires.*

54. Dominique Fernandez, *L'Arbre jusqu'aux racines,* p. 140.

55. Ibid., p. 125.

56. Ibid., p. 125.

57. Ibid., p. 128.

58. Ibid., p. 140 (italics in the text).

59. Ibid., p. 178 (italics in the text).

60. Preface by Jean-François Lyotard to Anton Ehrenzweig, *l'Ordre caché de l'art: Essai sur la psychologie de l'imagination artistique,* p. 2.

61. Nicolas Abraham, "Le temps, le rythme et l'inconscient," in *Entretiens sur l'art et la psychanalyse.*

62. Ismond Rosen, "Etude psychanalytique de la sculpture," in *Entretiens sur l'art et la psychanalyse.*

63. Anton Ehrenzweig, *l'Ordre caché de l'art,* p. 109.

64. We may add that, although Ehrenzweig's work is impressive by its originality, it nevertheless raises some theoretical problems that it does not resolve. Even if one admits the validity of his conception of the primary processes, one soon notices that his thesis, which is easily demonstrated in the case of modern painting, sculpture, and music, is less convincing in the case of "classical" music (despite a few examples) and applies barely if at all to literature (with the possible exception of the *nouveau roman*). Furthermore, Ehrenzweig does not quite succeed in explaining how, according to his system, "normal" artistic creation differs from the production of schizophrenics. Finally, one can ask why the presence of the "hidden order" at the heart of the primary processes did not give rise to serial music or abstract painting in the seventeenth century, for example, are we not obliged, in the end, to reinstruduce the structuring function of the ego as a determining element in artistic creation?

65. Fernandez, *L'Arbre jusqu'aux racines,* p. 181.

66. E. H. Gombrich, *Art and Illusion.*

67. Lucien Goldmann, *Pour une sociologie du roman,* pp. 86–87.

68.   This notion is similar to that of Leo Spitzer, who considered the "stylistic deviation" from the linguistic norm as an expression of the writer's personality; on the other hand, it is hard to see why Spitzer sought to interpret this deviation also as the sign of an evolution in the "collective soul." One remains unconvinced by his example of the use of the phrase "à cause de" in Charles-Louis Philippe's novel, *Bubu de Montparnasse* (see Leo Spitzer, *Linguistics and Literary History*, pp. 11–15).

69.   Jean-Paul Sartre, *Search for a Method,* trans. Hazel E. Barnes, pp. 62–63.

70.   Starobinski, *Le Relation critique,* p. 103.

71.   Ibid., p. 146.

72.   For a more detailed theoretical discussion, see Fred I. Greenstein, *Personality and Politics.* As its title indicates, Greenstein's book is concerned with the psychoanalytic bases of political behavior; he examines, in greater detail than I am able to do here, the problem of the relation between role and personality. Greenstein has also published an important volume of texts treating the influence of personality factors on political behavior; historians will find the theoretical discussions in the volume pertinent to their own concerns. (See Fred I. Greenstein and Michael Lerner, *A Source Book for the Study of Personality and Politics.*

73.   Raymond Aron, *Introduction à la philosophie de l'histoire,* p. 104.

74.   Aron, *Introduction à la philosophie de l'histoire,* p. 106.

75.   Stanley Hoffmann and Inge Hoffmann, "De Gaulle as Political Artist: The Will to Grandeur," in Stanley Hoffmann, *Decline or Renewal? France Since the 1930's,* p. 202.

76.   Hans Gerth and C. Wright Mills, *Character and Social Structure. The Psychology of Institutions,* p. 419.

77.   We could complicate the problem further: granted that the personality influences the mode of execution of a role considered from a subjective viewpoint—in other words, as a series of norms internalized by the individual who performs the role—that would not be the case if one considered the role in a broader perspective, not only in terms of internalized norms but also in terms of objective limits independent of individual will. We might add that it is precisely on the political level that these objective limits are most strongly felt, often leaving a very narrow margin of choice and maneuvering to the person who makes the decisions. This notion is reinforced by recent studies concerning the influence of bureaucratic organizations on decision making, notably in the field of foreign policy, where there appeared to be much more leeway for choice than in domestic policy. (See, for example, Graham T. Allison, *The Essence of Decision: An Analysis of the Cuban Missile Crisis.*) The reply to this kind of argument can be stated in brief and simple terms: the argument is not entirely false when the political process follows what can be called a "normal" course; but as soon as a crisis situation occurs, the limits imposed on individual decision-making by the weight of various objective factors, especially by organizational and bureaucratic constraints, are broadened, and the political leader finds himself free to choose between war and peace, resistance or submission, compromise or confrontation. Whether he finds support for his decision is another matter. Crisis situations allow one to see, more forcefully than ever, the essential role of personality factors in the context of political decision-making.

78.   Among the important works in this category, we may note the biographies of the English General Clinton and of the American politician, Charles Sumner. See William B. Wilcox, *Portrait of a General, Sir Henry Clinton, in the War of Independence*; David Donald, *Charles Sumner and the Coming of the Civil War.* .

79.   Besides the Georges' study on Wilson, we should mention Fawn M. Brodie, *Thomas Jefferson: An Intimate History*; Lewis J. Edinger, *Kurt Schumacher: A Study in Personality and Political Behavior*; Arnold Rogow, *James Forrestal: A Study of Personality, Politics and Policy*; Robert C. Tucker, *Stalin as Revolutionary, 1879–1929: A Study in History and Personality,* as well as the more limited but nevertheless very interesting study by Peter Loewenberg, "The Unsuccessful Adolescence of Heinrich Himmler," *American Historical Review* 76, no. 3 (1971), pp. 612ff.

80.   Sigmund Freud and William C. Bullitt, *Thomas Woodrow Wilson,* pp. 6–7.

81.   Alexander L. George and Juliette George, *Woodrow Wilson and Colonel House: A Personality Study*, p. 114.

82.   George and George, *Woodrow Wilson and Colonel House*, p. 12.

83.   This verification is made possible by the fact that a number of previously unpublished sources, notably the "deliberations of the Big Four," have been published since the Georges' study appeared.

84.   C. Seymour (ed.), *Intimate Papers of Colonel House*, p. 119.

85.   Sigmund Freud and William C. Bullitt, *Thomas Woodrow Wilson*, p. 116.

86.   *Intimate Papers of Colonel House*, p. 114.

87.   Ibid., pp. 126–127.

88.   Arthur S. Link, *Woodrow Wilson*, vol. 5, *Campaigns for Progressivism and Peace, 1916–1917*, p. 8.

89.   Ibid., vol. 2, *The New Freedom*, pp. 68–69.

90.   *Les Délibérations du Conseil des Quatre* (24 mars-28 juin 1919), vol. 1, p. 187.

91.   Ibid., p. 28.

92.   *Intimate Papers of Colonel House*, p. 120.

93.   Arthur S. Link, *Woodrow Wilson*, vol. 1, p. 8.

94.   See Freud and Bullitt, *Thomas Woodrow Wilson*, pp. 80–81.

95.   Edwin A. Weinstein, "Woodrow Wilson's Neurological Illness," p. 336.

96.   Ibid., pp. 339ff.

97.   Max Weber, *Theory of Social and Economic Organisation*, p. 358.

98.   Cited in Robert C. Tucker, "The Theory of Charismatic Leadership," *Daedalus* 97 (summer 1968), p. 745.

99.   Fred Weinstein and Gerald M. Platt, *Psychoanalytic Sociology*, pp. 68, 75, 112.

100.   Robert C. Tucker, "The Theory of Charismatic Leadership," p. 749.

101.   Peter Loewenberg, "Theodor Herzl: A Psychoanalytic Study in Charismatic Leadership," in Benjamin B. Wolman, *The Psychoanalytic Interpretation of History*, pp. 150ff.

102.   Erik H. Erikson, *Young Man Luther: A Study in Psychoanalysis and History*, p. 262.

103.   Erik H. Erikson, *Gandhi's Truth: On the Origins of Militant Non-Violence*, p. 401.

104.   Ibid., p. 408.

105.   Ibid., p. 412.

106.   Robert Coles, *Erik H. Erikson: The Growth of His Work*, p. 206.

107.   See *supra*, p.

108.   See *infra*, p.

109.   See, among many others, Harold D. Lasswell, *Psychopathology and Politics;* Theodore W. Adorno et al., *The Authoritarian Personality;* E. Victor Wolfenstein, *The Revolutionary Personality: Lenin, Trotsky, Gandhi;* James B. Barber, "Adult Identity and Presidential Style: The Rhetorical Emphasis," *Daedalus* 97 (summer 1968). For a detailed description of these typologies, see the previously cited works by Fred I. Greenstein.

110.   Milton Rokeach, *The Open and Closed Mind.*

111.   Stefan T. Possony, *Lenin: The Compulsive Revolutionary*, p. 398.

112.   Edward Shils, "Authoritarianism, Right and Left," in Richard Christie and Marie Jahoda, *Studies in the Scope and Method of "The Authoritarian Personality."*

113.   Harold D. Lasswell, *Psychopathology and Politics.*.

114.   Roger Stéphane, *Portrait de l'aventurier: T. E. Lawrence, Malraux, Von Salomon.*

115.   David McClelland, *The Roots of Consciousness.* "The Psychodynamics of the Creative Physical Scientist," pp. 146ff.

116. McClelland bases his argument on Robert Merton's theory—itself highly controversial—about the relationship between Puritanism and science (see R. K. Merton, *Social Theory and Social Structure*). In fact, if any religion is over-represented in the scientific domain in our day, it is the Jewish one.

117. Frank E. Manuel, *A Portrait of Isaac Newton*; and L. P. Williams, *Michael Faraday*, pp. 500ff.

118. Manuel, *A Portrait of Isaac Newton*, for example p. 99.

119. See Williams, *Michael Faraday*, pp. 8, 96, 99, 100, 358, and J. Agassi, *Faraday as Natural Philosopher*, p. 15, as well as Bernard S. Finn, "Views of Faraday," *Science* 176 (4035), pp. 665–667.

120. Ivor B. Evans, *Man of Power: The Life History of Baron Rutherford of Nelson*, pp. 221, 229.

121. Manuel, *A Portrait of Isaac Newton*, p. 104.

122. Agassi, *Faraday as Natural Philosopher*, pp. 59, 330.

123. See Manuel, *A Portrait of Isaac Newton*.

124. Williams, *Michael Faraday*, p. 3.

125. Evans, *Man of Power*, p. 25.

126. Agassi, *Faraday as Natural Philosopher*, p. 3; Williams, *Michael Faraday*, p. 3.

127. Manuel, *A Portrait of Isaac Newton*, p. 77.

128. See especially Frank E. Manuel's detailed discussion on this subject in *A Portrait of Isaac Newton.*.

129. Ibid.

130. For a summary of the research on this subject, see Kenneth W. Terhune, "The Effects of Personality in Cooperation and Conflict," in Paul Swingle, *The Structure of Conflict.*

131. On this subject, see Saul Friedländer and Raymond Cohen, "The Personality Origins of Belligerence in International Conflict: An Analysis of Historical Cases," *Journal of Comparative Politics,* January 1975.

132. This behavior pattern has often been studied; see in particular H. B. Biller and L. J. Borstelmann, "Masculine Development: An Integrative Review," *Merrill-Palmer Quarterly* 13 (1967); E. M. Hetherington, "A Developmental Study of the Effects of Sex of the Dominant Parent on Sex-role Preference, Identification and Imitation in Children," *Journal of Personality and Social Psychology* 2 (1965); D. B. Lynn and W. L. Sawrey, "The Effects of Father-absence on Norwegian Boys and Girls," *Journal of Abnormal and Social Psychology* 59 (1959).

Notes—Chapter Three

1.   Preface by Octavio Paz, to Jacques Lafaye, *Quetzalcoatl et Guadalupe: La Formation de la conscience nationale au Mexique,* pp. 24–25.

2.   Let us recall here the definition we gave in chapter 1 of the term "collective behavior," which is obviously linked to the notion of "collective phenomena": collective behavior consists of the shared perceptions, symbolic expressions, or modes of behavior attributable to the members of a group; at times, these perceptions or modes of behavior manifest themselves in an identical way, and over a long enough period to discount the effect of pure chance, even in individuals who do not belong to the same group (unless one defines the group as the abstract category created by the common denominator).

3.   More specifically, I have in mind here Freud's *Totem and Taboo, Civilization and Its Discontents,* and *Moses and Monotheism,* as well as Hebert Marcuse's *Eros and Civilization* and Norman O. Brown's *Life Against Death.* Erich Fromm's *Escape from Freedom* belongs in the same category.

4.   See William L. Langer, "The Next Assignment," in Bruce Mazlish, *Psychoanalysis and History;* E. R. Dodds, *Pagan and Christian in an Age of Anxiety;* Zevedei Barbu, *Problems of Historical Psychology.*

5.   According to Goffman's definition, the total institution isolates the individual from the outside world and places him in a particular context in which he is more or less absolutely, and for a more or less long period of time, bound by the rules of behavior decreed by the institution. Goffman distinguishes several categories of total institutions. To illustrate the notion in its general meaning, we can cite as examples the sanatorium, the prison or the concentration camp, the boarding school or the monastery. (See Irving Goffman, *Asylums: Essays on the Social Situation of Mental Patients and Other Inmates,* esp. p. 16.)

6.   As soon as a complementary group or a counter-group appears in the midst of a given group, the latter is no longer a homogeneous entity; that fact invalidates—at least in our present context—the principal argument used by Georges Devereux against the theories of Kardiner. (See Geroges Devereux, "La psychanalyse appliquée à l'histoire de Sparte," *Annales ESC,* January–February 1965, p. 38.)

7.   O. Mannoni, *Prospero and Caliban: The Psychology of Colonization.* It has been pointed out, however, that to treat the Malagasies as a homogeneous group is incorrect, given (among other reasons) the particular position of the dominant caste, the Hovas. (See Bruce Mazlish, "Group Psychology and Problems of Contemporary History," *Journal of Contemporary History* 3, no. 2 [1968].)

8.   John Demos, *A Little Commonwealth: Family Life in Plymouth Colony.*

9.   Stanley Elkins, *Slavery: A Problem in American Institutional and Intellectual Life.*

10.   Demos, *A Little Commonwealth,* pp. 135–139. In a previous study on the repetitive themes in the witchcraft of seventeenth-century New England, Demos found that aggressivity played the same central role, but his explanation in terms of the developmental model was more tentative. In fact, these aggressive themes are essentially linked to orality, which seems to lead back to the first stage in Erikson's model, unless one opts instead for a Kleinian interpretation. (See John Demos, "Underlying Themes in the Witchcraft of Seventeenth-Century New England," *American Historical Review* 75, no. 5 [1970].)

11.   Elkins' study provoked a great deal of controversy, the essential issues of which are summed up in Ann J. Lane, *The Debate over Slavery: Stanley Elkins and His Critics.* But on the whole the controversy was over the interpretation of the facts, not over the essential facts themselves. More recently, however, it is the basic data concerning black slavery in the United States that have been contested: the slave society has been described as a stratified society, with economic competition and a definite degree of individual development among its members. (See Robert William Fogel and Stanley L. Engerman, *Time on the Cross: The Economics of American Negro Slavery.*) Since the debate remains open and since Fogel's and Engerman's thesis is far from being accepted by most historians, we may consider that, in the absence of definite proof to the contrary, the traditionally accepted facts about the life of black slaves in the United States are correct.

12.   Elkins, *Slavery,* p. 82. To explain the formation of the Sambo personality, Elkins uses three convergent theories: the psychoanalytic theory of internalization, H. S. Sullivan's theory of interpersonal relations, and role theory.

13.   Elkins, *Slavery,* p. 130.

14.   In its most general form, this problem has not escaped the attention of other scholars. See especially Harold R. Isaacs, *The New World of Negro Americans,* and Charles Silberman, *Crisis in Black and White.*

15.   Every collective obsession requires a first gesture, a first narrative account, an initial setting in motion by a few magnetic personalities. See on this subject the clinical case histories reported in Georges Heuyer, *Psychoses collectives et suicides collectifs.*

16.   On this subject, see especially Norman Cohn, *The Pursuit of the Millenium.*

17.   Saul Friendländer, *L'Antisémitiseme nazi,* esp. pp. 146ff.

18.   See the general study by Julio Caro Baroja, *The World of Witches,* as well as Michel de Certeau's *La Possession de Loudun* and Chadwick Hansen's *Witchcraft of Salem.*

19.   From this point of view, the phenomenon closest to us, and perhaps the most astonishing one, is the quasi-disappearance of Nazism with the death of Adolf Hitler. But Norman Cohn already showed that the disappearance of the "prophets of the millenium" led to the disappearance of their sects. Similarly, possession as a phenomenon disappeared from Salem and Loudun practically overnight.

20.   Sigmund Freud, *Group Psychology and the Analysis of the Ego.*

21.   Ibid., p. 48.

22.   Ibid., p. 55.

23.   Ibid., p. 59.

24.   Friedländer, *L'Antisémitisme nazi,* pp. 173ff.

25.   Bruno Bettelheim, *The Informed Heart,* p. 109.

26.   Ibid., p. 172.

27.   We are obviously dealing here with phenomena that one would tend to qualify as forms of collective hypnosis—even though that term does not take us very far—or, in other times, as forms of "collective possession"—which takes us even less far. Hypnosis and possession are both described as phenomena that involve profound, but generally temporary, changes (even though in the case of possession the change can be, as we know, irreversible). In any event, the role of the historian is essential, for he alone is in a position to evaluate, in as strictly critical terms as

possible, all the documentary material needed for compartive studies (which must come first) and for theoretical explanation (which comes second).

28.   It is essential that we recall the relative character of the notions of homogeneity and heterogeneity that we are employing. Thus, if in a heterogeneous group all the young children experience the same traumatic events, certain similar tendencies can manifest themselves later in many of the members of that group as adults. In such a case the traumatic event produces a kind of *sui generis* homogeneity, as concerns a certain age group. For an interesting example, see Peter Loewenberg, "The Psychohistorical Origins of the Nazi Youth Cohort," *American Historical Review* 76, no. 5 (1971).

29.   Numerous studies of a similar nature exist in this field. We shall limit ourselves to discussing the classic work by David D. McClelland himself, *The Achieving Society.*

30.   Ibid., p. 3.

31.   Ibid., pp. 342, 345.

32.   Ibid., p. 353.

33.   Georges Devereux, *Essais d'ethnopsychiatrie générale,* p. 13.

34.   Ibid., p. 5.

35.   Ibid., p. 45.

36.   Ibid., p. 92.

37.   There exist numerous documentary sources for this kind of study: for example, the importance accorded to a particular symptom or disorder in the clinical literature, as well as in literature in general; hospital archives, especially those of psychiatric hospitals; the archives of various commissions or groups studying the mental health of a population; finally, the private archives of psychiatrists or psychoanalysts. In his *Madness and Civilization,* Michel Foucault has given us a brilliant history of the evolution of mental disorders and of the attitudes toward them in a given culture. One can envisage an additional psychohistorical dimension to a study of this kind.

38.   If one studies a particular group behavior involving a paroxystic collective phenomenon of short duration, one is in fact dealing with a temporary homogeneous group (as in the examples we mentioned earlier of witchcraft in Loudon or Salem). If, on the other hand, one considers the witchcraze as an irrational attitude that manifested itself over a period of close to two centuries, then one is studying an isolated phenomenon in the sense in which we are discussing it here.

39.   Hugh R. Trevor-Roper, *The European Witchcraze of the Sixteenth and Seventeenth Centuries,* p. 160.

40.   Henry Institoris and Jacques Sprenger, *Le Marteau des Sorcières* (with an introduction by Amand Danet).

41.   Danet, Introduction to *Le Marteau des Sorcières,* p. 8.

42.   Ibid.

43.   Trevor-Roper, *The European Witchcraze,* p. 170.

44.   See chapter 1, especially p. 20.

45.   For a discussion of the "identifying" role of marginal or deviant groups, see Kai T. Erikson, *Wayward Puritans: A Study in the Sociology of Deviance.*

46.   Georges Devereux, "La psychanalyse appliquée à l'histoire de Sparte," p. 32.

47.   Jean-Paul Sartre, *Portrait of the Anti-Semite,* trans. Mary Guggenheim, p. 11.

48.   Friedländer, *L'Antisémitisme nazi,* p. 50.

49.   The general psychological foundations of anti-Semitism have been analyzed in numerous studies, of which the best known are those of Ernst Simmel, *Antisemitism: A Social Disease*; Rodolphe Loewenstein, *Psychanalyse de l'antisémitisme*; Henry Loeblowitz-Lennart, "The Jew as Symbol," *Psychoanalytic Quarterly* 16, no. 1 (1947); Bela Grunberger, "The Antisemite and the Oedipal Conflict," *International Journal of Psycho-analysis* 45 (1964).

50. Nathan Ackermann and Marie Lazarsfeld-Jahoda, *Antisemitism and Emotional Disorder.*

51. G. H. Gough, "Studies in Social Intolerance: A Personality Scale for Antisemitism," *Journal of Social Psychology* 33 (1951), p. 253.

52. Loewenstein, *Psychanalyse de l'antisémitisme*, p. 17.

53. Friedländer, *L'Antisémitisme nazi*, pp. 27ff.

54. Iring Fetscher, "Zur Entstehung des politischen Antisemitismus in Deutschland," in Herman Huss and Andreas Schröder, *Antisemitismus: Zur Pathologie der Bürgerlichen Gesellschaft.*

55. Eva G. Reichmann, *Hostages of Civilization: The Social Sources of National-Socialist Anti-Semitism*, p. 164.

56. One point, however, deserves clarification. Anti-Semitism has been defined as an attitude allowing the anti-Semite to distinguish Good from Evil, the Pure from the Impure, and so on. In order for this function to be maintained, isn't the survival of the Jews essential to the non-Jewish society? But Nazism, the paroxystic form of anti-Semitism, made every effort to annihilate the Jews. Isn't there a fundamental contradiction implied in this? The answer is relatively simple: if the Nazis annihilated the Jews physically, they proceeded at the same time to elaborate a detailed and fantastic version of the myth of the Jew, in other words of the counter-ideal of the mythical "in-group." Furthermore, in a context of racial hierarchy other inferior races can fulfill the physical and concrete function of the visible counter-ideal, while the myth of the Jew preserves its function as the "ideal" incarnation of Evil.

57. Robert Nisbet, *Social Change*, pp. 1–2.

58. For a succinct and clear statement of this conception of social change, see Robert K. Merton, "A Paradigm for Functional Analysis in Sociology," in *Social Theory and Social Structure*, pp. 49ff.

59. Emphatically defended by Robert Nisbet (who borrowed some of his notions from Radcliffe-Brown), the theory of change through "rupture" is particularly well known and has been most often discussed in the context of scientific change, since the publication of Thomas S. Kuhn's *The Structure of Scientific Revolutions.*

60. Robert Nisbet, it is true, included several essays by historians in his volume on social change.

61. Emmanuel Le Roy Ladurie, *Le Territoire de l'historien*, p. 171.

62. See chapter 1, p. 35.

63. On this subject, see in particular David Schoenbaum, *Hitler's Social Revolution: Class and Status in Nazi Germany, 1933–1939.*

64. Neil J. Smelser,"Social and Psychological Dimensions of Collective Behavior," in *Essays in Sociological Explanation*, pp. 110ff.

65. Philippe Ariès, *Centuries of Childhood*, trans. Robert Baldick, p. 50.

66. Ibid.

67. Ibid., p. 30.

68. J. H. Van den Berg, *Metabletica ou la Psychologie historique*, pp. 32ff.

69. Kenneth Keniston, "Psychological Development and Historical Change," *The Journal of Interdisciplinary History* 2, no. 2 (1971), p. 342.

70. Keniston, ibid., p. 342. The same hypothesis has been formulated in particularly emphatic and univocal terms by Lloyd de Mause, in the framework of what he calls the "psychogenetic theory of History." According to de Mause, the specific traits of a culture depend on the particular configuration of childhood in that culture. This kind of theory, which is partially correct as far as homogeneous groups are concerned, becomes reductionistic when applied to heterogeneous groups, as we have shown. For a full statement of de Mause's views, see his introduction to the collective volume, *The History of Childhood.*

71.   David Hunt, *Parents and Children in History: The Psychology of Family Life in Early Modern France.*

72.   Ibid., p. 190.

73.   Ibid., p. 191.

74.   Ibid., p. 158. The qualification of "to some extent" is in this case essential, for once again we are not dealing with a homogeneous group.

75.   Ibid., p. 192.

76.   Karl Mannheim, "The Problem of Generations," in *Essays on the Sociology of Knowledge,* pp. 276ff.

77.   S. N. Eisenstadt, *From Generation to Generation: Age Groups and Social Structure,* p. 316.

78.   Philip Abrams, "Rites de passage: The Conflict of Generations in Industrial Society," *Journal of Contemporary History* 5, no. 1 (1970), p. 185.

79.   Kingsley Davis, "The Sociology of Parent-Youth Conflict," *American Sociological Review* 5 (1940), p. 535.

80.   Muzafer Sherif and Hadley Cantril, *The Psychology of Ego Involvements: Social Attitudes and Identifications,* pp. 205ff.

81.   See Robert Jay Lifton, "Protean Man," in *History and Human Survival.*

82.   See above, p. 103.

83.   Besides the various volumes of writings by members of the youth movements to which we shall be referring frequently in what follows, the two most complete historical studies on this subject are Howard Becker's *German Youth, Bond or Free,* and Walter Z. Laqueur's *Young Germany: A History of the German Youth Movement.*

84.   In 1911, the German youth movements counted around 15,000 members. (See George Mosse, *The Crisis of German Ideology,* p. 171.) According to Fritz Jungmann, the various youth movements that grew out of the *Wandervögel* had a total of 40,000 members in 1914. (See Fritz Jungmann, "Autorität und Sexualmoral in der Jugendbewegung," in Max Horkheimer, *Studien über Autorität und Familie,* p. 670.)

85.   Hans Blüher, "Geschichte des Wandervögels," in Werner Kindt, *Grundschriften der Deutschen Jugendbewegung,* p. 47.

86.   Kindt, *Grundschriften,* p. 10.

87.   Laqueur, *Young Germany,* pp. 92–93.

88.   Peter Gay, *Weimar Culture: The Outsider as Insider,* p. 78.

89.   The impact of a work such as *Helmut Harringa* was immense. Already before the first World War it had sold 400,000 copies. (See Fritz Jungmann, "Autorität und Sexualmoral in der Jugendbewegung," p. 671.)

90.   Elisabeth Busse-Wilson, "Liebe und Kameradschaft," in Kindt, *Grundschriften,* p. 329.

91.   Kindt, *Grundschriften,* p. 16.

92.   Gustave Wyneken, "Der Weltgeschichtliche Sinn der Jugendbewegung," in Kindt, *Grundschriften,* p. 153.

93.   Laqueur, *Young Germany,* p. 59.

94.   The role of active homosexuality in the German youth movements has been considerably overestimated, due to Blüher's books and to the practices of a deviant fraction within the movements, which drew public attention and provoked scandal. According to Jungmann, overt homosexuality within the movements was not more widespread than among German youth in general. On the other hand, the youth movement encouraged friendship with erotic overtones, or "sublimated" homosexuality between its members, and especially between the members and the leader. (See Fritz Jungmann, "Autorität und Sexualmoral in der Jugendbewegung," pp. 676–677.)

95.   Quoted in Howard Becker, *German Youth, Bond or Free,* p. 97.

96.   Wilhelm Stählin, "Der Neue Lebensstil," in Kindt, *Grundschriften,* p. 59.

97.   Quoted in Harry Pross, *Jugend, Eros, Politik: Die Geschichte der Deutschen Jugend-verbünde,* p. 286.

98.   Pross, *Jugend, Eros, Politik,* p. 288.

99.   Gay, *Weimar Culture,* pp. 102ff.

100.   For an extremely subtle thematic analysis of German films between the war and the Nazi seizure of power, see Siegfried Kracauer, *From Caligari to Hitler.*

101.   Ibid., pp. 84ff., 96ff. As concerns the youth movements, the instinctual freedom one finds in a group such as Muck-Lamberty's "Neue Schar" does not mean very much, given the limited and ephemeral character of the phenomenon. What seems far more significant was the rejection of expressionism and the choice of a highly stylized kind of painting, such as one finds from the very start in the illustrations of the youth movements' publications.

102.   One cannot fail to note that several of the psychological characteristics we have just mentioned have often been identified as being particular to the "fascist personality." Further-more, it has often been noted to what a great extent fascism idolized youth and was itself a "youth movement." George Mosse, who has placed particular emphasis on this aspect of fascism, notes that the fascist leaders themselves were for the most part men who were still young: "Mussolini was 39 when he became Prime Minister, Hitler 44 on attaining the Chancellorship. Léon Degrelle was in his early thirties, and Primo de Rivera as well as Codreanu were in their late twenties. . . . Indeed, when they inveighed against the bourgeoisie they meant merely the older generation which could never understand a movement of youth." (George L. Mosse, "The Genesis of Fascism," *Journal of Contemporary History* 1, no. 1 [1966], pp. 18–19). Robert Brasillach and Drieu La Rochelle practically equated youth with fascism; in the thirty-year old Brasillach, who has just discovered the marvels of fascism, we recognize all the major themes that inspired the adolescents of the *Wandervögel,* but in an extreme form. (See Robert Brasillach, "Notre avant-guerre," in *Une Génération dans l'orage,* p. 205ff.). A study of the deep psychological connections between fascism and youth remains to be written.

103.   See especially two articles by Walter Laqueur, "Reflections on Youth Movements" and "The Archeology of Youth," reprinted in his book, *Out of the Ruins of Europe.*

104.   This assertion is not based on a formal survey, but rather on an intuitive evaluation of the situation, based on my observation of various university settings both in the United States and in Europe.

105.   Daniel Bell, *The End of Ideology: On the Exhaustion of Political Ideas in the Fifties.*

106.   Kenneth Keniston, *The Uncommitted: Alienated Youth in American Society,* pp. 102–103. We should point out that in Keniston's study the totally "uncommitted" student appeared to be an exception. I am suggesting, however, that this is an "ideal type" which reflects the tendency of a very large segment, if not the majority, of American youth.

107.   Ibid., pp. 113, 117.

108.   Ibid., pp. 173ff., 199ff.

109.   Alexander Mitscherlich, *Society without a Father,* trans. Erich Mosbacher, p. 141.

110.   Jacques Le Goff, "Les mentalités: Une histoire ambiguë," in J. Le Goff and P. Nora, *Faire de l'histoire,* vol. 1, p. 80.

111.   Ibid., pp. 84, 91.

112.   Lucien Febvre, *Combats pour l'histoire,* p. 229.

113.   Alphonse Dupront, "L'histoire après Freud," *Revue de l'Enseignement supérieur,* nos. 44 45 (1969), p. 36.

114.   The reason for this qualification is clear: one can study, as Robert Mandrou has done, for example, French mentality in the seventeenth century as a global phenomenon (see Robert Mandrou, *Introduction à la France moderne, 1500–1640: Essai de psychologie historique*), or one can study a particular aspect of this mentality, such as religious mentality or peasant mentality.

115.   Despite their applicability to the general problems in the study of collective mentalities, we cannot take account here of the vast number of works and discussions devoted to the question of "national character." The debate over "national character" has in fact become a field unto itself; thus, the bibliography of a work published in 1960 on the study of national character lists close to a thousand titles, treating essentially of theoretical and methodological questions. See H. C. J. Duijker and N. H. Frijda, *National Character and National Stereotypes.*

116.   David Riesman, "Psychological Types and National Character," *American Quarterly,* no. 5 (1953), p. 329.

117.   Ibid., pp. 330–332.

118.   As examples of oversimplifications in this domain one can cite the numerous works of Geoffrey Gorer, the best known of which is *The People of Great Russia* (in collaboration with John Ryckmann).

119.   Louis Dumont, *Homo hierarchicus: Essai sur le système des castes,* p. 15.

120.   G. E. von Grünebaum, *L'Identité culturelle de l'Islam,* p. 1.

121.   Serge Moscovici, *Essai sur l'histoire humaine de la nature,* pp. 5–6.

122.   Devereux, *Essais d'ethnopsychiatrie générale,* p. 5.

123.   Febvre, *Combats pour l'histoire,* p. 235.

124.   Lafaye, *Quetzelcoatl et Guadalupe.*

125.   Le Goff, "Les mentalités," pp. 86ff.

126.   Devereux, *Essais d'ethnopsychiatrie générale.*

127.   Ernesto De Martino, *La Terre du remords,* especially pp. 303ff.

128.   Popular literature is perhaps more important in this instance than "great" literature. Robert Mandrou has provided an excellent demonstration of its importance in his book, *De la culture populaire aux XVIIe et XVIIIe siècles: La Bibliothèque de Troyes.*

129.   On this subject, see Anton Ehrenzweig's remarks on modern art in *L'Ordre caché de l'art,* pp. 102, 162ff. For the analysis of contemporary mentalities, the study of films is essential. The significance of a popular film is equal to that of the most widely read book, due to the direct impact of the image and the interaction between the spectator and the screen, which is just as deep as the one between the reader and the printed page. But only a thematic analysis of a great number of films can overcome the inherent obstacles posed by the composite nature of this mode of expression. For this reason, the conclusions drawn by Gregory Bateson from his analysis of the Nazi film, *Hitlerjunge Quex,* are not very convincing; the same can be said of Erikson's analysis of the Soviet film, *The Childhood of Maxim Gorky.* For a summary of Bateson's analysis, see Margaret Mead and Rhoda Metraux, *The Study of Culture at a Distance,* pp. 302ff.; for Erikson's study, see the last chapter of *Childhood and Society.* The comparative study by Martha Wolfenstein and Nathan Leites, presented in their book, *The Movies: A Psychological Study,* is methodologically far superior, despite some of the simplistic parallels the authors draw between the present and the distant past.

130.   Dupront, "L'histoire après Freud," p. 46.

131.   Johan Huizinga, *The Waning of the Middle Ages.*

132.   Michel Vovelle, *Mourir autrefois: Attitudes collectives devant la mort aux XVIIe et XVIIIe siècles,* p. 9.

133.   Marc Raeff, to cite one example, was not able to avoid this pitfall in his otherwise extremely suggestive study on the collective mentality of the Russian nobility in the eighteenth century, *Origins of the Russian Intelligentsia: The Eighteenth Century Nobility.* For a very pertinent critique of Raeff's work, especially in the perspective we are adopting here, see Michael Confino, "Histoire et psychologie: à propos de la noblesse russe au XVIIIe siècle," *Annales ESC,* vol. 22, November–December 1967.

134.   Alex Inkeles and Daniel J. Levinson, "National Character: the Study of Modal Personality and Sociocultural Systems," in Gardner Lindzey and Elliott Aronson, *The Handbook of Social Psychology,* vol. 4, p. 427.

135.   For this range of choices, see in particular Inkeles and Levinson, "National Character," p. 447. One of the chief weaknesses of the volume on culture and personality edited by Margaret Mead and Rhoda Metraux (see note 129) is precisely that the essays included in it are not comparative studies devoted to a few central problems, but rather dispersed monographs that do not allow one to draw any conclusion based on the only valid basis, which is intercultural comparison. It should be noted, however, that the problems posed by such intercultural comparisons are not easy to resolve; they have generated.a large number of methodological studies, not only in sociology and anthropology but in social psychology. We shall not enter into a detailed discussion of these technical questions.

136.   Le Roy Ladurie, *Le Territoire de l'historien, pp. 395, 402.*

137.   The comparative study edited by Margaret Mead and Martha Wolfenstein, *Childhood in Contemporary Cultures,* suffers from the absence of common points of reference. This notwithstanding, the analogous conclusions reached by several studies referring to the same general theme and presented by several co-authors of the volume—for example, Martha Wolfenstein's and Françoise Dolto's studies concerning the differences between French and American children—are not lacking in importance.

138.   For a particularly suggestive study on the relation between the global social context, the forms of child-rearing and certain characteristics of the American mentality, see David M. Potter, *People of Plenty: Economic Abundance and the American Character.*

139.   We could in fact add a fourth level of analysis, that of particular modes of thought (in the formal sense), which some scholars believe they have discerned through an analysis of the divergent structures of languages. See, for example, Benjamin L. Whorf, *Language, Thought and Reality*; Edward Sapir, *Language, Culture and Personality*; Hagime Nakamura, *The Ways of Thinking of Eastern Peoples.*

140.   Alain Besançon, *Le Tsarévitch immolé,* pp. 72ff.

141.   Ibid., p. 78.

142.   Ibid., p. 240.

143.   Ibid., p. 241.

144.   Ibid.

145.   In his contribution to the collective volume, *Faire de l'histoire,* Alain Besançon repeats this interpretation of Russian culture through an analysis of Chernyshevsky's *What Is To Be Done?* and Dostoevsky's *Notes from Underground.* (See Alain Besançon, "L'inconscient: L'épisode de la prostituée dans *Que faire?* et dans *Le Sous-Sol,*" in Le Goff and Nora, *Faire de l'histoire,* vol. 3, p. 31). But in a previous essay, Besançon implicitly reversed the roles of the mother and the father, so that it was the dangerous, castrating woman, the Oedipal mother, whom the Russian man had to confront. (See Alain Besançon, "Fonction du rêve dans le roman russe," in *Histoire et Expérience du moi.*)

Bibliography

Abraham, Nicholas. "Le temps, le rythme et l'inconscient," in *Entretiens sur l'art et la psychanalyse*. Paris-La Haye: Mouton, 1968.

Abrams, Philip. "Rites de passage. The Conflict of Generations in Industrial Society," *Journal of Contemporary History* 5, no. 1 (1970).

Ackermann, Nathan and Marie Lazarsfeld-Jahoda. *Antisemitism and Emotional Disorder*. New York: Harper & Bros., 1950.

Adorno, Theodore W. et al. *The Authoritarian Personality*. New York: Norton, 1969.

Agassi, J. *Faraday as Natural Philosopher*. Chicago: University of Chicago Press, 1971.

Allison, Graham T. *The Essence of Decision: An Analysis of the Cuban Missile Crisis*. Boston: Little, Brown & Co., 1971.

Allport, Gordon W. *The Use of Personal Documents in Psychological Science*. New York: Holt, 1942.

Arban, Dominique. *Dostoievski par lui-meme*. Paris: Ed. du Seuil, "Microcosme," 1962.

Ariès, Philippe. *Centuries of Childhood*. Trans. Robert Baldick. New York: Vintage Books, Random House, 1965. Orig. ed.: *L'Enfant et la vie familiale sous l'Ancien Régime*. Paris: Plon, 1960.

Aron, Raymond. *Introduction to the Philosophy of History*. Trans. George J. Irwin. London: Weindenfeld and Nicolson, 1961. Orig. ed. *Introduction à la philosophie de l'histoire*. Paris: Gallimard, 1948.

Aron, Raymond. *La Philosophie critique de l'histoire*. Paris: Vrin, 1969.

Bachelard, Gaston. *Lautréamont*. Paris: Corti, 1939.

Baldwin, Alfred L. "Personal Structure Analysis: A Statistical Method for Investigating the Single Personality." *Journal of Abnormal and Social Psychology* 37 (1942).

The most important works in psychohistory are followed by a letter in parentheses that indicates the field to which they make a special contribution:
(**T**) Psychoanalytic or psychohistorical theory
(**B**) Psychoanalytic biography
(**C**) Psychohistorical study of collective phenomena
Publication dates of works listed in the bibliography are those I have consulted and not necessarily the original publication dates.

Barber, James D. "Adult Identity and Presidential Style: The Rhetorical Emphasis." *Daedalus*, no. 97 (summer 1968).

Barbu, Zevedei. *Problems of Historical Psychology.* London: Routledge and Kegan Paul, 1960.

Baroja, Julio Caro. *The World of the Witches.* Trans. Nigel Glendinning. London: Weindenfeld and Nicolson, 1964. Orig. ed. *Las brujas y su mundo.* Madrid: Revista de Occidente, 1961.

Barthes, Roland. *Michelet.* Paris: Ed. du Seuil, 1954.

Barzun, Jacques. "The Muse and Her Doctors." *The American Historical Review* 77, no. 1 (1972). (**T**)

Bastide, Roger. *Sociologie et Psychanalyse.* Paris: Presses universitaires de France, 1950.

Becker, Howard. *German Youth, Bond or Free.* London: Paul, Trench, Trubner, & Co., 1946.

Bell, Daniel. "National Character Revisited." In Edward Norbeck et al., *The Study of Personality.* New York: Holt, Rinehart and Winston, 1968.

Bell, Quentin. *Virginia Woolf.* 2 vols. London: Hogarth Press, 1972–1973.

Bellah, Robert N. *Beyond Belief: Essays on Religion in a Post-Traditional World.* New York: Harper & Row, 1970.

Bellak, Leopold. "Somerset Maugham: A Thematic Analysis of Ten Short Stories." In Robert W. White, *The Study of Lives.* New York: Aldine, 1969.

Berkhofer, Robert F. *Behavioral Approach to Historical Analysis.* New York: The Free Press, 1969.

Besançon, Alain. *Le Tsarévitch immolé.* Paris: Plon, 1967. (**C**)

———. *Histoire et Expérience du moi.* Paris: Flammarion, 1971. (**T,C**)

Bettelheim, Bruno. *The Informed Heart.* New York: Free Press, 1967.

———and Morris Janowitz, *Social Change and Prejudice.* New York: Free Press, 1964.

Biller, H. B. and L. J. Borstelmann. "Masculine Developement: An Integrative Review." *Merrill-Palmer Quarterly* 13 (1967).

Binion, Rudolph. *Frau Lou: Nietzsche's Wayward Disciple.* Princeton: Princeton University Press, 1968.

———. "Research Note." *Newsletter: Group for the Use of Psychology in History* 1, no. 3 (July 1972).

Binswanger, Ludwig. "The Case of Ellen West: An Anthropological-Clinical Study." In Rollo May et al., *Existence: A New Dimension in Psychiatry and Psychology.* New York: Basic Books, 1958.

———. *Henrik Ibsen und das Problem der Selbstrealisation in der Kunst.* Heidelberg, 1949.

Bluher, Hans. "Geschichte des Wandervogels." In Werner Kindt, *Grundschriften der Deutschen Jugendbewegung.* Düsseldorf-Cologne: Dietrichs, 1963.

Blum, Gerald S. *Psychodynamics: The Science of Unconscious Mental Forces.* Belmont: Brooks/Cole, 1966.

Bonaparte, Marie. *The Life and Works of Edgar Allan Poe: A Psychoanalytic Interpretation.* Trans. John Rodker. London: Imago Pub. Co., 1959. French ed. *Edgar Poe, sa vie, son oeuvre: Etude analytique.* Paris: Presses universitaires de France, 1958, 3 vols. (**B**)

Bowlby, John. "The Nature of the Child's Tie to Its Mother." *International Journal of Psycho-analysis* 39 (1958).

Brasillach, Robert. "Notre avant-guerre." In *Une génération dans l'orage*. Paris: Plon, 1968.

Brenner, Charles. *An Elementary Textbook of Psychoanalysis*. New York: Double-day, 1957.

Brodie, Fawn M. *Thomas Jefferson: An Intimate History*. New York: Norton, 1971. (B)

Brown, Norman O. *Life against Death*. London: Rutledge & Kegan Paul, 1959.

Burke, R. "Histoire sociale des rêves." *Annales ESC* 28 (March–April 1973).

Bushman, Richard L. "On the Uses of Psychology: Conflict and Conciliation in Benjamin Franklin." *History and Theory* 6, no. 1 (1966).

Busse-Wilson, Elisabeth. "Liebe und Kameradschaft." In Werner Kindt, *Grund-schriften der Deutschen Jugendbewegung*. Düsseldorf-Cologne: Dietrichs, 1963.

Bychowski, Gustav. *Dictators and Disciples*. New York: International Universities Press, 1948.

Certeau, Michel de. *La Possession de Loudun*. Paris: Julliard, 1970.

Chasseguet-Smirgel, Janine. *Pour une psychanalyse de l'art et de la créativité*. Paris: Payot, 1971. (T)

Les Chemins actuels de la critique. Paris: Plon, 1966.

Christiansen, Björn. "The Scientific Status of Psychoanalytic Clinical Evidence." *Inquiry* 7 (1964).

Clancier, Anne. *Psychanalyse et Critique littéraire*. Paris: Privat, 1973.

Clark, Kenneth. *Civilisation: A Personal View*. London: Phaidon, 1969.

Cohn, Norman. *The Pursuit of the Millenium*. London: Secker and Warburg, 1957.

Coles, Robert. *Erik H. Erikson: The Growth of His Work*. Boston: Little, Brown & Co., 1970.

———. "How Good is Psychohistory?" *The New York Review of Books,* March 8, 1973.

Confino, Michael. "Histoire et psychologie: à propos de la noblesse russe au XVIIIe siècle." *Annales ESC 22* (Nov.-Dec. 1967).

Dadoun, Roger. *Géza Roheim et l'Essor de l'anthropologie psychanalytique*. Paris: Payot, 1972.

Davis, Kingsley. "The Sociology of Parent-Youth Conflict." *American Sociological Review* 5 (1940).

Delay, Jean. *The Youth of André Gide*. Trans. June Guicharnaud. Chicago: University of Chicago Press, 1963. Orig. ed. *La Jeunesse d'André Gide*. Paris: Gallimard, 1956–1957, 2 vols.

———. "Névrose et création." In *Aspects de la psychiatrie moderne*. Paris: Presses universitaires de France, 1956.

De Martino, Ernesto. *La Terre du remords*. Paris: Gallimard, 1966.

De Mause, Lloyd. *The History of Childhood*. New York: Psychohistory Press, 1974.

Demos, John. "Underlying Themes in the Witchcraft of Seventeenth-Century New England." *American Historical Review* 75, no. 5 (1970).

———. *A Little Commonwealth: Family Life in Plymouth Colony*. New York: Oxford University Press, 1971. (C)

Devereux, Georges. *Essais d'ethnopsychiatrie générale.* Paris: Gallimard, 1966.

————. *From Anxiety to Method in the Behavioral Sciences.* Paris-La Haye: Mouton, 1967 (**T**)

————. "La psychanalyse appliquée à l'histoire de Sparte." *Annales ESC* 20 (Jan.-Feb. 1965). (**C**)

Dicks, Henry V. *Licensed Mass Murder.* New York: Basic Books, 1972.

Dodds, E. R. *The Greeks and the Irrational.* Berkeley-Los Angeles: University of California Press, 1951.

————. *Pagan and Christian in an Age of Anxiety.* Cambridge: Cambridge University Press, 1965.

Donald, David. *Charles Sumner and the Coming of the Civil War.* New York: Knopf, 1960.

Dostoevsky, Fyodor. *The Diary of a Writer.* Trans. Boris Brasol. New York: Octagon, 1973.

————. *Crime and Punishment.* Trans. Constance Garnett. New York: F. Watts, 1969.

Doubrovsky, Serge. *The New Criticism in France.* Trans. Derek Coltman. Chicago: University of Chicago Press, 1973. Orig. ed. *Pourquoi la nouvelle critique? Critique et Objectivité.* Paris: Mercure de France, 1966.

Dufrenne, Mikel. *La Personnalité de base.* Paris: Presses universitaires de France, 1966. (**T**)

Duijker, H. C. J. and G. H. Frijda. *National Character and National Stereotypes.* Amsterdam: North-Holland, 1960.

Dumont, Louis. *Homo Hierarchicus: An Essay on the Caste System.* Trans. Mark Sainsbury. Chicago: University of Chicago Press, 1970. Orig. ed. *Homo Hierarchicus: Essai sur le système des castes.* Paris: Gallimard, 1966.

Dupront, Alphonse. "Problèmes et méthodes d'une histoire de la psychologie collective." *Annales ESC* 16 (Jan. 1961).

————. "L'histoire après Freud." *Revue de l'Enseignement supérier,* 44–45 (1969). (**T**)

Edel, Leon. *Henry James.* 4 vols. Philadelphia: J. B. Lippincott, 1953–1972 (**B**)

Edinger, Lewis J. *Kurt Schumacher: A Study in Personality and Political Behavior.* Stanford: Stanford University Press, 1965. (**B**)

Ehrenzweig, Anton. *L'Ordre caché de l'art: Essai sur la psychologie de l'imagination artistique.* Paris: Gallimard, 1974. (**T**)

Eisenstadt, S. M. *From Generation to Generation: Age Groups and Social Structure.* New York: The Free Press, 1964.

Eissler, Kurt R. *Leonardo da Vinci: Psychoanalytic Notes on the Enigma.* London: International Universities Press, 1961.

————. *Medical Orthodoxy and the Future of Psychoanalysis.* New York: International Universities Press, 1965.

Elkins, Stanley. *Slavery: A Problem in American Institutional and Intellectual Life.* Chicago: University of Chicago Press, 1968.

Eliot, T. S. *Selected Essays.* London: Faber and Faber, 1932.

Erikson, Erik H. *Childhood and Society.* New York: Norton, 1950. (**T,C**)

———. *Young Man Luther: A Study in Psychoanalysis and History.* New York: Norton, 1962.

———. *Gandhi's Truth. On the Origins of Militant Non-Violence.* New York: Norton, 1969. **(B)**

———. *Identity, Youth and Crisis.* New York: Norton, 1968.

———. "On the Nature of Psychohistorical Evidence: In Search of Gandhi." *Daedalus* 97 (summer 1968). **(T,B)**

Erikson, Kai T. *Wayward Puritans: A Study in the Sociology of Deviance.* New York: Wiley, 1966.

Escalona, Sibylle K. and Grace Heider. *Prediction and Outcome: A Study in Child Development.* New York: Basic Books, 1959.

Evans, Ivor B. *Man of Power: The Life History of Baron Rutherford of Nelson.* London: Stanely-Paul, 1939.

Eysenck, H. J. *Crime and Personality.* London: Routledge and Kegan Paul, 1970.

Febvre, Lucien. *Combats pour l'histoire.* Paris: Colin, 1953.

———. *Un Destin: Martin Luther.* Paris: Presses universitaires de France, 1973.

Fernandez, Dominique. *L'Echec de Pavese.* Paris: Grasset, 1967. **(B)**

———. *L'Arbre jusqu'aux racines: Psychanalyse et Création.* Paris: Grasset, 1972. **(T,B)**

———. "Introduction a la psychobiographie." *Incidences de la psychanalyse* 1 (1970).

Festinger, Leon. *A Theory of Cognitive Dissonance.* Evanston, White Plains: Row, Peterson, 1957.

Fogel, Robert William and Stanley L. Engerman. *Time on the Cross: The Economics of American Negro Slavery.* Boston: Little, Brown, 1974.

Foucault, Michel. *Madness and Civilisation: A History of Insanity in the Age of Reason.* Trans. Richard Howard. New York: New American Library, 1965. Orig. ed. *Histoire de la folie à l'âge classique.* Paris: Plon, 1961.

Frankl, Victor E. *Man's Search for Meaning; An Introduction to Logotherapy.* New and enlarged edition of *From Death-Camp to Existentialism.* New York: Simon & Schuster, 1970.

Freud, Anna. *The Ego and the Mechanisms of Defence.* Trans. Cecil Baines. New York: International Universities Press, 1957. **(T)**

Freud, Sigmund. *Group Psychology and the Analysis of the Ego.* Trans. James Stachey. London: Hogarth Press, 1948.

———. *The Standard Edition of the Complete Psychological Works of Sigmund Freud.* Published by James Strachey (with the collaboration of Anna Freud). London: Hogarth Press, 1953. **(T,B,C)**

———. *The Origins of Psychoanalysis: Letters to Wilhelm Fliess, Drafts and Notes: 1887–1902.* Trans. Erich Mosbacher and James Strachey. London: Imago, 1954.

Freud, Sigmund and William C. Bullitt. *Thomas Woodrow Wilson, Twenty-Eighth President of the United States: A Psychological Study.* Boston: Houghton Mifflin, 1966.

Friedländer, Saul. *L'Antisémitisme nazi: Histoire d'une psychose collective.* Paris: Ed. du Seuil, 1971. (**B,C**)

Fromm, Erich. *Escape from Freedom.* New York: Holt, Rinehart and Winston, 1941.

Gallie, W. B. *Philosophy and the Historical Understanding.* London: Chatto & Windus, 1964.

Garraty, John A. *The Nature of Biography.* London: Jonathan Cape, 1957.

Gatzke, Hans W. "Hitler and Psychohistory." *American Historical Review* 78, no. 2 (1973).

Gay, Peter. *Weimar Culture: The Outsider as Insider.* London: Secker & Warburg, 1969.

George, Alexander L. and Juliette L. George. *Woodrow Wilson and Colonel House: A Personality Study.* New York: John Day, 1964 (**B**)

Gerbner, George et al. *The Analysis of Communication Content.* New York: Wiley, 1969.

Gerth, Hans and C. Wright Mills. *Character and Social Structure: The Psychology of Institutions.* New York: Harcourt-Brace, 1964.

Gill, Merton and G. S. Klein. *The Collected Papers of David Rapaport,* New York: Basic Books, 1967 (**T**)

Goffman, Irving. *Asylums: Essays on the Social Situation of Mental Patients and Other Inmates.* Chicago: Aldine, 1961.

Goldmann, Lucien. *The Hidden God.* Trans. Philip Thody. London: Routledge and Kegan Paul, 1964. Orig. ed. *Le Dieu caché. Etude de la vision tragique dans les Pensées de Pascal et dans le théâtre de Racine.* Paris: Gallimard, 1955.

———. *Towards a Sociology of the Novel.* Trans. Alan Sheridan. London: Tavistock, 1975. Orig. ed. *Pour une sociologie du roman.* Paris: Gallimard, 1964.

———. *Structures mentales et Création culturelle.* Paris: Anthropos, 1970.

Gombrich, E. H. *Art and Illusion.* London: Phaidon, 1972.

Gorer, Geoffrey and John Ryckmann. *The People of Great Russia.* London: Cresset Press, 1949.

Gottschalk, Louis, Clyde Kluckhohn and Robert Angell. *The Use of Personal Documents in History, Anthropology and Sociology.* New York: Social Science Press, 1945.

Gough, G. H. "Studies in Social Intolerance: A Personality Scale for Antisemitism." *Journal of Social Psychology* 33 (1951).

Gough, Harrison H. "Clinical versus Statistical Prediction in Psychology." In Leo Postman, *Psychology in the Making.* New York: Knopf, 1968.

Greenstein, Fred I. *Personality and Politics: Problems of Evidence, Inference and Conceptualization.* Chicago: Markham, 1969. (**T,B,C**)

Greenstein, Fred I. and Michael Lerner. *A Source Book for the Study of Personality and Politics.* Chicago: Markham, 1971 (**T,B,C**)

Grunberger, Bela. "The Antisemite and the Oedipal Conflict." *International Journal of Psycho-analysis* 45 (1964).

Grünebaum, G. E. von. *L'Identité culturelle de l'Islam.* Paris: Gallimard, 1973.

Guttmacher, M. S. *America's Last King: An Interpretation of the Madness of George III.* New York: Scribner, 1941.

Hamblin, Robert L. "Group Integration During a Crisis." In J. David Singer, *Human Behavior and International Politics: Contributions from the Social Psychological Science.* Chicago: Rand McNally, 1965.

Hansen, Chadwick. *Witchcraft of Salem.* New York: G. Braziller, 1969.

Harrison, Saul E. "Is Psychoanalysis 'Our Science'? Reflections on the Scientific Status of Psychoanalysis." *Journal of the American Psychoanalytic Association* 18 (1970).

Hartmann, Ernest. "The Psychophysiology of Free Will: An Example of Vertical Research." In Rudolf M. Loewenstein et al., *Psychoanalysis as a General Psychology.* New York: International Universities Press, 1966.

Hartmann, Heinz. *Essays on Ego Psychology: Selected Problems is Psychoanalytic Theory.* New York: International Universities Press, 1965. (**T**)

———. *Ego Psychology and Problems of Adaptation.* Trans. by David Rappaport. New York: International Universities Press, 1958.

———, Ernst Kris and Rudolf Loewenstein. "Some Psychoanalytic Comments on Culture and Personality." In George H. Wilbur and Werner Muensterberger, *Psychoanalysis and Culture: Essays in Honor of Géza Roheim.* New York: International Universities Press, 1965.

Hassoun, Jacques. "Avant-propos" to Theodor Reik. *Le Rituel, psychanalyse des rites religieux.* Paris: Denoel, 1974.

Hempel, Carl. "The Function of General Laws in History." In Patrick Gardiner, *Theories of History.* New York: The Free Press, 1965.

Heuyer, Georges. *Psychoses collectives et Suicides collectifs.* Paris: Presses universitaires de France, 1973.

Hetherington, E. M. "A Developmental Study of the Effects of Sex of the Dominant Parent on Sex-Role Preference, Identification and Imitation in Children." *Journal of Personality and Social Psychology* 2 (1965).

Hilgard, Ernest L. "Psychoanalysis: Experimental Studies." In D. L. Sills, *International Encyclopaedia of the Social Sciences,* vol. 13. New York: Macmillan, 1968.

L'Historien entre l'éthnologue et le futurologue. Paris-La Haye: Mouton, 1971.

Hoffmann, Stanley. *Decline or Renewal? France since the 1930's.* New York: Viking Press, 1974.

Horkheimer, Max and Theodore W. Adorno. *Dialectics of Enlightenment.* Trans. John Cumming. New York: Herder and Herder, 1972.

Hospers, John. "Free Will and Psychoanalysis," in Wilfrid Sellers and J. Hospers, *Readings in Ethical Theory.* New York: Appleton-Century Crofts, 1970.

Hughes, H. Stuart. "The Historian and the Social Scientist." *American Historical Review* 66, no. 3 (1960).

———. *History as Art and as Science.* New York: Harper & Row, 1964. (**T**)

Huizinga, Johan. *The Waning of the Middle Ages: A Study of Forms of Life, Thought and Art in France and the Netherlands in the 14th and 15th Centuries.* Trans. F. Hopman. New York: St. Martin's Press, 1967.

Hundert, E. J. "History, Psychology and the Study of Deviant Behavior." *The Journal of Interdisciplinary History* 2, no. 4 (1972).

Hunt, David. *Parents and Children in History. The Psychology of Family Life in Early Modern France.* New York: Basic Books, 1970. (C)

Huss, Hermann and Andreas Schroder. *Antisemitismus: Zur Pathologie der Bürgerlicher Gesellschaft.* Frankfurt am Main: Europäische Verlagsanstalt, 1965.

Immergluck, Ludwig. "Determinism versus Freedom in Contemporary Psychology: An Ancient Problem Revisited." *American Psychologist* 19 (1964).

Inkeles, Alex. "Personality and Social Structure." In Robert K. Merton, et al., *Sociology Today: Problems and Prospects.* 2 vols. Glencoe: The Free Press, 1949.

Inkeles, Alex and Daniel J. Levinson. "National Character: The Study of Modal Personality and Sociocultural Systems." In Gardner Lindzey and Elliot Aronson, *The Handbook of Social Psychology*, vol. 4. Reading: Addison-Wesley, 1968–1969. (C)

Institoris, Henry and Jacques Sprenger. *Le Marteau des sorcières.* Paris: Plon, 1973.

Isaacs, Harold R. *The New World of Negro Americans.* New York: Viking Press, 1963.

Jaspers, Karl. *Strindberg und Van Gogh: Versuch einer Pathographischen Analyse unter vergleichenden Heranziehung von Swedenborg und Hölderlin.* Berne: Bircher, 1922.

Jones, Ernest. *The Life and Works of Sigmund Freud.* New York: Basic Books, 1961.

———. *Essays in Applied Psychoanalysis.* London: Hogarth Press, 1951.

Jungmann, Fritz. "Autorität und Sexualmoral in der Jugendbewegung." In Max Horkheimer, *Studien über Autorität und Familie.* Paris: Alcan, 1936.

Kafka, Franz. *Diaries.* Ed. by Max Brod. Trans. by Joseph Kresh. New York: Schocken, 1965.

Kaplan, Abraham. *The New World of Philosophy.* New York: Random House, 1961.

———. *The Conduct of Inquiry: Methodology for Behavioral Sciences.* San Francisco: Chandler, 1964. (T)

Kaplan, Bert. "Cross-cultural use of Projective Techniques." In Francis L. K. Hsu. *Psychological Anthropology.* Cambridge: Schenkman, 1972.

Kardiner, Abram and Ralph Linton. *The Individual and His Society.* New York: Columbia University Press, 1939. (T,C)

Kaufmann, Walter. *Nietzsche, Philosopher, Psychologist, Antichrist.* Princeton: Princeton University Press, 1950.

Keniston, Kenneth. *The Uncommitted: Alienated Youth in American Society.* New York: Harcourt-Brace, 1965 (C)

———. "Psychological Development and Historical Change." *The Journal of Interdisciplinary History* 2, no. 2 (1971).

Klein, Melanie. *Contributions to Psychoanalysis, 1921–1941.* London: Hogarth Press and Institute of Psycho-Analysis, 1948.

Knight, R. P. "Determinism, Freedom and Psychotherapy." *Psychiatry* 9 (1946).

Kofman, Sarah. *L'Enfance de l'art: Une interprétation de l'esthétique freudienne.* Paris: Payot, 1970.

Kohut, Heinz. *The Analysis of the Self: A Systematic Approach to the Psychoanalytic*

Treatment of Narcissistic Personality Disorders. New York: International Universities Press, 1972. (**T**)

Kracauer, Siegfried. *From Caligari to Hitler: A Psychological History of the German Film.* Princeton: Princeton University Press, 1947.

Kretschmer, Ernst. *Physique and Character.* Trans. W. J. H. Sprott, London: Routledge & Kegan Paul, 1949.

Kris, Ernst. *Psychoanalytic Exploration in Art.* New York: International Universities Press, 1964. Orig. ed. London: Allen & Unwin, 1953.

Kuhn, Thomas S. *The Structure of Scientific Revolutions.* Chicago: University of Chicago Press, 1970.

Kurth, Gertrud M. "The Jew and Adolf Hitler." In Sandor Lorand, *The Yearbook of Psychoanalysis* 4 (1949).

Lafaye, Jacques. *Quetzalcoatl et Guadalupe: La Formation de la conscience nationale au Mexique.* Paris: Gallimard, 1974.

Lagache, Daniel. *La Psychanalyse.* Paris: Presses universitaires de France, 1969.

Lane, Ann J. *The Debate over Slavery: Stanley Elkins and His Critics.* Chicago: University of Illinois Press, 1971.

Lange-Eichbaum, W. *The Problem of Genius.* London: Kegan Paul, 1931.

Langer, Walter C. *The Mind of Adolf Hitler: The Secret Wartime Report.* New York: New American Library, 1973.

Langer, William L. "The Next Assignment." In Bruce Mazlish, *Psychoanalysis and History.* Englewood Cliffs: Prentice-Hall, 1963. (*AHR* 63 [Jan. 1958], pp. 283–304.) (**T**)

Laplanche, Jean. *Hölderlin et la Question du père.* Paris: Presses universitaires de France, 1961.

Laplanche, Jean and J. B. Pontalis. *The Language of Psychoanalysis.* Trans. Donald Nicholson-Smith. London: Hogarth Press, 1973. Orig. ed. *Vocabulaire de la psychanalyse.* Paris: Presses universitaire de France, 1967.

Laqueur, Walter Z. *Young Germany: A History of the German Youth Movement.* London: Routledge and Kegan Paul, 1962.

———. *Out of the Ruins of Europe.* New York: Library Press, 1971.

Lasswell, Harold D. *Psychopathology and Politics.* Chicago: University of Chicago Press, 1930.

Leach, Edmund. *Genesis as Myth and Other Essays.* London: Jonathan Cape, 1969.

———. *Lévi-Strauss.* New York: Viking Press, 1970.

Le Goff, Jacques. "Les mentalités. Une histoire ambiguë." In Jacques Le Goff and Pierre Nora, *Faire de l'histoire.* Vol. III, *Nouveaux Objets.* Paris: Gallimard, 1974.

——— and Pierre Nora. *Faire de l'histoire.* 3 vols. Paris: Gallimard, 1974.

Leites, Nathan Constantin. *The New Ego: Pitfalls in Current Thinking about Patients in Psychoanalysis.* New York: Science House, 1971.

Le Roy Ladurie, Emmanuel. *Le Territoire de l'historien.* Paris: Gallimard, 1973.

Lévi-Strauss, Claude. "Discours de réception à l'Académie Française." *Le Monde,* June 28, 1974.

———. "Introduction à l'oeuvre de Marcel Mauss." In Marcel Mauss, *Sociologie et Anthropologie.* Paris: Presses universitaires de France, 1968.

Lewy, E. "Responsibility, Free Will and Ego Psychology." *International Journal of Psycho-analysis* 42, no. 3 (1961).

Lifton, Robert Jay. *History and Human Survival*. New York: Random House, 1971. (**T,C**)

Link, Arthur S. *Woodrow Wilson*. 4 vols. Vol. 1, *The Road to the White House*. Princeton: Princeton University Press, 1947.

Lipset, Seymour M. and Leo Loewenthal. *Culture and Social Character*. New York: Free Press, 1961.

Lipton, Samuel D. "A Note on the Compatibility of Psychic Determinism and Freedom of Will." *International Journal of Psychoanalysis* 36, no. 2 (1955).

Loeblowitz-Lennart, Henry. "The Jew as a Symbol." *Psychoanalytic Quarterly* 16, no. 1 (1947).

Loewenberg, Peter. "The Psychohistorical Origins of the Nazi Youth Cohort." *American Historical Review* 76, no. 5 (1971). (**C**)

———. "Theodor Herzl: A Psychoanalytic Study in Charismatic Leadership." In Benjamin B. Wolman, *Psychoanalytic Interpretation of History*. New York: Basic Books, 1971.

———. "The Unsuccessful Adolescence of Heinrich Himmler." *American Historical Review* 76, no. 3 (1971). (**B**)

Loewenstein, Rudolf. *Psychanalyse de l'antisémitisme*. Paris: Presses universitaires de France, 1952.

Lukács, Georges. *L'Ame et les formes*. Paris: Gallimard, 1974.

Lynn, D. B. and W. L. Sawrey. "The Effects of Father Absence on Norwegian Boys and Girls." *Journal of Abnormal and Social Psychology* 59 (1959).

MacAlpine, Ida and Richard Hunter. *George III and the Mad Business*. New York: Pantheon Books, 1970.

Maisonneuve, Jean. *Introduction à la psychosociologie*. Paris: Presses universitaires de France, 1973.

Malinowski, Bronislaw. *Sex and Repression in Savage Society*. London: K. Paul, Trench, Trubner & Co., 1927.

Mandelbaum, Maurice. *The Problem of Historical Knowledge*. New York: Harper & Row, 1967.

Mandrou, Robert. *Introduction à la France moderne (1500–1640). Essai de psychologie historique*. Paris: Albin Michel, 1961.

———. *De la culture populaire aux XVIIe et XVIIIe siècles. La Bibliothèque de Troyes*. Paris: Stock, 1964.

Mannheim, Karl. "The Problem of Generations." In *Essays on the Sociology of Knowledge*. London: Routledge and Kegan Paul, 1952.

Mannoni, Octave. *Prospero and Caliban; the Psychology of Colonization*. Trans. Pamela Powesland. New York: Praeger, 1965. Orig. ed. *Psychologie de la colonisation*. Paris: Eds. du Seuil, 1950.

Manuel, Frank E. *A Portrait of Isaac Newton*. Cambridge: Harvard University Press, 1968.

———. "The Use and Abuse of Psychology in History." *Daedalus* 100 (winter 1971). (**T**)

Marcuse, Herbert. *Eros and Civilization: A Philosophical Inquiry into Freud.* London: Sphere, 1969.

Marrou, H.-I. *The Meaning of History.* Trans. Robert Olsen. Baltimore: Helicon, 1966. Orig. ed. *De la connaissance historique.* Paris: Ed. du Seuil, 1959.

Martin, Michael. "The Scientific Status of Psychoanalytic Evidence." *Inquiry* 7 (1964).

Maser, Werner. *Hitler: Legend, Myth and Reality.* Trans. Peter and Betty Ross. New York: Harper and Row, 1973. Orig. ed. *Adolf Hitler, Legende, Mythos, Wirklichkeit.* Munich: Bechtle, 1971.

Maslow, Abraham H. *Toward a Psychology of Being.* New York: Van Nostrand-Reinhold, 1968.

Mauron, Charles. *Des métaphores obsèdantes au mythe personnel. Introduction à la psychocritique.* Paris: Corti, 1962 (**B**)

————. "Les origines d'un mythe personnel chez l'écrivain." In *Critique sociologique et critique psychanalytique.* Brussels, 1970.

Mauss, Marcel. *Sociologie et Anthropologie.* Paris: Presses universitaires de France, 1968.

May, Rollo. *Psychology and the Human Dilemma.* New York: Van Nostrand-Reinhold, 1966.

Mazlish, Bruce. *Psychoanalysis and History.* Englewood Cliffs: Prentice-Hall, 1963. (*T,B,C*)

————. "Clio on the Couch." *Encounter* 31, no. 3 (1968).

————. "Group Psychology and Problems of Contemporary History." *Journal of Contemporary History* 3, no. 2 (1968). (**T,C**)

————. "Autobiography and Psychoanalysis: Between Truth and Self-Deception." *Encounter* 34, no. 4 (1970).

————. *In Search of Nixon: A Psychological Inquiry.* New York: Basic Books, 1973.

McClelland, David C. *The Roots of Consciousness.* New York: Van Nostrand-Reinhold, 1964.

————. *The Achieving Society.* New York: The Free Press, 1967. (**C**)

McKeachie and C. L. Doyle. *Psychology.* Reading: Addison-Wesley, 1970.

Mead, Margaret and Rhoda Metraux. *The Study of Culture at a Distance.* Chicago: University of Chicago Press, 1953.

Mead, Margaret and Martha Wolfenstein. *Childhood in Contemporary Cultures.* Chicago: University of Chicago Press, 1955. (**C**)

Meehl, Paul E. *Clinical versus Statistical Prediction: A Theoretical Analysis and a Review of Evidence.* Minneapolis: University of Minnisota Press, 1954.

Mendel, Gérard. *La Révolte contre le père.* Paris: Payot, 1968. (**T**)

————. *La Crise des générations.* Paris: Payot, 1969.

Merton, Robert K. *Social Theory and Social Structure.* New York: The Free Press, 1968.

———— et al. *Sociology Today: Problems and Prospects.* 2 vols. New York: Harper and Row, 1972.

Meyer, Bernard C. *Joseph Conrad: A Psychoanalytic Biography.* Princeton: Princeton University Press, 1967.

Meyerhoff, Hans. "On Psychoanalysis and History." *Psychoanalysis and the Psychoanalytic Review* 49, no. 2 (1962).

Mitscherlich, Alexander. *Society Without a Father.* Trans. Erich Mosbacher. New York: J. Aronson, 1974.

Mitzman, Arthur. *The Iron Cage: An Historical Interpretation of Max Weber.* New York: Knopf, 1970.

Moran, Lord. *Winston Churchill: The Struggle for Survival, 1940–1965.* London: Constable, 1966.

Moscovici, Serge. *Essai sur l'histoire humaine de la nature.* Paris: Flammarion, 1968.

Mosse, George. "The Genesis of Fascism." *Journal of Contemporary History* 1, no. 1 (1966).

————. *The Crisis of German Ideology.* New York: Grosset & Dunlap, 1964.

Munroe, Ruth L. V. *Schools of Psychoanalytic Thought.* New York: Holt, Rinehart and Winston, 1955. (T)

Murphy, Gardner. "Psychological Views of Personality and Contributions to Its Study." In Edward Norbeck, Douglas Price-Williams and William M. McCord, *The Study of Personality: An Interdisciplinary Appraisal.* New York: Holt, Rinehart and Winston, 1968.

Nagel, Ernest. "Methodological Issues in Psychoanalytic Theory." In Sidney Hook, *Psychoanalysis, Scientific Method and Philosophy.* New York: New York University Institute of Philosophy, 1959.

Nakamura, Hagime. *The Ways of Thinking of Eastern Peoples.* Honolulu: University of Hawaii Press, 1964.

Namier, Lewis. *Personalities and Powers.* London: Hamish Hamilton, 1955.

Namier, Lewis and John Brook. *Charles Townshend.* London: Macmillan, 1964.

Neumann, Erich. *Art and the Creative Unconscious.* New York: Princeton University Press, 1959.

Nisbet, Robert. *Social Change.* New York: Harper & Row, 1972.

Norbeck, Edward, Douglas Price-Williams and William M. McCord. *The Study of Personality: An Interdisciplinary Appraisal.* New York: Holt, Rinehart and Winston, 1968.

Novey, Samuel. *The Second Look: The Reconstruction of Personal History in Psychiatry and Psychoanalysis.* Baltimore: John Hopkins University Press, 1968.

Nunberg, Herman and Ernst Federn. *Minutes of the Vienna Psychoanalytic Society.* New York: International Universities Press, 1962, vol. 1; 1967, vol. 2.

Painter, George D. *Proust.* Boston: Little, Brown & Co., 1959. (B)

Parsons, Anne. "Is the Oeidpus Complex Universal?" In Werner Muensterberger and Sidney Axelrad, *The Psychoanalytic Study of Society.* New York: International Universities Press, 1960–1972; 1964, vol. 2. (T)

————. *Social Structure and Personality.* Glencoe: The Free Press of Glencoe, 1964. (T)

Parsons, Talcott. "Psychoanalysis and the Social Structure." *Psychoanalytic Quarterly* 19, no. 3 (1950).

Piaget, Jean. *Epistémologie des sciences de l'homme.* Paris: Gallimard, 1970.

————. "Le problème de l'explication." In Leo Apostel et al., *L'Explication dans les sciences.* Paris: Flammarion, 1973.

Picard, Raymond. *New Criticism or New Fraud?* Trans. Frank Towne. Washington State University Press, 1969. Orig. ed. *Nouvelle critique ou nouvelle imposture.* Paris: Pauvert, 1965.

Plumb, J. H. "The Wolf's Clothing." *The New York Review of Books,* Dec. 14, 1972.

Popper, Karl R. *Conjectures and Refutations: The Growth of Scientific Knowledge.* London: Routledge and Kegan Paul, 1969.

————. "Philosophy of Science: A Personal Report." In C. A. Mace, *British Philosophy in the Midcentury.* Cambridge: Cambridge University Press, 1957.

Possony, Stefan T. *Lenin: The Compulsive Revolutionary.* Chicago: Regnery, 1964.

Potter, David M. *People of Plenty: Economic Abundance and the American Character.* Chicago: University of Chicago Press, 1954. (C)

Pross, Harry. *Jugend, Eros, Politik, Die Geschichte der Deutschen Jugendverbände.* Berne: Scherz, 1964.

Pumpian-Mindlin, E. *Psychoanalysis as Science.* Westport, Conn.: Greenwood Press, 1952.

Raeff, Marc. *Origins of the Russian Intelligentsia: The Eighteenth-Century Nobility.* New York: Harcourt-Brace, 1966.

Rapoport, Anatol. "Various Meanings of Theory." *The American Political Science Review* 52, no. 4 (1958).

Rattner, Sidney. "The Historian's Approach to Psychology." *Journal of the History of Ideas* 2, no. 1 (1941).

Reich, Wilhelm. *The Mass Psychology of Fascism.* New York: Farrar, Strauss & Giroux, 1970.

Reichenbach, Hans. "Probability Methods in Social Science." In Daniel Lerner and Harold D. Lasswell, *The Policy Sciences: Recent Developments in Scope and Method.* Stanford: Stanford University Press, 1951.

Reichmann, Eva G. *Hostages of Civilisation: The Social Sources of National-Socialist Anti-Semitism.* London: V. Gollanz, 1950.

Ricoeur, Paul. *Finitude and Guilt.* Trans. Charles Kellbey. Chicago: Gateway Editions, 1969. Orig. ed. *La Symbolique du mal. II. Finitude et Culpabilité.* Paris: Aubier-Montaigne, 1960.

————. *Freud and Philosophy.* Trans. Dennis Savage. New Haven: Yale University Press, 1970. Orig. ed. *De l'interprétation: Essai sur Freud.* Paris: Ed. du Seuil, 1965.

Rieff, Philip. *Freud: The Mind of the Moralist.* New York: Doubleday, 1961.

————. "The Meaning of History and Religion in Freud's Thought." In Bruce Mazlish, *Psychoanalysis and History.* Englewood Cliffs: Prentice-Hall, 1963.

Riesman, David. "Psychological Types and National Character." *American Quarterly* 5 (1953).

Riesman, David et al. *The Lonely Crowd: A Study of Changing American Character.* New York: Doubleday, 1953.

Robert, Marthe. "Vincent VanGogh, le génie et son double." *Preuves,* Feb. 1968.

Rogers, Carl E. "Toward a Science of the Person." In T. W. Wann, *Behaviorism and Phenomenology: Contrasting Bases of Modern Psychology.* Chicago: University of Chicago Press, 1964.

Rogow, Arnold. *James Forrestal: A Study of Personality, Politics, and Policy.* New York: Macmillan, 1963 (**B**)

Roheim, Géza. *The Origin and Function of Culture.* New York: Nervous and Mental Disease Monographs, 1943.

Rokeach, Milton. *The Open and Closed Mind.* New York: Basic Books, 1960.

Rosen, Ismond. "Etude psychanalytique de la sculpture." In *Entretiens sur l'art et la psychanalyse.* Paris-La Haye: Mouton, 1968.

Rossi, Ino. "The Unconscious in the Anthropology of Claude Lévi-Strauss." *American Anthropologist* 25 (1973).

Rousset, Jean. "Les réalités formelles de l'oeuvre." In *Les Chemins actuels de la critique.* Paris: Plon, 1966.

Rycroft, Charles. *Psychoanalysis Observed.* London: Constable, 1966.

Sachs, Hans. "The Delay of the Machine Age," *Psychoanalytic Quarterly* 4, no. 2 (1933).

Sapir, Edward. *Language, Culture and Personality.* Berkeley: University of California Press, 1956.

Sarnoff, I. *Testing Freudian Concepts: An Experimental Social Approach.* New York: Springer, 1972.

Sartre, Jean-Paul. *Baudelaire.* Trans. Martin Turnell. New York: New Directions, 1967. Orig. ed. *Baudelaire.* Paris: Gallimard, 1947.

———. *Critique of Dialectical Reason: Theory of Practical Ensembles.* Trans. Alan Sheridan-Smith. London: NLB, 1976. Orig. ed. *Critique de la raison dialectique.* Paris: Gallimard, 1060.

———. *Portrait of the Anti-Semite.* Trans. Mary Guggenheim. New York: Partisan Review, 1946. Orig. ed. *Réflexions sur la question juive.* Paris: Gallimard, 1962.

———. *L'Idiot de la famille.* Paris: Gallimard, 1971–75, 3 vols.

———. *Search for a Method.* Trans. Hazel E. Barnes. New York: Alfred A. Knopf, 1967.

Saussure, Raymond de. "Psychoanalysis and History." In Géza Roheim, *Psychoanalysis and the Social Sciences.* New York: 1950, vol. 2.

Schafer, Roy. *Aspects of Internalization.* New York: International Universities Press, 1968.

Schapiro, Meyer. "Leonardo and Freud: An Art Historical Study." *Journal of the History of Ideas* 17 (1956).

Schmidl, Fritz. "Psychoanalysis and History." *Psychoanalytic Quarterly* 31, no. 4 (1962).

Schoenbaum, David. *Hitler's Social Revolution: Class and Status in Nazi Germany, 1933–1939.* New York: Doubleday, 1966.

Schorske, Carl E. "Politique et parricide dans *l'Interprétation des rêves* de Freud." *Annales ESC* 28 (March-April 1973).

Shapiro, David. *Neurotic Styles.* New York: Basic Books, 1965.

Sears, Robert R. *Survey of Objective Studies of Psychoanalytic Concepts.* New York: Social Science Research Council, 1943.

Sherif, Muzafer and Hadley Cantril. *The Psychology of Ego Involvements: Social Attitudes and Identifications.* New York: Wiley, 1947.

Shils, Edward. "Authoritarianism, Right and Left." In Richard Christie and Marie Jahoda, *Studies in the Scope and Method of "the Authoritarian Personality."* Glencoe: The Free Press of Glencoe, 1954.

Silberman, Charles. *Crisis in Black and White.* New York: Random House, 1964.

Simmel, Ernst. *Antisemitism: A Social Disease.* New York: International Universities Press, 1946.

Singer, Milton. "A Survey of Culture and Personality Theory and Research." In Bert Kaplan, *Studying Personality Cross-Culturally.* New York: Harper & Row, 1961.

Smelser, Neil J. *Theory of Collective Behavior.* New York: The Free Press, 1963.

———. *Essays in Sociological Explanation.* Englewood Cliffs: Prentice-Hall, 1968. (**T,C**)

Smith, Page. *The Historian and History.* New York: Knopf, 1964.

Soriano, Marc. *Les Contes de Perrault: Culture savante et traditions populaires.* Paris: Gallimard, 1968. (**B**)

Sperber, Dan. *Rethinking Symbolism.* Trans. Alice L. Morton. London: Cambridge University Press, 1975.

Spitzer, Leo. *Linguistics and Literary History.* Princeton: N.J.: Princeton University Press, 1948.

Starobinski, Jean. *La Relation critique.* Paris: Gallimard, 1970. (**B**)

Stahlin, Wilhelm. "Der Neue Lebensstil." In Werner Kindt, *Grundschriften der Deutschen Jugendbewegung.* Düsseldorf-Cologne: Dietrichs, 1963.

Stéphane, Roger. *Portrait de l'aventurier: T. E. Lawrence, Malraux, Von Salomon.* Paris: Grasset, 1965.

Stern, Fritz. *The Varieties of History from Voltaire to the Present.* New York: World Publishing Co., 1956.

Storr, Anthony. "The Man." In A. J. P. Taylor et al. *Churchill Revised: A Critical Assessment.* New York: Dial Press, 1969.

———. *The Dynamics of Creation.* New York: Atheneum, 1972.

———. *Human Destructiveness.* New York: Basic Books, 1973.

———. *Jung.* London: Fontana Books, 1973. (**T**)

Strout, Cushing. "Ego Psychology and the Historian." *History and Theory* 7, no. 3 (1968). (**B**)

Terhune, Kenneth W. "The Effects of Personality in Cooperation and Conflict." In Paul Swingle, *The Structures of Conflict.* New York: Academic Press, 1970.

Thomas, Keith. *Religion and the Decline of Magic.* London: Scribner, 1971.

Thompson, Clara. *Psychoanalysis: Evolution and Development.* New York: Gross Press, 1957.

Trevor-Roper, Hugh R. *The European Witchcraze of the 16th and 17th Centuries.* New York: Harper & Row, 1969.

Tucker, Robert C. "The Theory of Charismatic Leadership." *Daedalus* 97 (summer 1968).

———. *Stalin as Revolutionary, 1879–1929: A Study in History and Personality.* New York: Norton, 1973. (**B**)

Van den Berg, J. H. *Metabletica ou la Psychologie historique.* Paris: Buchet-Chastel, 1962.

Vernon, Philip E. *Personality Assessment: A Critical Survey.* London: Methuen, 1964.

Veyne, Paul. *Comment on écrit l'histoire.* Paris: Ed. du Seuil, 1971.

Vovelle, Michel. *Mourir autrefois: Attitudes collectives devant la mort aux XVIIe et XVIIIe siècles.* Paris: Gallimard, 1974.

Waelder, Robert. *Basic Theory of Psychoanalysis.* New York: International Universities Press, 1962.

Waite, Robert G. L. "Adolf Hitler's Antisemitism." In Benjamin B. Wolman, *The Psychoanalytic Interpretation of History.* New York: Basic Books, 1971.

Wallerstein, Robert S. and Neil J. Smelser. "Psychoanalysis and Sociology: Articulations and Applications." *International Journal of Psycho-analysis* 50 (1969).

Weber, Max. *Theory of Social and Economic Organisation.* New York: The Free Press, 1947.

Wehler, Hans-Ulrich. *Geschichte und Psychoanalyse.* Cologne: Kiepenheur und Witsch, 1971.

Weinstein, Edwin A. "Woodrow Wilson's Neurological Illness," *Journal of American History* 57 (1970–1971).

Weinstein, Fred and Gerald M. Platt. *The Wish to Be Free: Society, Psyche and Value Change.* Berkeley: University of California Press, 1969. (**T,C**)

———. "History and Theory: The Question of Psychoanalysis." *The Journal of Interdisciplinary History* 2, no. 4 (spring 1972).

———. *Psychoanalytic Sociology: An Essay on the Interpretation of Historical Data and the Phenomena of Collective Behavior.* Baltimore: Johns Hopkins University Press, 1973. (**T,C**)

Whiting, John W. M. and Irving L. Child. *Child Training and Personality: A Cross-Cultural Study.* New Haven: Yale University Press, 1953.

Whorf, Benjamin L. *Language, Thought and Reality.* Edited by J. B. Carroll. Cambridge, Mass.: MIT Press, 1956.

Whyte, Lancelot L. *The Unconscious before Freud.* London: Tavistock, 1962.

Wilcox, William B. *Portrait of a General, Sir Henry Clinton, in the War of Independence.* New York: Knopf, 1964.

Williams, Leslie P. *Michael Faraday: A Biography.* New York: Basic Books, 1965.

Wolfenstein, Martha and Nathan Leites. *The Movies: A Psychological Study.* New York: Atheneum Press, 1950.

Wolfenstein, E. Victor. *The Revolutionary Personality: Lenin, Trosky, Gandhi.* Princeton: Princeton University Press, 1967.

Wolff, P. "The Developmental Psychology of Jean Piaget and Psychoanalysis." *Psychological Issues* 2, no. 1 (1960).

Wolman, Benjamin B. *The Psychoanalytic Interpretation of History.* New York: Basic Books, 1971.

Wyneken, Gustav. "Der Weltgeschichtliche Sinn der Jugendbewegung." In Werner Kindt, *Grundschriften der Deutschen Jugendbewegung.* Düsseldorf-Cologne: Dietrichs, 1963.

Index

.

Index

DATE DUE
